Food Cultures of Great Britain

Recent Titles in The Global Kitchen

Food Cultures of China: Recipes, Customs, and Issues
Qian Guo
Food Cultures of Japan: Recipes, Customs, and Issues
Jeanne Jacob
Food Cultures of Mexico: Recipes, Customs, and Issues
R. Hernandez-Rodriguez

Food Cultures of Great Britain

Cuisine, Customs, and Issues

Victoria R. Williams

BLOOMSBURY ACADEMIC
NEW YORK • LONDON • OXFORD • NEW DELHI • SYDNEY

BLOOMSBURY ACADEMIC

Bloomsbury Publishing Inc, 1359 Broadway, New York, NY 10018, USA
Bloomsbury Publishing Plc, 50 Bedford Square, London, WC1B 3DP, UK
Bloomsbury Publishing Ireland, 29 Earlsfort Terrace, Dublin 2, D02 AY28, Ireland

BLOOMSBURY, BLOOMSBURY ACADEMIC and the Diana logo are trademarks of Bloomsbury Publishing Plc

First published in the United States of America 2024

Copyright © Bloomsbury Publishing, Inc., 2026

For legal purposes the Acknowledgments on p. vii constitute an extension of this copyright page.

Cover image © ingusk/Adobe Stock

All rights reserved. No part of this publication may be: i) reproduced or transmitted in any form, electronic or mechanical, including photocopying, recording or by means of any information storage or retrieval system without prior permission in writing from the publishers; or ii) used or reproduced in any way for the training, development or operation of artificial intelligence (AI) technologies, including generative AI technologies. The rights holders expressly reserve this publication from the text and data mining exception as per Article 4(3) of the Digital Single Market Directive (EU) 2019/790.

Bloomsbury Publishing Inc does not have any control over, or responsibility for, any third-party websites referred to or in this book. All internet addresses given in this book were correct at the time of going to press. The author and publisher regret any inconvenience caused if addresses have changed or sites have ceased to exist, but can accept no responsibility for any such changes.

Library of Congress Cataloging-in-Publication Data
Names: Williams, Victoria, author.
Title: Food cultures of Great Britain : cuisine, customs, and issues / Victoria R. Williams.
Description: New York : Bloomsbury Academic, 2024. | Series: The global kitchen | Includes bibliographical references and index. |
Summary: "There's far more to British food than fish and chips. Discover the history and culture of Great Britain through its rich culinary traditions"– Provided by publisher.
Identifiers: LCCN 2023034030 (print) | LCCN 2023034031 (ebook) | ISBN 9781440877414 (hardback) | ISBN 9798765114131 (paperback) | ISBN 9798765110096 (epub) | ISBN 9781440877421 (ebook)
Subjects: LCSH: Food habits–Great Britain–History. | Gastronomy–Great Britain–History. | Great Britain–Social life and customs.
Classification: LCC GT2853.G7 W53 2024 (print) | LCC GT2853.G7 (ebook) | DDC 394.1/20941–dc23/eng/20230721
LC record available at https://lccn.loc.gov/2023034030
LC ebook record available at https://lccn.loc.gov/2023034031

ISBN: HB: 978-1-4408-7741-4
PB: 979-8-7651-1413-1
ePDF: 978-1-4408-7742-1
eBook: 979-8-7651-1009-6

Series: The Global Kitchen

Typeset by Newgen KnowledgeWorks Pvt. Ltd., Chennai, India

For product safety related questions contact productsafety@bloomsbury.com.

To find out more about our authors and books visit www.bloomsbury.com
and sign up for our newsletters.

Contents

Series Foreword		vi
Acknowledgments		vii
Introduction		ix
Chronology		xv
1	Food History	1
2	Influential Ingredients	27
3	Appetizers and Side Dishes	57
4	Main Dishes	71
5	Desserts	95
6	Beverages	111
7	Holidays and Special Occasions	137
8	Street Food and Snacks	159
9	Dining Out	173
10	Food Issues and Dietary Concerns	189
Glossary		207
Selected Bibliography		215
Index		229

Series Foreword

Imagine a typical American breakfast: bacon, eggs, toast, and home fries from the local diner. Or maybe a protein-packed smoothie, sipped on the go to class or work. In some countries in Europe, breakfast might just be a small cookie and a strong coffee, if anything at all. A South African breakfast might consist of a bowl of corn porridge with milk. In Japan, breakfast might look more like dinner, complete with rice, vegetables, and fish. What we eat varies from country to country, and even region to region. The *Global Kitchen* series explores the cuisines of different cultures around the world, from the history of food and food staples to main dishes and contemporary issues. These volumes will delight readers by discovering other cultures through the lens of a treasured topic: food.

Each volume focuses on the culinary heritage of one country or one small group of countries, covering history and contemporary culture. Volumes begin with a chronology of major food-related milestones and events in the area, from prehistory to the present. Chapters explore the key foods and meals in the country, covering the following topics:

- Food History
- Influential Ingredients
- Appetizers and Side Dishes
- Main Dishes
- Desserts
- Beverages
- Holidays and Special Occasions
- Street Foods and Snacks
- Dining Out and
- Food Issues and Dietary Concerns

Sidebars, a glossary of important terms, and a selected bibliography round out each volume, providing readers with additional information and resources for their personal and scholarly research needs. The *Global Kitchen* series will allow readers to fully immerse themselves in other cultures, giving a taste of typical daily life and tradition.

Acknowledgments

I would like to thank the following people for their help in the writing of this book:

First, my editor, Maxine Taylor, senior acquisitions editor at ABC-CLIO, for her unceasing enthusiasm for the project and her encouragement. Second, Kevin Downing, editorial director of Books at ABC-CLIO for his guidance on the project during the strange days of lockdown. Also, my great thanks to Kaitlin Ciarmiello, former senior acquisitions editor at ABC-CLIO, for assigning me the project. I would also like to thank Bloomsbury for taking on the project. Lastly, "thank you" to my parents for instilling in me a love of food.

Introduction

The earliest Britons lived as hunter-gatherers who ate the plants and wild animals indigenous to Britain. Then, during the Neolithic period, Britons started to domesticate animals and cultivate crops to eat. While most Britons grew crops on a subsistence basis, some Britons became crop farmers. At the same time, however, Britons continued to forage for food.

The Roman invasion of Britain heralded the arrival of myriad new foods to Britain as well as wine. Importantly, the Romans built numerous roads around Britain that allowed foods to be transported easily. Consequently, new foods became available across Britain, and market gardens and orchards became established in British cities. As well as introducing new foods, the Romans also imported some of the first cookbooks to Britain. The Romans' introduction of new foods to Britain resulted in the development of a new British farming system as Britons began to create enclosures around their farms. When the Romans left Britain, they abandoned these farms. This allowed the farm animals to interbreed with indigenous British animals or become wild themselves, while Roman crops self-seeded in the British landscape.

After the Romans, Britain was invaded by the Anglo-Saxons and then by the Vikings. The Vikings settled across Britain, and Britons soon adopted the Vikings' love of fish. The Vikings also developed a British fish trade. After the Norman Conquest in 1066, Britain developed close cultural ties with France, and it was under Norman rule that Britain was introduced to the Mediterranean and Arab foods eaten in other Norman colonies. When English soldiers returned from the Crusades, the popularity of Persian food increased further in Britain. The same soldiers also brought the first sugar to England. During this time, spices such as cloves, ginger, and saffron became popular in Britain too.

During the Middle Ages, bread and the thick stew-soup known as pottage were the staple foods. Peasants supplemented this diet with pork as pigs were cheap to keep and represented a year-round source of meat. As medieval villages tended to be located near rivers, fish represented another reliable food source. Britons living in cities lacked land on which to grow or forage for food, however, so cities imported food from the countryside. Over time, this meant that cities such as London became home to numerous eateries, food shops, and markets.

The food and drink of Elizabethan Britain was extremely varied. Diets were rich in meat and fish while stews and sauces were both flavored and colored by the presence of spices and flowers. Elizabethan food preservation methods were limited so most Elizabethans either grew their own food or bought food at local markets though wealthy landowners were self-sufficient. At this time, most foods were boiled, roasted, or fried over open fires or baked in brick ovens. Wealthy Elizabethans also had a penchant for sweet treats made using sugar from the Americas. In the 1590s, crop failures and poor harvests led to starvation among many poor Britons and meant grain had to be imported. The fact that much British farmland was given over to sheep farming rather than food production exacerbated the situation as there was less land for food production. The land enclosure system reduced further the amount of land available to peasant farmers leading many agricultural laborers to relocate to towns.

During the eighteenth to mid-nineteenth century, Britain experienced much immigration from Northern Europe. The migration influenced British food immensely for French fruit and vegetable varieties were introduced to Britain as were German sausages and Dutch pancakes. Moreover, many English aristocrats sent their chefs to France in order to broaden their repertoire. Meanwhile, many English peasants found employment in newly established city factories and lived on starchy foods washed down by gin.

By this time, tea had become Britain's national drink. Additionally, breakfast was now an important meal as increasing numbers of Britons needed to eat before starting work and so foods such as kippers became popular breakfast dishes. As there was usually a long wait between breakfast and dinner, wealthier Britons started to enjoy the mid-afternoon meal of afternoon tea as a way to fend off pre-dinner hunger. Meanwhile, the coming of the railways allowed regional foods to be transported across Britain quickly. Similarly, in the Victorian era, the development of steam ships meant foods could be moved faster across longer distances. Likewise, from the 1880s, refrigerated meat transportation was possible so Britain could import meat from the United States. This made meat affordable to more Britons, and thus, for the first time, meat became a regular feature of all British diets.

The continuing growth of the British Empire influenced British food immeasurably. For example, by the 1840s, curry had become hugely popular in Britain, while kedgeree became a popular Victorian breakfast dish. The Victorian era also saw the popularity of the "full English" cooked breakfast grow. Another Victorian food innovation was the opening of Britain's first fish-and-chip shop, the dish having been popularized by European Jewish migrants living in London. New food preservation methods evolved during Victorian times too, and kitchen gadgets became extremely popular. This was also the era when women chefs and food writers came to the fore and ushered in a new era of domesticity.

The outbreak of the First World War led to food shortages that were compounded when British crops failed. With food becoming scarce, the British government introduced food rationing that meant Britons were permitted only certain amounts of certain foods.

Some foods continued to be in short supply even after the end of the war with butter rationed until 1920. The start of the Second World War signaled a return to food rationing and as fruit and vegetables were often in short supply, the British government encouraged Britons to grow their own under the famous scheme known as "Dig for Victory." Rationing continued in peacetime for in 1946, the British government rationed bread in order to prevent a famine in postwar Germany. Only in 1954 did foods such as bacon become freely available in Britain.

In the 1950s, British food tended to be frugal as Britain experienced postwar debt. Nonetheless, the 1950s saw restaurateurs start to cater for a new British demographic—teenagers—when burger chains started to open in London. Postwar, immigration also led to an increasing number of new restaurants serving various global cuisines. In particular, the 1960s saw the opening of numerous Indian restaurants in London, southeast England, and elsewhere. By the end of the 1960s, the British economy boomed meaning Britons could afford to holiday abroad and so encounter new foods.

In the 1970s, societal changes meant convenience became highly prized when food shopping, and so supermarkets started to monopolize British food shopping. At the same time, developments in canning and freezing techniques and the invention of chemical additives and preservatives meant food lasted longer. The 1980s saw another major convenience food innovation when the retailer Marks & Spencer introduced prepacked sandwiches to Britain.

More recent British food history has been dominated by food scares including the 1988 salmonella egg scandal that forced thousands of British chicken farmers into bankruptcy and led, ultimately, to the Lion Quality Mark Scheme that requires all hens to be vaccinated against *Salmonella enteritidis*. Shortly after the egg crisis, an outbreak of bovine spongiform encephalopathy (BSE) began that resulted in offal being banned for human consumption in Britain. The bovine spongiform encephalopathy epidemic peaked in 1992–3 and saw over four million cattle slaughtered in an effort to stop the disease. The outbreak caused many countries to stop the importation of British beef, with China ending their ban only in 2018.

In 2001, Britain suffered an outbreak of foot-and-mouth disease that caused the British government to cull more than six million pigs, cattle, and sheep in order to stop the disease. Other diseases to affect British food supplies recently include avian flu, bluetongue, and African swine fever. In 2021, Britain suffered its largest outbreak of avian flu resulting in millions of farm birds being culled, while in 2022, the British government ordered that all bird keepers keep their birds indoors and uphold strict biosecurity measures. In 2007, the bluetongue virus that affects mostly sheep but also cattle and deer was first detected in England. Since then, in Britain, the virus has spread, with the virus' transmission helped by rising global temperatures that means the geographical distribution of the midge that transmits the disease has moved northwards. While a vaccine against bluetongue has prevented major outbreaks, were bluetongue to become established in Britain, it would cause a decline in British lamb and beef exports and cause the price of the meats to rise.

At the start of 2013, routine food testing discovered horsemeat in beef products sold throughout Britain in what became known as the horsemeat scandal. The scandal dominated the British media and led to many Britons either reducing their meat consumption or giving up meat-eating altogether. The horsemeat scandal also caused British food retailers to become much more transparent about foods' origin. The scandal caused many Britons to focus on buying foods produced locally, a move that still continues today.

More recently still, Britain has seen a steep rise in food bank use. In 2021, the so-called cost of living crisis began that has seen food prices in Britain rise faster than household income. The rising cost of food has exacerbated the need for food banks. That some Britons find it difficult to eat regularly and healthily is reflected by the fact that in 2019, poor diets were blamed for an estimated 64,000 deaths every year in England, while more than half of all over the age of 45 were found to be living with diet-related health conditions.

The Covid-19 pandemic, Brexit (Britain's withdrawal from the European Union [EU]), and Russia's invasion of Ukraine have shaped the most recent

British food history. At various times during the pandemic, authorities instigated lockdowns that closed eateries which meant that Britons could only leave home for essential reasons, such as buying food. The lockdowns were found to have exacerbated the food insecurity felt by many Britons as food banks experienced a rapid rise in demand. The lockdowns also saw some food banks experience compromised supply chains as panicked wealthier Britons stockpiled food. The lockdowns also changed British food shopping habits as increasing numbers of older Britons started to shop online for food.

Britain's reliance on food from the EU means that British food imports have been impacted by new trade regulations brought in post-Brexit. Many small food businesses report that the new rules are time-consuming bureaucracy, delay deliveries, and add to costs. Similarly, Brexit has also reduced the availability of crop-pickers and lorry drivers from EU countries working in Britain, which in turn has impacted British food supply chains. That EU foods are now more difficult and expensive to import, does, however, mean that British-made food is experiencing a rise in demand, thereby accelerating the trend for buying local, seasonal foods.

Russia's invasion of Ukraine has not had a significant impact on the availability of food in Britain, though the supply of cooking oil has been disrupted, for most sunflower oil used in Britain comes from Ukraine. Moreover, the invasion worsened Brexit-induced labor shortages for the invasion meant Ukrainian men who would normally work in Britain were fighting in their homeland. Despite such challenges, food and soft drinks represent Britain's largest manufacturing sector and is the fourth largest such sector in the world.

Climate change, soil depletion, and loss of biodiversity represent the most severe medium- to long-term risks to British food production. Climate change will cause Britain to suffer hotter, drier summers followed by warmer, wetter winters. Such climactic change will reduce British crop yields and endanger livestock through excessively high temperatures and increased risk of disease. For this reason, Britain is putting much emphasis on sustainable farming methods and drought-prevention measures. Some British farmers have also started to grow new crops more suited to drier conditions.

British agriculture relies on the health of the soil, so soil degradation poses an underlying threat to Britain's food security. At present, estimates suggest soil degradation, erosion, and compaction cost the British economy over £1 billion annually while reducing the amount of land viable for food production. Just as deforestation damages British soil by removing the organic matter that makes soil resilient to weathering, so habitat loss together with climate change and the use of pesticides have caused a decline in Britain's biodiversity, especially populations of pollinating insects. That many species of pollinating insects in Britain are in decline puts Britain's long-term food security at risk because fewer pollinating insect species means there will be fewer insects to pollinate crops. As much of British land is used for farming, the management of farmland is hugely important to maintaining pollinator populations. At present, British farming employs various methods to try to improve the number of pollinating insects in Britain, including growing seasonal food sources such as oilseed rape, leaving grasslands wild, and providing wildflower margins that provide insects with food year-round.

Chronology

Britain's history has been shaped by successive periods of invasion, war, empire-building, and immigration. The Romans, Vikings, and Norman French brought new ingredients and food techniques to Britons, as did British soldiers returning home from the Crusades and British India. Wartime exploits abroad widened Britons' culinary knowledge as did foreign leisure travel. Rationing during the First and Second World Wars forced Britons to become inventive in the kitchen, while refugees and migrants from across the globe have influenced British food immeasurably. The 1990s saw food become part of the zeitgeist as "Cool Britannia" brought an air of optimism to Britain, chefs became superstars, and London became a leading foodie destination. More recently, war has again influenced food in terms of availability and price rises. Meanwhile, Britain is experiencing both rising levels of obesity and of food bank use as some Britons struggle to afford food.

252–201 million years ago: inland seas cover England and create layers of salt.
10,000–4,000 BCE: early Britons live as hunter-gatherers.
4000–2200 BCE: Britons begin to domesticate livestock and cultivate crops.
3800 BCE: salt-making occurs in Cleveland, northeast England.
3000 BCE: wheat introduced to Britain.
1500 BCE: Britain's earliest field systems established.
1200 BCE: Britain's oldest fish trap used in Wales.
43 CE: Romans invade Britain.
fourth/fifth century: *De Re Coquinaria* by Apicius become the first cookery books to arrive in Britain.
410: Romans leave Britain allowing their crops to self-seed and their farm animals to either interbreed with indigenous British animals or become wild.

450: the Anglo-Saxons colonize Britain.

650–890: fish weirs used in west London.

eighth century: Vikings start to raid Britain and introduce fish smoking and drying techniques. The Vikings also develop a British fish trade.

1066: Britain is invaded by Norway and by William, duke of Normandy. William's invasion creates close cultural ties between Britain and France.

1070–1: the Normans squash a rebellion in Cheshire and lay waste to the area's salt industry.

1095–1270: Britons returning from the Crusades introduce sugar and Persian ingredients to England.

twelfth century: British land enclosure system forces peasant farmers to find work in towns.

1152: English king Henry II marries French queen Eleanor of Aquitaine allowing imports of French salt to enter England.

1199: King John allows the city of Preston to host a cheese festival and so starts Lancashire's cheese-making industry.

1361: first Alban buns are distributed to the poor.

1362: the first beer to include hops imported from the Netherlands to Britain.

Early fourteenth century to the mid-nineteenth century: the Little Ice Age makes some vitamin-rich foods become scarce in Britain. The fourteenth century also sees Britons start to fish in Icelandic waters.

1390: publication of *The Forme of Cury* recipe collection.

1394: salt merchants in London form the Fraternity of Salters.

1441: beer becomes subject to an official maximum price per gallon.

1445: Britain's first pancake race held.

1494: first record of whisky in Scotland.

1520: cultivation of hops begins in Britain.

1530s: the Dissolution of the Monasteries causes the British cheese-making industry to decline.

1563: Queen Elizabeth I enshrines in law that Britons must eat fish (or possibly poultry, game, and veal) on certain days of the week, as well as during Lent.

1575: the Netherlands starts to export gin to England.

1585: first recipe for trifle is printed.

1590s: crop failures and poor harvests lead to starvation among poor Britons yet the British wool trade booms.

1592: Queen Elizabeth I bans the eating of hot cross buns except on specific days.

1599: Oliver Cromwell taxes salt and salt-making heavily.

1601: the Poor Law consolidated earlier acts and laws of poor relief to help those impacted by the ill-effects of the land enclosure system.

1637: coffee arrives in England.

1650: England's first coffeehouse opens.

Late 1600s: English aristocrats send their chefs to France in order to broaden their repertoire.

1660: the British monarchy is restored with the salt tax abolished by King Charles II. The king's wife, Catherine of Braganza, introduces tea to the English aristocracy.

1664: Scotland introduces a whisky tax.

1685: powdered coffee becomes available for home consumption.

1688: Queen Mary reinstates the salt tax. The Wine Act imposes heavy duty on French wine.

1689: tea becomes subject to customs duty.

1690: the Act for the Encouraging of the Distilling of Brandy and Spirits from Corn is introduced giving tax breaks for grain farming.

1702: extension of the Salt Act stops the opening of new coastal salt refineries outside of Cheshire.

1714: start of the Georgian era sees Hanoverian kings rule Britain and elements of Northern European food introduced to British kitchens.

1730: the salt tax is repealed again. Britain establishes a coffee plantation in Jamaica. Commercial whisky production begins in earnest in the Scottish Lowlands.

1732: the salt tax is reintroduced.

1736: the Gin Act introduces a retail tax on gin.

1738: Fortnum & Mason invents the Scotch egg.

1739: the Gin Act is repealed after social unrest.

1747: Hannah Glasse publishes a recipe for Yorkshire pudding in her book *The Art of Cookery Made Plain and Simple*.

Mid-1700s: French and Italian artisans open ice-cream shops in London.

1751: a new Gin Act increases the tax on imported gin.

1757: the East India Company's rule over India begins and so Indian cuisine starts to influence British food.

1759: Fry's chocolate company is founded.

1783: Prime Minister William Pitt the Younger slashes tax on tea.

1786: the government halves the duty on French wine.

1791–2: first abolitionist campaign to reject Caribbean sugar in Britain begins.
1793: a new salt refinery is built near Liverpool.
1809: the world's first cooking apple, the Bramley, grows in Nottinghamshire.
1810: the canning process is patented allowing for the preservation of a wider range of foods.
1814: Colman's of Norwich starts to sell its English mustard powder.
1817: the forcing process is invented at London's Chelsea Physic Garden.
1820s: rock salt from Continental Europe floods the British market.
1823: Scotland's Excise Act is passed.
1825: the salt tax is repealed. Clarence Birdseye invents the double belt freezer that allows for the quick freezing of fish at sea meaning Britain's long-distance fishing fleet can catch and freeze cod. British Army officers in India invent the gin and tonic cocktail.
1830: the Beerhouse Act allows more inns to open. The Patent Still is invented thereby industrializing whisky production.
1831: commercial production of Melton Mowbray pork pies begins.
1837: the term "ploughman's lunch" first appears in print.
1839: the East India Company starts to import tea from India. Digestive biscuits are invented in Scotland.
1840s: development of the railways in Britain. The concept of afternoon tea is invented.
1843: Britain's first harvest festival is held.
1844: Britain's first rock salt mine opens in Cheshire.
1845: Eliza Acton's *Modern Cookery for Private Families* becomes a best-selling cookbook.
1848: the Metropolitan Commission of Sewers in London is established to clean up the city's water supply.
1849: end of a cholera epidemic due to contaminated water that kills over 14,000 Londoners.
1850: British salt brine pits become exhausted. Cox's Orange Pippin apple is introduced.
1853: the tax on tea is cut further. The first blended whiskies are produced. Fry's introduces the first filled chocolate bar.
1855: laws are introduced to restrict pub-opening hours.
1860: the British government enacts the Adulteration of Food and Drink Act to combat the issue of food adulteration.

1861: Isabella Beeton's best-selling *Mrs Beeton's Book of Household Management* ushers in a new era of Victorian domesticity.
1862: Britain's earliest combined roller and stone mill opens in Ipswich.
1863: a fish-and-chip shop opens in Mossely and claims to be the first fish-and-chip shop in the world.
1865: Britain's first large-scale, meat-canning factory opens.
1866: Fry's launches the world's first mass-produced chocolate bar.
1868: combined roller and stone mills open in Bristol and Liverpool.
1870s: the introduction of the triple expansion engine means ships can bring foods to Britain over longer distances. Meanwhile, the introduction of steam trawlers allows British fishers to trawl greater depths using larger nets.
1872: the British government establishes official food inspectors invested with the power to fine food producers who adulterate food and drink.
1874: import duty on sugar ends.
1875: Cadbury produces their first chocolate Easter egg.
1877: the first forced rhubarb is cultivated.
1878: first dictionary entry for Cumberland sauce.
1880s: refrigerated meat transportation means Britain can import meat from the United States.
1881: Britain's first purpose-built lager brewery opens in London.
1885: Jacobs' Cream Crackers launch.
1888: most British saltworks merge to create the Salt Union.
1889: kippers debut on the breakfast menu of London's Savoy hotel.
1894: J. Lyons & Co opens its first teashop in London's Piccadilly.
1904: medics report the deaths of 30,000 British children due to outbreaks of diseases linked to milk.
1908: first Chinese restaurant opens in London.
1914: the First World War begins and impedes Britain's food supplies.
1916: England and Scotland experience a poor wheat harvest, and the potato crop fails.
1917: Germany declares a policy of unrestricted submarine warfare meaning British merchant ships carrying food imports are at risk of being destroyed. The Women's Land Army forms to provide extra voluntary farm labor to replace farm workers fighting overseas. Voluntary food rationing begins.
1918: the government introduces food rationing with sugar as the first food rationed.
1919: British agriculture falls into depression.

1920: butter rationing ends.

1929: the British government begins to survey fishing grounds in the western Barents Sea.

1930s: the Norwegian government claims a 4-mile territorial limit on its waters.

1933: the creation of various government reports into the fishing industry results in the Sea Fishing Industry Act.

1935: milkshake bars begin to open in British seaside resorts.

1940: the British government reintroduces food rationing as the Second World War rages.

1942: government introduces regulated brown bread called the National Loaf. Scottish distilleries close temporarily when war disrupts grain supplies.

1944: Iceland gains independence from Denmark and annuls the Anglo-Danish Territorial Waters Agreement of 1901. Consequently, the Icelandic government extends its territorial limit to 4 miles and sparks a lengthy dispute between Britain and Iceland known as the Cod Wars.

1946: the British government introduces bread rationing in order to prevent a famine in Germany.

1947: North Sea fish stocks fall due to increased fishing post–Second World War.

1948: British bread rationing ends.

1949: a postwar boom in fish prices collapses.

1952: tea rationing ends.

1953: rationing of eggs, cream, sugar, and sweets ends. Britain's first espresso bar opens in London. Coronation chicken invented.

1954: rationing of cheese, butter, cooking oil, fresh meat, and bacon ends. The first Wimpy Bar opens in London.

1955: Britain's Cheese Bureau is established to represent British and Commonwealth cheese producers.

1956: The Organisation of European Economic Co-operation forces Britain to accept Iceland's 4-mile limit.

1958: the United Nations holds the first International Conference on the Law of the Sea at which Iceland extends the limit of its territorial waters to 12 miles. Britain refuses to recognize this claim.

1961: Britain agrees to Iceland's 12-mile limit.

1960s: steep increase in the number of Indian restaurants in Britain.

1968: first Christingle orange given out in Britain.

1970: the European Economic Community introduces the Common Fisheries Policy that allows member nations equal access to community waters.
1971: banoffee pie is invented in East Sussex.
1972: Icelandic fishermen start to sabotage British trawlers.
1973: Britain joins the European Economic Community. Britain and Iceland agree that for the next 2 years, some British trawlers can operate within Iceland's 12-mile limit.
1975: Iceland declared a 200-mile territorial limit, which Britain refuses to recognize.
1976: Britain recognizes Iceland's 200-mile territorial limit, effectively ending Britain's long-distance fishing industry.
1980s: Marks & Spencer introduces the first prepacked sandwich.
1983: the European Union's Common Fisheries Policy comes into force meaning fish are classed as a common resource for EU member states.
1988: Politician Edwina Currie claims most British eggs are contaminated with salmonella and caused a 60 percent slump in egg sales.
1998: the government introduces the Lion Quality Mark Scheme that requires all hens to be vaccinated against *Salmonella enteritidis*.
1989: the sale of offal is banned for human consumption due to an outbreak of bovine spongiform encephalopathy (BSE).
1992–3: 180,000 cattle are infected with BSE. About 4.4 million cattle are slaughtered in order to try to stop the disease.
1993: London restaurant Quaglino's opens.
1994: *Ready Steady Cook* television show first broadcast.
1995: triple-cooked chips first served at The Fat Duck restaurant. Marco Pierre White becomes both the first British chef to be awarded three Michelin stars and the youngest chef to achieve three stars.
1996: Stilton cheese and Jersey Royal potatoes are given the European Protected Designation of Origin (PDO) status.
2000: The Trussell Trust opens its first food bank.
2001: an outbreak of foot-and-mouth disease infects around 2,000 British animals. The British foreign secretary Robin Cook hails chicken tikka masala as representative of multicultural Britain.
2007: another outbreak of foot-and-mouth disease is stopped before it becomes widespread. West Country Farmhouse Cheddar is awarded PDO status. First British case of bluetongue virus is detected.
2008: Melton Mowbray pork pies are given PDO status.
2009: Sipsmith, London's first copper pot distillery for 189 years, opens.

2010: the first British Street Food Awards are held. The Food Hygiene Rating Scheme launches. The Waterside Inn becomes the only restaurant outside of France to hold three Michelin stars for 25 years.

2011: the EU grants the Cornish pasty Protected Geographical Indication status in Europe.

2013: horsemeat is found in beef products sold by major food retailers throughout Britain and Ireland.

2015: last recorded case of BSE in Wales.

2016: Britain votes to leave the European Union in the so-called Brexit Referendum impacting British food companies' relationship with suppliers.

2018: last recorded case of BSE in Scotland, and China ends its ban on British beef imports. The Marine Conservation Society calls on Britons to eat different fish thereby easing pressure on cod and haddock stocks.

2019: the British government launches the Seasonal Worker visa allowing migrant workers to enter Britain temporarily.

2020: Britain enters its first lockdown due to the global Covid-19 pandemic sparking the temporarily closure of "non-essential" businesses including restaurants, cafés, and pubs. In August, the government launches the Eat Out to Help Out scheme aimed at encouraging Britons to frequent their local eateries.

2021: a post-Brexit trade deal allows some EU member states' boats to fish in the waters off Britain. Millions of farm birds are culled due to an outbreak of avian flu.

2022: Russia invades Ukraine and causes food prices to rise as trade and fertilizer supplies are disrupted. Cumbrian restaurant L'Enclume is awarded a third Michelin star.

2023: the British government gives emergency authorization for the use of the banned insecticide thiamethoxam despite dangers to pollinating bees. The coronation quiche is invented to commemorate the coronation of King Charles III and Queen Camilla.

1

Food History

Historically, British food has been influenced by periods of war and invasion, immigration, colonialism, and expanded travel options that have brought a variety of flavors, ingredients, and traditions to the British dining table. More recently, rising living costs, the Covid-19 pandemic, Brexit, and Russia's invasion of Ukraine have impacted Britons' access to food.

Prehistoric British Food

During the Mesolithic period (10,000–4,000 BCE), the earliest Britons existed as hunter-gatherers foraging leaves, shoots, roots, and fruits from edible plants and hunting the wild animals indigenous to Great Britain.

Aurochs—the Prehistoric Cattle of Britain

The landscape of prehistoric Britain was covered in a patchwork of plains, shrublands, and forests, which was an ideal habitat for aurochs—wild European oxen. In summer, the aurochs moved between open plains and sunny glades before migrating to shrublands and woodlands in autumn and winter where they could eat woody vegetation. As human habitation spread throughout Britain, there was less open land for aurochs to roam and eventually they became extinct. Nevertheless, aurochs are the ancestors of Britain's hardier breeds of cattle including the Scottish Highland cattle, which are known for their long horns and shaggy coat, and the English Longhorn, which have curved horns.

Later, the Neolithic period (4000–2200 BCE) saw Britons begin to domesticate cattle, pigs, and sheep, and cultivate crops including wheat and barley. Evidence from Stonehenge, the Neolithic site in Wiltshire, southwest England, shows that flint tools were used to cut beef while pigs were roasted on spits. By the end of the Neolithic period, Britons had become experts at raising animals for meat and milk. Consequently, meat and milk became fundamental to the people's diets and economy. As crop farmers, Neolithic Britons created permanent fields and operated small-scale cereal-processing schemes (Great Britain's earliest field systems date from around 1500 BCE). Despite growing crops, the people still foraged for food and hunted wild animals to eat.

The Food of Roman Britain

When the Romans invaded Great Britain in 43 CE, they brought with them a variety of foods including game animals (rabbits and pheasants), vegetables (onions, garlic, celery), fruits (grapes, figs, olives, dates), and nuts and seeds (walnuts, pine nuts, almonds). The Romans also introduced lentils, pepper, and herbs including thyme, basil, and dill; they also introduced wine to Great Britain.

Before Roman colonialization, Britons had grown crops on a largely subsistence basis. Now, the building of Roman roads allowed food to be transported easily around Great Britain. Consequently, under Roman rule, new foods became widely available. Not only did this availability revolutionize British diets but market gardens and orchards growing cash crops became commonplace in urban areas. However, the new ingredients were adopted far more quickly among wealthier city dwellers than among the rural poor. Uptake was slowest in the remotest parts of Roman Britain, particularly northwestern Britain, though military communities in these areas did eat Roman foods.

Under Roman rule, Britons consumed meat widely with households often owning pigs and prospering from sheep farming. The introduction of new animals, fruits, vegetables, and herbs resulted in the development of a new British farming system as people started to create enclosures around their farms. These enclosures were often in the form of leporaria, gardens in which Romans kept rabbits as food. As well as importing new ingredients, the Romans also brought some of the first recipes to Great Britain including those in *De Re Coquinaria* by Apicius, a set of ten cookery books dating from the fourth or fifth century.

The Middle Ages (476–1500)

Following the departure of the Romans in 410, the Anglo-Saxons (migratory Germanic tribes) arrived in Great Britain around 450 CE. Their arrival meant that Roman villas, farms, and orchards were abandoned allowing animals imported by the Romans to either interbreed with indigenous animals or became wild themselves. Meanwhile, crops grown by the Romans self-seeded and spread across the British landscape.

Recent research suggests that Anglo-Saxon diets were largely cereal-based but included small amounts of meat and cheese though Anglo-Saxon royals were predominantly vegetarian. In the late eighth century, raids by the Vikings (seafaring Scandinavian invaders) began on various sites in Great Britain. Over time, Viking raiders settled across Great Britain, mainly in the east and north of England as well as in the Orkney Isles off Scotland. In these areas, the Vikings became farmers and fishermen. Indeed, the Vikings introduced a Scandinavian love of fish to Great Britain as well as fish-smoking and -drying techniques. This history is evident today for Arbroath Smokies, a smoked haddock that is a specialty of the fishing village of Auchmithie are reputed to have originated among Viking settlers who lived along the coasts of Scotland. The Vikings also developed a British fish trade.

In 1066, Great Britain suffered separate invasions by Harald Hardrada, the king of Norway, and William, the duke of Normandy (also called William the Conqueror) who was descended from Scandinavian settlers in northern France. The Norman Conquest, as William's invasion was known, created close cultural ties between Britain and France. Norman nobles were used to lavish foods that included elements of Mediterranean and Arab cuisines eaten in other areas under Norman rule, and richly spiced Persian food continued to be a favorite of Normans living in Britain. The popularity of Persian food increased further in Britain with the introduction of ingredients brought back to England by soldiers returning from the Crusades (a series of religious wars in the Middle East, 1095–1270). Soldiers returning from the Crusades also brought with them the first sugar to England. Subsequently the use of sugar spread throughout Britain though, initially, sugar was employed predominantly as a spice or medicine rather than as a sweetener. During the reign of John, king of England (1166–1216), spices such as cloves, ginger, and saffron became popular ingredients in British food. While these ingredients had been eaten in Great Britain during Roman times, they vanished from British kitchens under Viking rule. Only with the Normans did these ingredients reappear in Britain.

Bread and cereals were the staple foods of the Middle Ages. The poor tended to eat barley, oats, and rye as wheat was used to make white bread and porridge, which were eaten by the rich. Wheat was reserved for the rich as it was expensive to produce, thriving only in manure-rich soil. Manchet or Pandemain (lord's bread) was the finest leaven bread of the Middle Ages. However, as manchet was made of stoneground wheat sieved twice through a cloth, it was labor-intensive to create and thus extremely expensive to produce. Therefore, manchet was eaten only by the highest echelons of society and thus became a status symbol among those able to afford it.

Meanwhile, the medieval poor had to settle for growing rye and barley that produced dark, heavy bread. Maslin bread made from a combination of grains such as rye and barley was a commonly eaten bread of the Middle Ages. The bread, which derived its name from the French word *miscelin* (mixture), was eaten by servants and poorer families. Slices of stale maslin bread were also used as a type of plate called a trencher. When a poor grain harvest occurred, the poor Britons would include peas and foraged acorns in their bread.

Pottage, a thick stew-soup, was another staple food of the Middle Ages. The ingredients of pottage depended on which crops a peasant was able to grow on the land around their home.

The main meat of peasants of the Middle Ages was pork. This is because pigs were cheap to keep as they were able to find their own food in the form of foraged acorns. Also, pigs could be slaughtered throughout the year, meaning they were a year-round source of meat. Peasants did not waste any part of the animals they killed including the blood, which they used to make black pudding (blood sausage). Deer, boar, and rabbits lived in woodland surrounding most peasant villages, but these animals tended to be the property of local landowners, and peasants were not allowed to hunt them legally. Many nobles did, however, allow peasants to hunt on their land for small animals such as hedgehogs and squirrels, as well as to fish for small fish such as dace from rivers flowing through their estates. As most medieval villages were located near rivers, fish represented a reliable food source. Many nobles owned fishponds stocked with trout and salmon, but these fish were eaten only by the nobility. Meanwhile, Britons living in cities lacked land on which to cultivate or forage for food. Consequently, cities had to import their food from the countryside and this in turn led to the development of the public eating-houses and food shops in cities such as London.

Elizabethan Food

In Elizabethan Britain (1558–1603), food and drink were remarkably diverse. Diets were rich in meat, and people enjoyed intensely flavored sauces made using Asian ingredients, as well as pastries and cakes that were often eaten between the savory courses. As food storage and preservation were still problematic, fresh produce was either grown at home or bought at local markets. Large estates were usually self-sufficient, however, for they produced their own meat, fish, bread, and dairy products. Wealthier Elizabethans were better equipped to store their food for they could store grains and preserved foods in airtight chests as well as in pantries (boxes with air-holes used for foods such as cheese). The wealthiest Elizabethans also employed cooks to prepare their food unlike most Elizabethans who either cooked their own food in their home kitchen or used communal ovens to cook bread-dough they had prepared at home. People also used the communal ovens to cook pottage. Elizabethan home kitchens often comprised a brass cooking pot, iron pan, and spit that were used to boil, roast, or fry food over an open fire, as well as utensils and serving dishes made from wood, clay, or pewter. Food was also sometimes baked in a closed brick oven much like the modern pizza oven.

Most poorer Elizabethans worked in agriculture and had their own plot of land that they used to grow vegetables and fruit and rear poultry though they also bought food at local markets. In London, there were markets throughout the city, so people did not have to travel far for their daily food shopping. The markets were open six days per week, from 6 a.m. to 11 a.m. and 1 p.m. to 5 p.m. On Sundays, the shoppers could only buy such perishable foods as fruit and vegetables.

The diets of the upper and lower classes varied in the amount of meat eaten for the upper classes had access to fresh meat for much of the year as well as salted, smoked, dried, cured, and pickled meat in winter. Preserving meat was important for animals were often slaughtered before winter as it was difficult to feed them during winter months. The upper classes also had a greater range of meats to eat including beef, pork, lamb, duck, goose, pigeon, venison, and pheasant. Elizabethans also ate swan, blackbird, and peacock. Almost all parts of slaughtered animals were eaten including the trotters and heads. Fish such as cod, mackerel, and herring were eaten frequently by all Elizabethans as were eels, mussels, crabs, shrimps, and oysters. In coastal areas, seafood was a cheap food whereas in inland areas seafood was considered a luxury eaten only by the rich. Usually, fish was fried or poached or was preserved by salting.

In a move to support the fishing industry, in 1563, Queen Elizabeth I made it the law that Elizabethans eat fish on Wednesdays, Fridays, and Saturdays as well as during all of Lent. If a person wished to eat meat on a day designated for fish, then they could buy a "flesh-eater's licence" in order to circumvent the law though these did not permit the consumption of beef or veal between Michaelmas and May 1. To prevent Britons from becoming bored of fish, the definition of "fish" was extremely broad and encompassed poultry, game, and veal. When meat was eaten, it was often cooked in ale, almond milk, wine, or verjuice (a highly acidic liquid made from unripe fruit such as crab apples or grapes). Stews made from meat and fish were popular and tended to be flavored with mustard or spices such as cloves, ginger, mace, and cinnamon. Other popular stew ingredients included onions, fennel, woody herbs, and thickening ingredients such as barley or oats. Flowers such as marigolds, violets, and primroses were used to add color and flavor. In 1585, the law against eating meat on Wednesdays was repealed while simultaneously people began to eat more meat and less fish. By 1593, most Elizabethans began to eat meat during Lent and on Fridays and Saturdays.

It was usual for Elizabethan diners to eat cheese, honey, or nuts such as hazelnuts and walnuts after their main course. Elizabethans enjoyed cherries, plums, apples, pears, mulberries, and raspberries but rarely ate fruit raw. The rich also enjoyed expensive fruits such as peaches and pomegranates.

Wealthy Elizabethans also enjoyed buttery pastries, biscuits, and gingerbread, made using refined sugar now available from the Americas. Often banquets featured spectacular dishes that let nobles display their wealth. These dishes included jellies dyed using natural colorings such as sandalwood, saffron, and boiled blood. Elaborate ornamental sugar sculptures called sotiltees (or subtleties) shaped as castles, ships, and celebrities were also popular with wealthy hosts. Elizabethans also used sugar to make jam, marzipan, and candy. Wealthy Elizabethans tended to eat a sit-down breakfast consisting of porridge, bread, cheese, fruit, and meat while the poor ate leftovers or bread with butter. An Elizabethan dining table was set with a large wooden plate, a food bowl, a bowl for waste, and a serving spoon. Forks were not yet used as most food was cut up before being served. Diners brought their own knives to meals.

The climatic event known as the Little Ice Age (a period of regional cooling from the early fourteenth century to the mid-nineteenth century that resulted in prolonged cold winters) meant some vitamin-rich foods became scarce, so people ate foraged vegetables and fruits. Crop failures and poor harvests, as occurred in the 1590s, led to starvation among the poor in many areas of Britain as scarcity meant grain had to be imported and consequently tripled in price. The situation was compounded by the fact that the booming wool trade meant British farming had come to focus on sheep farming. The focus on sheep farming increased hunger among the poor as fields were dedicated to rearing sheep rather than growing crops. At the same time, land enclosure became more common. In earlier times, farming revolved around large, open fields that allowed tenant farmers to use random strips of land. From the twelfth century onward, however, farmland became enclosed, meaning land holdings were amalgamated into fields owned or rented by individuals. The land enclosure system came to replace the traditional open field system: thus, the fields once owned by peasant farmers morphed into smaller enclosed tracts of land operated as profitable farming units. Thus, the enclosures forced the poorest members of rural society, agricultural laborers, to leave the countryside and seek work in towns. The ill-effects of land enclosed resulted in the enactment of the Poor Law of 1601 that consolidated earlier acts and laws of poor relief.

Georgian Food

The Georgian era (1714 to around 1837) was named after Kings George I, George II, George III, and George IV each of whom belonged to the House of Hanover, a royal house that originated in Germany. The foreignness of the royal family reflected that during this period, Great Britain experienced a great deal of immigration from Northern Europe. The immigration caused a cultural shift that filtered down to the foods eaten by all classes. French seed companies started to send catalogs to Britain so that estate owners could grow foreign varieties of fruit, vegetables, and edible flowers in kitchen gardens and orchards. Continental Europe also influenced British food in ways that are still felt today such as the eating of French *ris-de-veau* (sweetbreads), German sausages, and Dutch pancakes. From the late 1600s onward, many English aristocrats sent their cooks to France in order to broaden their culinary repertoire and explore French ingredients. The Georgian era was also a time of increasing domestic migration as landowners began to enclose more land for use in commercial farming. Consequently, peasants struggled to find land to grow food and had to move to cities in order to find work in newly created factories. Often these factories were located in the Midlands area of England or in the south of the country. Here, the workers lived in overcrowded slums where their diet consisted chiefly of bread, potatoes, and oats washed down with gin and other spirits.

Despite the trend for Continental European food, much of the British middle class preferred plainer food and opted for roast meats. During the Georgian era, various types of meat were eaten, sometimes in the same meal, with beef, venison, mutton, bacon, rabbit, goose, pigeons, duck, and partridge all being popular. Fish was also eaten, with lobster and oysters being cheap foods because they were so numerous in the waters around Britain. It was also at this time that a huge range of puddings, both sweet and savory, became prevalent in British cuisine. Often the puddings, which were usually baked or boiled, were filled with meat or game and came in pasty made with suet or butter, even though butter was expensive. Soups and stews were also popular. One popular dish was white soup made from veal stock, cream, almonds, and rice, while London's street food sellers sold pea soup. Meanwhile, pease pudding became traditional in northeast England. The Georgians also enjoyed desserts such as syllabub, a wine or cider drink sweetened with nutmeg, milk, and cream, while ice cream, which had been available in Britain since the late 1600s, was popularized during the mid-1700s by French and Italian artisans who established shops in London. Favorite Georgian ice cream flavors included brown bread, elderflower, jasmine, and barberry.

Georgian breakfasts were accompanied by either tea, which was now the national drink, or hot chocolate. Previously, people would eat a late morning meal of tea or coffee, bread, meat, and eggs. As the working and middle classes became more established in society, the timing of mealtimes changed so that a meal at 8 a.m. or 9 a.m. was needed to allow tradesmen and professionals to eat before leaving home for work. This morning meal was eaten in a household's drawing room or dining room and featured fruity spiced breads, cakes, or hot, buttered caraway seed buns though from the 1770s people in northern England also started to eat English-style muffins for breakfast. Kippers (smoked herrings) were also a popular breakfast dish. There tended to be a long gap between breakfast and dinner so wealthier Georgians developed the concept of afternoon tea for this allowed them both to satisfy their hunger and exhibit their ornate tea sets.

New winter livestock feeding systems together with improved breeding methods meant that meat became more plentiful and cheaper to buy. Meanwhile, improved transport networks allowed regional foods and seafood such as oysters to be carried across the country. Sugar and spices were also transported, allowing people to invent pickles and preserves. Sugar was also used to sweeten drinks such as tea, coffee, hot chocolate, and wine.

The Georgians' rich diet resulted in a variety of health issues particularly gout, which was linked to wealthy Georgians' love of foods rich in purine (gout-causing chemical compounds) such as caviar, anchovies, shellfish, and offal as well as sugary food and drink. Also detrimental to Georgian health was that many of their foods contained poisonous substances. For example, copper and lead were added to pickles, cheese, and chocolate, and alum, a mineral salt, was added to bread to made it appear whiter despite the fact it could cause respiratory issues. Floor sweepings were used to bulk out ground pepper, while soil was added to coffee for the same reason. Food adulteration continued to be a problem into the nineteenth century prompting the British government to pass the Adulteration of Food and Drink Act (1860). Although the act was largely resisted by food producers, in 1872, the government established official inspectors invested with the power to test food and impose substantial fines on producers who adulterated food and drink.

Victorian Food

The Victorian era was a time of industrial and scientific development. The growth of steam railways allowed people to move from the countryside to cities where the migrants worked in factories producing foods and other goods. The railways also made it possible for food to be transported easily. The development of steam ships meant that Victorian Britons could enjoy a far wider range of food than had been available to previous generations for food could now be moved quicker across longer distances. In the 1800s, British merchant ships carried goods across the British Empire, and by the 1870s, the introduction of the more energy-efficient triple expansion engine propelled ships over longer distances meaning they could bring foods to Britain from even further afield. From the 1880s, refrigerated meat transportation was possible so Britain could import meat from the United States. Consequently, meat became much cheaper, and for the first time, it became a regular feature of British diets across the class spectrum. The earliest combined roller and stone mill in Britain was probably that used by Fison and Co. of Ipswich in 1862, though by 1868, similar mills were used in Bristol and Liverpool. The advent of roller mills allowed white flour, and thus white bread, to be made as well as the first British flour to be exported to America.

The growth of the British Empire continued to influence British food. For instance, kedgeree, a British take on the Indian rice and lentil dish *Khichri*, was brought to Britain by the staff of the East India Company, an English company that was granted a royal charter to exploit Britain's trade with Asia, especially

India, and which ruled the Indian subcontinent from 1757 to 1858. Subsequently, kedgeree became a traditional British breakfast meal.

By the 1840s, Indian food was hugely popular in Britain, and curry was the popular way for Britons to use up cold meat. Kedgeree was not the only Victorian breakfast innovation. At the start of the Victorian era, breakfasts often comprised cold meats and cheese, but later in the era, these breakfast foods were replaced by fish dishes, porridge, or by eggs and bacon—what is now considered a "full English." By the end of the era, however, these dishes had themselves been superseded by breakfast cereals. As well as developing breakfast as a meal, the Victorians also introduced the concept of the two- or three-course meal—starter, main course, dessert—during which courses arrive one at a time in a certain order (previously all courses arrived simultaneously).

Cheap, seasonal vegetables such as onions, cabbages, carrots, and turnips were sold at Victorian markets while the main fruits sold were apples in winter and cherries in summer. The Victorians also enjoyed eating nuts, particularly chestnuts that were roasted and sold by street vendors who also sold rice milk, ginger beer, and sheep trotters. In cities, fishmongers, milkmen, and greengrocers delivered straight to people's homes but as this service was unavailable in rural areas, country folk continued to live off the land. Victorians living in coastal areas ate fish and seafood including herrings, eels, oysters, cockles, and whelks. At some point during Victorian times, Great Britain's first fish-and-chip shop opened. In 1863, while a fish-and-chip shop that opened in Mossely in northern England claimed to be the first in the world, in London's East End, a Jewish immigrant, Joseph Malin, is also reputed to have opened his fish-and-chip shop in the 1860s.

As home refrigeration was not common, Victorians tended to eat either fresh, seasonal vegetables or ones that had been preserved. The patenting of the canning process in 1810 allowed for the preservation of a wide range of produce including stews, fruit, soups, and vegetables without the need for salting or pickling. By the 1860s, tinned meat was widely available. At first, this tinned meat was predominantly fat with chunks of meat incorporated into it. This meat was sold as a cheap meat option and was eaten by the poor. Other long-life products also evolved during this period including condensed milk, dried eggs, and bottled sauces. The advent of new food preservation methods led to the invention of new kitchen gadgets, and numerous types of kitchen equipment were developed during the Victorian era. For example, after Britain's first large-scale meat-canning factory opened in 1865, the tin opener became ubiquitous in middle-class British kitchens. Cast iron and tin-plated kitchen equipment became popular, and kitchens were crammed with mass-produced gadgets including graters, potato peelers, jelly molds, and mincers.

Victorian kitchens were often large and equipped with coal-fired ovens that for the first time allowed cooks to control the temperature at which foods were cooked. Temperature regulation meant that home cooks could now make dishes that required nuanced cooking. One consequence of this development in home cookery was that celebrity chefs such as Marie-Antoine Carême (1783–1833, the pioneer of haute cuisine) became revered. Moreover, middle-class families started to acquire cookbooks. Two of the most successful cookbooks of the era were by the English writers Eliza Acton and Isabella Beeton.

Acton's *Modern Cookery for Private Families* (1845) was a bestseller running through thirteen editions by 1853. However, its success was eclipsed by Beeton's *Mrs Beeton's Book of Household Management* (1861), which was innovative for giving specific quantities and precise cooking times for recipes. The huge success of *Mrs Beeton's Book of Household Management* is notable for initiating a new cult of domesticity that shaped middle-class Victorian life.

Meanwhile, many people lived in slums without ovens and existed on diets comprising mostly bread, gruel, and broth made from boiled bones. Unsurprisingly, many slum children were malnourished, anemic, and suffered from stunted growth. Many poorer Victorians ate meat only on Sundays, a habit that led to the tradition still enjoyed today of the "Sunday roast" whereby a joint of meat such as beef or pork is roasted, then shared with family. The meat is accompanied by vegetables, especially roast potatoes, and gravy. The poorest Victorian families could not usually afford a roasting joint, however, so they instead ate offal, such as liver, tongue, or heart. Disparities in diet depended not

---

Mrs. Beeton

Born Isabella Mayson in London in 1836, Beeton was educated in Germany. In 1856, she married Samuel, a wealthy publisher, and started to write articles on cookery and household management for his publications. In 1861, the first part of *Mrs Beeton's Book of Household Management* was published in Samuel's publication *Englishwoman's Domestic Magazine* to immediate success. In its first year of publication *Mrs Beeton's Book of Household Management* sold more than 60,000 copies, and by 1868, it had sold almost two million copies. In 1865, Beeton died of an infection following the birth of her fourth child.

just on class, but also on location for Victorians living in rural area tended to eat better than city dwellers as they had greater access to fresh meat, vegetables, and milk.

Wartime Food

When the First World War erupted in 1914, Britain imported over 60 percent of its food and 80 percent of its wheat. Before the war began, the cultivation of the American plains and the falling costs of steam ship transportation meant grain prices were low. Consequently, it made sense for Britain to import American grain for this allowed British farmers to switch from arable agriculture to more profitable dairy and meat farming. However, when Germany began to sink commercial, food-laden ships, Britain's reliance on imported food led to food shortages. These shortages worsened in 1916 when the wheat harvest was poor and potato crops failed in Scotland and England. The low crop yields caused food prices to rise rapidly meaning some foods became unaffordable to many people. The food situation worsened when, in 1917, Germany declared a policy of unrestricted submarine warfare. The policy was intended to create a food crisis in Great Britain for it left British merchant ships carrying food imports at increased risk of being destroyed. The shortages of imported food were exacerbated by the fact that at the outbreak of the war, many British men working in the farming industry had entered the armed services thereby leaving the country short of agricultural workers. In response to the shortage of farm workers, in 1917, the Women's Land Army was formed to provide extra voluntary farm labor, with so-called Land Girls replacing the absent farm workers. Food shortages were exacerbated further by the fact that some food available in Britain was sent away to feed soldiers fighting overseas. To combat the food shortages, the British government began propaganda campaigns that urged Britons to grow their own food as a patriotic act that would bolster the nation's food reserves. The campaigns led to an increase in the amount of public land given over to allotments for the growing of food. Since many city dwellers did not know how to grow vegetables, "model allotments" were established in such London parks as Regent's Park and Kensington Gardens. The model allotments saw an experienced horticulturist show how a small plot of land could produce fresh vegetables all year round. Allotments were intended to produce easy-to-grow, bulky crops with high nutritional and calorific content. Fruit-growing was not encouraged on the basis that it can take time for fruit trees to produce fruits.

The year 1917 also saw the introduction of a voluntary food rationing campaign intended to reduce people's food consumption and food wastage. To this end, Britons became creative in the kitchen, inventing meals such as potted cheese, which consisted of cheese scraps combined with mustard, then baked and served on toast. At the same time, filling dishes such as toad-in-the-hole, mutton stew, fish pie, and treacle pudding became favorites. Since 1906, many schools have served pupils filling lunches, but schools were impacted by wartime food shortages and so had to reduce the amounts of food they could give to children. This meant some children went hungry because for most of the week many poor families could only afford one meal per day and so children existed by eating bread and jam washed down with tea.

Under the voluntary rationing scheme, bread, cakes, meat, poultry, and sugar were all rationed. However, the scheme was not enough to stop food shortages, and while wealthier people could still afford food, the poor were becoming increasingly malnourished. In order to make the situation fairer, in 1918, the government introduced rationing that meant all people were only allowed certain amounts of certain foods. Under the scheme, everyone in Britain was issued with a ration book and had to register with local food shops. Despite the rationing, fresh fruit and vegetables, meat and bread were difficult to buy, and there were often long lines outside food shops. While this rationing meant that some wealthier Britons had less food than usual, many poor people found they had more food than in prewar times. In January 1918, sugar became the first food to be rationed. By the end of April that year, however, meat, butter, cheese, and margarine had also been rationed. Some foods continued to be in short supply even after the end of the war. For example, butter was rationed until 1920.

The advent of the Second World War (1939–44) signaled a return to food rationing for in 1940, the British government reintroduced food rationing in order to make sure everyone had their fair share of food at a time when some foods were in short supply. Initially, basic foods such as sugar, meat, fat, bacon, and cheese were rationed but the list of rationed foods grew throughout the war. The scheme was overseen by the Ministry of Food, which issued all adults and children with a ration book filled with an allowance of coupons. The coupons had to be presented when food was bought. Once food was bought, the shopkeeper marked the purchase in the customer's ration book. Special dispensation was given to people who might require extra food including mine workers, members of the Women's Land Army and members of the armed forces. Some foods, such as tinned goods, dried fruits, cereals, and biscuits, were rationed under a points system—the number of points allocated to each of these food items changed according to their availability and consumer demand. Allowances of milk and eggs were prioritized to the neediest, especially children and pregnant women. Rationing was enforced strictly, and anyone caught cheating the system faced a fine or imprisonment. Nonetheless, a food black market evolved as people paid greatly inflated prices to unscrupulous shopkeepers who kept back supplies for those prepared to pay for them. Additionally, petty criminals known as "spivs" traded in foods obtained by dubious means.

Some foods were not rationed, however. Whale meat was available to buy without a ration book ("off ration") but it was unpopular with Britons as it tasted bland and smelled unpleasant. Similarly, the National Loaf was introduced across Britain in 1942. This was a government-regulated brown bread made from National Wheatmeal Flour. White bread was banned under rationing, but while the National Loaf was praised by nutritionists, Britons had by now become accustomed to white bread and did not enjoy the National Loaf's gritty texture. Fruit and vegetables were never rationed but they were often in short supply, with imported foreign fruits particularly hard to find. To combat a shortage of vegetables, the government encouraged Britons to grow them at home and in allotments, many of which were created in public parks, as in the First World War. This grow-your-own scheme became known as "Dig for Victory." Bananas were one of the foods that were not available at all during the Second World War, and there are many anecdotal stories of British children eating bananas with the skin on postwar because having never seen a banana, they did not know that banana skins should be removed before eating. Oranges, lemons, pineapples, and grapes were also imported and so, like bananas, many wartime children did not get to try these fruits until after the war.

The end of wartime did not see an end to rationing. Indeed, bread, which had not been rationed during the war, was rationed in July 1946 when the British government introduced bread rationing in order to prevent a famine in Germany. Post–Second World War, Germany lay in ruins and Berliners had difficulty in finding food amid the destruction. In order to start rebuilding Germany, the Allies split the country between the United States, Great Britain, and Russia while Berlin was divided into zones—the Soviets controlled the eastern zone while the United States, UK, and France controlled the west. In June 1948, the United States and Great Britain introduced a new currency, the Deutschmark, to the zones that they controlled. This led to the Soviets blockading all routes into Allied-controlled areas of Berlin, thereby cutting off food supplies. By rationing bread, Britain reduced its grain imports meaning American grain could be diverted to feed Berlin. Ultimately, British bread rationing ended in

July 1948. In 1952, tea came off ration, and eggs, cream, sugar, and sweets were off ration from 1953. From 1954, cheese, butter, cooking oil, fresh meat, and bacon were freely available.

Despite the food shortages Britain experienced during the World Wars, it is generally believed that Britons have never eaten more healthily than during these periods. This is because Britons who had plentiful food previously were forced to eat less fat and sugar than before while people who had suffered a poor diet previously were now able to increase their intake of protein and vitamins as they received the same food as the rest of the population. At the same time, the government intervened to make Britons healthier through food—pregnant women and children were given free cod liver oil and milk, and calcium was added to flour in order to stop rickets. Additionally, all schoolchildren were given a weekly dose of VIROL, a nutrient-rich malt extract.

Postwar Food

In the 1950s, British food tended to be plain and thrifty, with the so-called meat and two veg (a meal consisting of meat and two types of vegetables) being the staple diet of most families. With Britain experiencing postwar debt, most British families did not eat out often at restaurants. This situation started to change in 1954, however, when the first Wimpy Bar opened in London. As a British chain of eateries akin to American burger bars, Wimpy Bars catered for the newest consumer group—teenagers. Increased immigration also led to the opening of restaurants that served food from various minority communities. While the first Chinese restaurant had opened in London in 1908, a wave of refugees from Hong Kong led to a slew of Chinese restaurants opening in the late 1950s and 1960s. The food served at such restaurants was a world away from the plain food Britons ate ordinarily. The 1960s also saw a steep rise in the number of Indian restaurants in Britain, especially in London and southeast England. At the end of the 1960s, the British economy boomed, and people experienced a dramatic rise in their standard of living. Consequently, Britons began to holiday in Europe as package holidays made overseas travel affordable to people of all classes. During their travels, British holidaymakers encountered new foods and ingredients. Toward the end of the 1960s, dinner parties became popular in Britain as these allowed people to feature foreign dishes they had encountered on holiday. Around this time, restaurant chains such as the Berni Inns began to open across Britain. These restaurants served staple 1970s meals of melon or prawn cocktail to start, steak or a mixed grill for a main course, and Black Forest gâteau for dessert. By the mid-1970s, Britons had begun to eat out regularly.

Since the 1970s, societal changes have seen an increase in the number of single-person households, one-parent families, and women working outside of the home. Such changes have influenced people's eating and food shopping habits with convenience becoming highly prized. For this reason, supermarkets monopolized British food shopping, most households came to own a microwave, and ready-meals became a cornerstone of British diets. Developments in canning and freezing techniques were accompanied by the creation of new ways to preserve food, such as the invention of chemical additives, enhancers, and preservatives. These innovations allowed shoppers to buy food that lasted for a conveniently long time. Faster transport also meant that imported food could reach shoppers more quickly and from further afield.

Another major food innovation arrived in the 1980s when the high street retailer Marks & Spencer introduced prepacked sandwiched in its stores, a move that revolutionized British lunches. The first sandwiches available were salmon and tomato, salmon and cucumber, and egg and cress with prices starting at 43p (around 52¢). Originally, shop staff made the sandwiches, but within one year, demand was so strong that Marks & Spencer had to ask three suppliers to industrialize the sandwich-making process. In response to the sandwiches' success, other food retailers soon launched their own sandwich ranges. By 1990, the British sandwich industry was worth £1 billion. On the back of the prepacked sandwich success, in the early 1990s, Marks & Spencer opened its first dedicated "food to go" section equipped with its own tills and checkouts. This innovation prefigured the layout of most contemporary supermarkets. During the 1990s, the sandwich industry trebled in size and nowadays, Britons buy around four billion sandwiches per year. The sandwich remains the main driver of the UK's £20 billion food-to-go industry, which is the largest in Europe.

In recent years, Britain has weathered several food scares. For instance, in 1988, the undersecretary of state for health, Edwina Currie, claimed that most British eggs were contaminated with the salmonella bacteria, something that angered farmers, politicians, and egg producers. Currie's pronouncement sparked public outcry and caused a 60 percent slump in egg sales. Currie resigned from government, but as a result of her comment, hundreds of millions of eggs were destroyed and two million hens were slaughtered. The controversy also meant that thousands of British chicken farmers faced bankruptcy while some Britons became uneasy about eating egg-based foods. Amid the crisis, the British government mounted a major compensation package for egg producers, and in 1998, the Lion Quality Mark Scheme was introduced that requires all hens to be vaccinated against *Salmonella enteritidis*. Today, all Class A British eggs (i.e., eggs sold intact in their shells) have to be marked with a "red lion" stamp and a code that shows the type of farming system that produced the eggs (such as organic or free-range), the eggs' country of origin, and the farm production unit from which they came. Almost all British eggs fall under the British Lion Scheme, which is now considered Britain's most successful food safety scheme for it is responsible for a dramatic reduction in the presence of salmonella in British eggs. The scheme's success means the Food Standards Agency deems eggs stamped with the red lion to be safe to eat runny, or even raw, by vulnerable groups including pregnant women, the elderly, and children. Previously, these groups were advised not to eat undercooked or raw eggs because the potential salmonella bacteria in eggs could cause them serious illness.

In the late 1980s, an outbreak of bovine spongiform encephalopathy (BSE, a usually fatal disease of the central nervous system sometimes referred to as mad cow disease) began that led, in 1989, to offal being banned for human consumption. The human form of BSE, known as variant Creutzfeldt-Jakob disease (vCJD), is fatal for it attacks the brain gradually, often remaining dormant for decades. The contraction of vCJD can be linked to eating contaminated meat. The BSE epidemic peaked in 1992–3 when 180,000 cattle were infected with BSE and 4.4 million cattle were slaughtered in order to try to stop the spread of the disease. Since 1995, when vCJD was identified, 178 deaths have been attributed to the disease, and it is believed that one in 2,000 Britons carry the disease. Once the link between BSE and vCJD was discovered, strict controls were introduced to protect the public from BSE. For instance, since the BSE crisis came about because British cattle were fed meat and bonemeal infected with the disease, today brain and spinal cord are not included in cattle feed. Additionally, it was made illegal to sell certain cuts of beef. As a result of these measures, only a few cases of BSE occur in Britain with the last recorded case in Wales being in 2015 and one in Scotland in 2018. Nevertheless, many countries stopped importing British beef, with China only ending their ban in 2018.

In 2001, Britain suffered a disastrous outbreak of foot-and-mouth disease, a highly infectious, often fatal illness that affects cloven-footed animals such as cattle, sheep, and pigs. In total, there were around 2,000 cases of the disease in farms across Britain with Cumbria in the far north of England being the worst affected area. The first case of foot-and-mouth disease was detected in an abattoir in Essex, eastern England, in February 2001. Over subsequent days, several more cases were found across England. Later, it was discovered that pigs involved in each case originated from the same farm. Over the next few weeks, more cases were discovered in England, Wales, and Scotland, and so the Ministry of Agriculture, Fisheries and Food (MAFF) adopted a policy of contiguous cull meaning all animals within 3,000 m (1.9 miles) of a known case had to be slaughtered. The MAFF policy was that if an infected carcass from a cull could not be disposed on-site, then it had to be taken to a central rendering plant. However, this meant infected corpses were taken through disease-free areas. Soon the disease reached a peak, and MAFF decided to try to stop the spread of the disease by banning the sale of British pigs, sheep, and cattle until the disease was eradicated, continued the cull, and burning the resultant animal carcasses. There were also extensive measures to prevent humans carrying the disease on their clothing and vehicles.

Ultimately, it took over 7 months of culling to control the disease . The disease devastated British farming because to bring the disease under control, more than six million pigs, cattle, and sheep had to be culled on over 10,000 farms. The outbreak's total cost to Britain was estimated to be more than £8 billion. Many lessons were learned from the outbreak, however. For example, today it is forbidden to feed farm animals with swill (untreated kitchen waste and scraps) as this is thought to have been the cause of the outbreak. Also, livestock movement is strictly recorded and controlled. Crucially, the development of gene-sequencing technology means scientists can track the movement of viruses and thus deduce patterns of infection. The ability to track a disease proved vital in 2007 when foot-and-mouth disease reappeared. This time the outbreak was halted before it could become widespread.

At the start of 2013, following routine food testing by the Food Safety Authority of Ireland, horsemeat was discovered in beef products sold by major food retailers throughout Britain and Ireland. This became known as the horsemeat scandal. In February that year, British company Findus and two leading supermarkets reported that horsemeat had been found in various meat products, all of which were produced by a French supplier. Following these revelations, the European Union (EU) launched a random testing program to check for horsemeat in processed beef products. The results showed that around 5 percent of samples contained horse DNA, thus indicating the problem was EU-wide. However, the scandal dominated the British media particularly as the consumption of horsemeat is generally considered culturally unacceptable in Britain unlike in some EU states where horsemeat is eaten routinely. In the weeks after the discovery, British consumer trust in beef products plummeted as did trust in processed meat products in general. Indeed, 7 percent of British shoppers stopped buying meat altogether. Six months after the crisis broke, the British government commissioned an independent review into the scandal. The review produced many recommendations and suggested that food fraud should become a crime when the fraud constitutes an organized activity rather than random acts by individuals.

The horsemeat scandal prompted a dramatic change in British food retailers' attitudes for they now take great pride in the transparency of food production. For example, supermarkets provide information on their meat product testing regime, and in many instances, food packaging indicates the name of meat suppliers. Since the horsemeat scandal, there has not been another major meat-related crisis in British food. However, there have been other food fraud incidents involving herbs, spices, and honey. Perhaps as a result of such food scandals, it is unsurprising that in the last few years Britain has seen a strong trend toward eating seasonal, locally produced food.

In recent years, the use of food banks has become widespread in Britain. Food banks are organized by various volunteers, churches, and charities so there is no comprehensive dataset on food banks in Britain. In 2000, the anti-poverty charity Trussell Trust opened its first food bank and now runs over half of food banks across Britain, providing food parcels to people who are referred to it by health professionals, social services, and other agencies. The Independent Food Aid Network represents the rest of Britain's food banks. Across the UK, there are over 1,400 Trussell Trust food banks while there are also at least 1,172 independent food banks. Traditionally, food banks receive most of their food in three ways: surplus food redistributed directly by supermarkets or indirectly via organizations such as FareShare (a national network of charitable food redistributors); items donated by people using in-shop donation baskets, directly to food banks, or through organizations such as church groups; and food purchased wholesale by the food bank themselves.

Both the number of food banks and the quantity of food parcels they distribute has generally increased over recent years: for instance, between April 2018 and March 2019, Trussell Trust's food banks distributed 1.6 million food parcels, which was 26 times more than in 2010. During the period 2021–2, the highest distribution of Trussell Trust food parcels was in London, followed by the southeast and northwest of England. Much of the use of food banks can be attributed to cuts in social security initiated by the British government in 2010.

2020 Onward

The most recent British food history is dominated by the Covid-19 pandemic, Brexit, Russia's invasion of Ukraine, and the so-called cost of living crisis (the ongoing period, started in 2021, in which prices for many essential goods in Britain started to increase faster than household income).

At various times during the Covid-19 pandemic, the British government instigated lockdowns to combat the virus. England entered its first national lockdown on March 23 with similar measures implemented simultaneously in Scotland, Wales, and Northern Ireland. Restrictions varied across the countries that comprise Great Britain for health is an issue devolved to each of the home nations. Consequently, restrictions were imposed separately by each government though the central British government acted on behalf of England. At various times, the lockdowns saw all "non-essential" businesses closed including restaurants, cafés, and pubs, and people were ordered to leave home only for essential reasons, such as food shopping.

According to a government report, lockdown-exacerbated food insecurity in Britain for the number of adults who were food insecure quadrupled during the lockdown, and more than three million Britons reported that someone in their household experienced hunger during the first 3 weeks of the first lockdown. This period also saw British food banks experience a rapid rise in demand. The Food Standards Agency found that food insecurity was particularly problematic for younger age groups, households that included at least one a child, and people who had a physical or mental health condition. Indeed, the Trussell Trust reported an 89 percent increase in need for emergency food parcels in April 2020, compared to the same time the year before, including a 107 percent increase in food parcels given to children. Meanwhile, food banks within the IFAN experienced a 175 percent increase in food request during this period. However, food charities and food banks found their supply chains were challenged because at the start of the pandemic, some Britons panic-bought goods and stockpiled food. The stockpiling jeopardized the food security of low-income households as they were financially unable to hoard food and so found that when they went to buy groceries only premium versions of products that they could not afford were available in the shops. Poor availability of budget-friendly supermarket foods forced many low-income households to obtain food from food banks or forego food entirely. Researchers from the Food Foundation healthy eating charity found 14 percent of those asked said a household member had reduced their food intake or missed meals because they could not access or afford food during lockdown. Adults with young children were among the groups most affected by this issue for lockdown food shortages together with school closures meant children who were eligible for free school meals (all infants in education as well as those whose parents receive certain state benefits) did not receive food at school. Low-income families with children were provided with vouchers to buy food from supermarkets, but the usefulness of the vouchers depended on the availability of food in those shops.

Under lockdown, Britons made fewer grocery trips but when did they go shopping, they spent more on groceries and bought different foods as they adapted to lockdown life. Indeed, in the 4 weeks to April 19, 2020, grocery sales in Britain increased by 5.5 percent year-on-year. The lockdown also brought about changes in Britain's consumer behavior for many people spent more time home baking with such a craze for baking banana bread that by the end of April 2020, British web searches for banana bread has risen by 525 percent, and there were more than 45,000 Instagram posts about baking banana bread. Banana bread fever was centered around London and southeast England, where 45 percent of people asked said they had baked the cake, compared with less than 25 percent in northwest England. Banana bread baking was also more popular with women than men. Lockdown baking mania also resulted in a surge in sales of suet (up 115 percent) and sugar (up 46 percent) over the four-week to April 19, 2020.

Another lockdown behavior change was a boom in online grocery shopping. The greatest increase was among older shoppers with Britons aged over 65 years spending 94 percent more on online food deliveries than they did the year before. Sales of alcohol also increased, as Britons replaced pub visits with virtual socializing. Researchers have discovered that Britons who drank alcohol most often pre-lockdown drank more alcohol more often during lockdown while Britons who already drank the least cut down their alcohol consumption the most.

One especially controversial episode after the first lockdown was Eat Out to Help Out (EOtHO). EOtHO was a government scheme to boost the hospitality industry that had been forced to shut down during lockdown and saw the government subsidize food and non-alcoholic drinks ordered at participating restaurants, cafés, pubs, at 50 percent up to the value of £10 per person per order. The scheme ran weekly (Monday to Wednesday) during August 2020. While the scheme was popular with many diners and hospitality business owners, it was controversial as it cost the government around £500 million yet produced only short-lived economic benefits. Some public health experts also suggest that EOtHO may have contributed to a rise in Covid infections in August and

September 2020 as people flocked to hospitality venues to take advantage of the discounts.

The pandemic revealed not only stark inequalities in the availability of food in Britain but also food distribution issues including an overdependence on just-in-time supply chains (which move produce just before it is needed) that source produce from overseas. The pandemic highlighted how heavily reliant Britain is on food from overseas especially from EU countries, such as Spain and Italy. Britain produces less than half of its own food—while Britain exports meat and dairy, it imports 46 percent of its fresh vegetables and 84 percent of its fresh fruit. Britain's reliance on food from EU countries means that British food imports have been affected by Brexit for the post-Brexit era has seen new trade regulations for EU food imports. The Federation of Small Businesses found the extra, time-consuming bureaucracy impacted small food businesses in particular for it acted as a trade barrier to firms that need to import small and frequent quantities of foods such as cheese, cooked meat, and fish. The new regulations also delay deliveries and added to costs.

On the plus side, however, with EU foods more difficult and expensive to import, British-made food experienced a rise in demand, thereby accelerating the trend for shopping locally and supporting British food producers. However, the ramifications of Brexit may in time hinder British food companies wishing to expand internationally as Brexit issues could prove a barrier to entering export markets. Certainly, a combined impact of Brexit and the Covid-19 pandemic meant that during the first three-quarters of 2021, British exports to the EU fell by almost 24 percent compared to pre-pandemic levels. As well as affecting food imports and exports, Brexit has also changed migration patterns and, consequently, the availability of labor including crop-pickers and lorry drivers. This impacted British food supply chains as there were fewer people available to harvest crops and transport foods.

In April 2022, the think tank UK in a Changing Europe concluded that post-Brexit trade barriers had caused a 6 percent increase in British food prices between 2020 and 2021 with the sharpest price increase coming after the Brexit trade deal came into force on May 1, 2021. The worse affected foods were fresh pork, tomatoes, and jams, which were largely imported from the EU. Products with low EU import shares, for example, tuna and pineapple, were less affected by price rises. The price increases exacerbated the rising financial pressure on Britons at a time when they were warned to expect the worst squeeze on living standards since the 1950s due to soaring inflation driven by the rising price of food, energy, and fuel triggered by Russia's invasion of Ukraine on February 24, 2022. A survey published in April 2022 found that 85 percent of Britons have been impacted by food price rises while food bank organizers warned the hike in prices was hitting the poorest the hardest and pushing many people into hardship they had not known before. These finding were borne out by data from the Trussell Trust that showed food banks had experienced a 14 percent increase in use since the period before the Covid-19 pandemic.

Russia's invasion of Ukraine has challenged Britain's food supply, especially in relation to the rising price of fertilizer from Russia, as well as animal feed and energy. While the British government did not expect any significant impact on the availability of food in Britain, it acknowledged that food prices would probably rise even further as trade and fertilizer supplies were disrupted. However, the fragility of global food chains was demonstrated in April 2022 when the crisis in Ukraine caused most major British supermarkets to ration the amount of cooking oil that consumers could buy. Most sunflower oil used in Britain comes from Ukraine so when the Russian invasion prevented Ukraine from exporting oil as usual, food production companies were forced to source other vegetable oils, such as rapeseed oil, causing the price of cooking oil in shops to rise by around 20 percent. At the same time, the price increase caused the price of chips and crisps made with sunflower oil to rise too.

The shortage of labor caused by Brexit was worsened by the Russian invasion of Ukraine for between April 2020 and the end of March 2022, Ukrainians made up 67 percent of temporary workers issued with a Seasonal Worker visa. Therefore, once the Ukrainian government stopped men of fighting age from leaving their homeland, there were fewer Ukrainians who were able to work in Britain. The British government had already launched the Seasonal Worker visa (2019) in order to alleviate the shortage of agricultural labor by allowing migrant workers to enter Britain to work for up to 6 months. The scheme was initially launched as a pilot and limited to 2,500 places. It has since been extended and has a quota of 30,000 places for 2022, with the potential to increase by another 10,000 if needed. The scheme should remain in place until the end of 2024, but authorities have said that in the long term, British farming must make greater use of mechanization and recruit more British workers in order to reduce its reliance on labor from overseas.

Further Reading

Barber, Harriet. "Britain is one shock away from a food crisis, experts warn." *The Telegraph: News: Global Health Security* (June 1, 2022). https://www.telegraph.co.uk/global-health/terror-and-security/britain-one-shock-away-food-crisis-experts-warn/ (accessed August 21, 2022).

Barrie, Josh. "Banana bread had a serious moment in lockdown, and it might be about to have another one." *INews: Lifestyle* (September 25, 2020). https://inews.co.uk/inews-lifestyle/food-and-drink/banana-bread-baking-craze-lockdown-second-wave-660901 (accessed August 22, 2022).

BBC. "Cambridge University study finds Anglo-Saxon kings were mostly vegetarian." *BBC News: UK: Cambridgeshire* (April 22, 2022). https://www.bbc.co.uk/news/uk-england-cambridgeshire-61178452 (accessed August 17, 2023).

BBC. "How to eat like a Victorian." *BBC News* (October 16, 2016). https://www.bbc.co.uk/news/magazine-37654373 (accessed August 17, 2023).

BBC. "'Mad cow disease': What is BSE?" *BBC News: UK* (October 18, 2018). https://www.bbc.co.uk/news/uk-45906585 (accessed August 17, 2023).

Brooks, Stephanie, Christopher T. Elliott, Michelle Spence, Christine Walsh, and Moira Dean. "Four years post-horsegate: An update of measures and actions put in place following the horsemeat incident of 2013." *npj Science of Food* 1, no. 5 (2017). https://doi.org/10.1038/s41538-017-0007-z (accessed August 17, 2023).

Buettner, Elizabeth. "'Going for an Indian': South Asian restaurants and the limits of multiculturalism in Britain." *Journal of Modern History* 80, no. 4 (2008): 865–901. https://doi.org/10.1086/591113 (accessed August 17, 2023).

Coe, Sarah, Xameerah Malik, Felicia Rankl, Paul Bolton, and Iona Stewart. "House of Commons Library: The effect of the war in Ukraine on UK farming and food production" (July 18, 2022). https://researchbriefings.files.parliament.uk/documents/CDP-2022-0147/CDP-2022-0147.pdf (accessed August 17, 2023).

Davey, James. "Life in lockdown Britain means fewer shopping trips but bigger bills." *Reuters: Business News* (April 28, 2020). https://www.reuters.com/article/uk-health-coronavirus-britain-supermarke/life-in-lockdown-britain-means-fewer-shopping-trips-but-bigger-bills-idUKKCN22A0V7?edition-redirect=uk (accessed August 21, 2022).

DEFRA. "Foot and mouth disease control strategy for Great Britain" (November 2011). https://assets.publishing.service.gov.uk/government/uploads/system/uploads/attachment_data/file/69456/fmd-control-strategy111128.pdf (accessed February 2, 2023).

Eating Better. Ready Meals Snapshot Survey 2020. https://www.eating-better.org/uploads/Documents/2019/ready-meal-survey-final.pdf (accessed August 17, 2023).

Fetzer, Thiemo. *Subsidizing the spread of COVID19: Evidence from the UK's Eat-Out-to-Help-Out scheme* (October 29, 2020). https://warwick.ac.uk/fac/soc/economics/research/centres/cage/manage/publications/wp.517.2020.pdf (accessed August 21, 2022).

The Grocer. "Pandemic bake-offs, banana bread fever and social recipes: 10 charts explaining UK attitudes to home baking" (May 11, 2021). https://www.thegrocer.co.uk/trend-reports/pandemic-bake-offs-banana-bread-fever-and-social-recipes-10-charts-explaining-uk-attitudes-to-home-baking/655954.article (accessed August 22, 2022).

The Herald Scotland. "Runny eggs declared safe to eat 30 years after Edwina Currie's salmonella scare" (October 11, 2017). https://www.heraldscotland.com/news/15587982.runny-eggs-declared-safe-eat-30-years-edwina-curries-salmonella-scare/ (accessed September 26, 2022).

Irvine, Susannah, Aleksandra Gorb, and Brigid Francis-Devine. *House of Commons Library: Food banks in the UK* (July 14, 2022). https://researchbriefings.files.parliament.uk/documents/CBP-8585/CBP-8585.pdf (accessed August 21, 2022).

Jane Austen's World. "Food—to die for: Food preparation in the Georgian era." (August 5, 2012). https://janeaustensworld.com/2012/08/05/food-to-die-for-food-preparation-in-the-georgian-era/ (accessed August 17, 2023).

Knight, Sam. "How the sandwich consumed Britain." *The Guardian: News: The Long Read* (November 24, 2017). https://www.theguardian.com/news/2017/nov/24/how-the-sandwich-consumed-britain (accessed August 17, 2023).

Liverpool John Moores University. *Direct and indirect impacts of COVID-19 on health and wellbeing. Rapid Evidence Review* (Version 2) (July 2020). https://www.ljmu.ac.uk/~/media/phi-reports/2020-07-direct-and-indirect-impacts-of-covid19-on-health-and-wellbeing.pdf (accessed August 17, 2023).

Mason, Laura. *Food Culture in Great Britain: Food Culture around the World*. Edited by Ken Albala. Westport, CT: Greenwood Press, 2004.

Mortimer, Ian. *The Time Traveller's Guide to Elizabethan England*. London: The Bodley Head, 2012.

Mukherjee, Debabrata. "The British curry." *History Magazine: History UK: Culture UK* (November 2, 2017). https://www.historic-uk.com/CultureUK/The-British-Curry/ (accessed August 17, 2023).

Power, Madeleine, Bob Doherty, Katie Pybus, and Kate Pickett. "How COVID-19 has exposed inequalities in the UK food system: The case of UK food and poverty." *Emerald Open Research* 2, no. 11 (May 13, 2020). doi: 10.35241/emeraldopenres.13539.2. PMCID: PMC7219559 (accessed August 21, 2022).

Rivard, Christopher, Jeffrey Thomas, Miguel A. Lanaspa, and Richard J. Johnson. "Sack and sugar, and the aetiology of gout in England between 1650 and 1900." *Rheumatology*, 52, no. 3 (March 2013): 421–6. https://doi.org/10.1093/rheumatology/kes297 (accessed August 17, 2023).

Speciality Food. "How Brexit will impact the food sector in 2022." *Speciality Food Magazine: Brexit* (January 13, 2022). https://www.specialityfoodmagazine.com/news/brexit-impact-food-sector-in-2022 (accessed August 22, 2022).

Spencer, Colin. *British Food: An Extraordinary Thousand Years of History*. London: Grub Street, 2002.

Yates, Annette. *English Traditional Recipes: A Heritage of Food and Cooking*. London: Hermes House, 2010.

2

Influential Ingredients

As an island nation, Britain is surrounded by waters rich in seafood while the land provides cereals, fruits, and vegetables, as well as grazing land for animals. Historical trade routes mean ingredients such as sugar have long been used too.

From the Sea

Salt

Salt is one of the Earth's most abundant minerals. In Britain, it is used not just to flavor and preserve food but also in activities such as freezing ice cream, road gritting, and water softening. Salt is an essential part of the food manufacturing process for it is included in such foods as bread, cheese, meat and fish products, and preserves. In Britain, both table salt and sea salt are readily available as are specialty salts such as pink Himalayan rock salt.

Over 200 million years ago, England was covered by inland seas that created layers of salt that are today mined as rock salt. Most British rock salt is mined from salt deposits in Cleveland in Teesside, northeast England, and Winsford in Cheshire, northern England. The names of four of the towns surrounding Winsford—Middlewich, Nantwich, Northwich, and Leftwich—reveal their historic association with salt production for the "-wich" suffix derives from the Anglo-Saxon word *wych*, meaning "brine town." The Winsford rock salt mine, which opened in 1844, is Britain's largest and oldest working salt mine. It is located roughly 492 feet under the Cheshire countryside.

Salt making in Britain dates back to pre-Roman times. In 2021, researchers claimed salt deposits in Cleveland represent Britain's earliest salt-making site for they discovered there ceramic salt pans dating from around 3800 BCE. When the Roman Conquest of Britain took place in 43 CE, salt creation had been long established at several coastal sites as well as in the English counties of Cheshire and Worcestershire. Salt was such a valuable commodity in Roman Britain that soldiers of the Roman army were paid partly in salt via a monthly salt allowance called a *salarium argentum*, from which the word salary derives (the Latin word for "salt" being *sal*). For this reason, a soldier who did not perform his duties well was said to be "not worth their salt," a saying still used today in Britain to describe something subpar.

The Roman Army's advance to northern England reached Cheshire around 60 CE, and here the Romans established military bases at the towns of Chester and Middlewich. At Middlewich, the Romans founded military saltworks next to the River Croco near an existing Celtic salt-making settlement. The military saltworks provided salt for the army's own needs, while Romano-British salt-makers used the existing Celtic salt production site to supply local people with salt.

Salt-making methods stayed much the same for thousands of years after the Romans left Britain. The first account of Anglo-Saxon salt production in Cheshire occurs in the *Domesday Book* (1086). At this time, Cheshire's salt industry was recovering from being laid waste by the Normans following a rebellion in 1070–1. The *Domesday Book* also reveals that several manors owned coastal salt-making plants (salterns) between Lincolnshire and Cornwall, especially in the fenlands of Lincolnshire and East Anglia, and along England's south coast. One area of England that still produces sea salt is Maldon, a town in the eastern county of Essex. Maldon salt production dates back to at least the eleventh century for the *Domesday Book* records that the town had forty-five salt pans. Today, Maldon salt is generally considered Britain's best salt. Early coastal salt production relied on solar evaporation and so tended to be a seasonal pursuit. Today in Maldon, seawater is evaporated in salt pans held over flames in order to create salt crystals that are hand-harvested.

The demand for salt grew in line with Britain's increasing population—from 1066 to the mid-fourteenth century, England's population doubled in size, and salt experienced a corresponding rise in demand. As well as saltworks in Cheshire and Worcestershire, numerous coastal saltworks evolved in the counties of Lincolnshire, Norfolk, and Sussex that drove a sizeable salt export trade to Continental Europe.

Outside of the local area, only the wealthy could afford salt transported overland for carriage costs were high. For this reason, some English salt was brought to London by boat from coastal saltworks. However, London's primary source of salt was the coast of the Bay of Biscay, which lies along the western coast of France and northern Spain. When English king Henry II married French queen Eleanor of Aquitaine in 1152, much of southwestern France came under English rule, and a market for Biscay salt began that prospered through the thirteenth century. Imports of Biscay salt arrived in England via ports in London and southern England. In London, salt merchants were located in the Bread Street area where they formed the Fraternity of Salters, which was granted a license in 1394. Here the salt merchants (salters) replaced Bread Street's original tenants—bread traders after whom the street was named. As well as trading in salt, the Fraternity of Salters were experts in the salting of fish and meat for preservation. As salt trading became more important in large cities and around ports involved in salt importation, by the seventeenth century, the Fraternity of Salters in London had united with salt traders in eastern and southern English coast towns to look after their trading interests and setting industry-wide standards.

Salt pans was first produced in Scotland in the twelfth century by monks who made salt in pans on the seashore of their village east of Edinburgh. In time, the village became so associated with salt making that its name evolved from Prieststown, to Salt Prieststown, then Salt Preston, and ultimately Prestonpans. During the twelfth century, Prestonpans received a royal warrant to produce salt, which lasted until 1959. Prestonpans salt was notorious, however, for the evaporation process created an acrid smoke that smelled bad because animal blood was added to the pans so that the blood's albumen could draw impurities from the heated brine. Local women were especially important to the Scottish salt industry for women known as "salt-wives" used to carry the salt to market in Edinburgh using creels (wicker fish baskets). By the sixteenth century, Scotland had developed a true salt industry for coal from Fife was used to heat seawater. From the sixteenth to the nineteenth centuries, Scottish salt production was concentrated around the Firth of Forth on Scotland's east coast near Edinburgh. Here the settlements of Culross, St. Monans, and Joppa developed into important centers of salt making. The Scottish salt-making industry peaked in the eighteenth century when the Act of Union allowed Scottish salt to flood the English market. The Act of Union also led to salt being smuggled out of Scotland to England where taxes were higher. However, Scotland's salt industry was all but destroyed in the 1820s, when rock salt from Continental Europe flooded the British market.

Under Oliver Cromwell (1599–1658, head of state for England, Scotland, and Ireland, following the execution of King Charles I), salt and salt making were heavily taxed in order to fund the government. However, following the

Restoration of the British monarchy in 1660, the salt tax was abolished by King Charles II. In 1688, however, Queen Mary and her husband William reinstated the tax. Subsequently, the salt tax was amended so that the tax on salt made in England was cut, while the tax on imported Europe salt rose to compensate. In 1730, the salt tax was repealed for it was felt to bring great hardship to the poor. At this time, salt was used for seasoning and food preservation, as well as for leather and fertilizer production. Salt was especially important to the British fishing industry as it was used to preserve herring. The salt tax put the British fishing industry at a disadvantage for it made it impossible for British fishers to compete with the Dutch fishing industry. In 1732, however, Prime Minister Sir Robert Walpole reintroduced the salt tax for 3 years, with proceeds from the tax given to the British royal family. Throughout the rest of the eighteenth century, the rates of salt tax fluctuated depending on the government's need for revenue, with the rate at its highest when Britain was at war. By 1815, the salt tax generated at least £1.6 million per year in revenue. After the Napoleonic Wars, the salt tax remained as it helped the British government pay its residual war debts and was only reduced in 1822. The tax was repealed completely in 1825. By this time, salt had become an important mineral in the manufacturing processes that evolved during the Industrial Revolution.

During the seventeenth century, coastal salt making had come to flourish. This was true particularly in areas where there were coastal coalfields such as Cumberland and Tyneside in northern England. A 1702 extension of the Salt Act prevented the opening of new coastal refineries outside of Cheshire though in 1793, a new refinery was built near Liverpool. Throughout the eighteenth century, the size of salt pans increased while pumping technology improved thereby allowing deeper brine shafts to be constructed that yielded stronger brine from brine pits. By 1850, however, these brine pits were exhausted.

Following the abolition of the salt tax, entrepreneurs sought to take advantage of the salt industry's financial opportunities as well as new salt-based chemical innovations. The growth of new saltworks led to overcapacity in the industry, however, and ultimately, in 1888, almost all Britain's saltworks merged to create the Salt Union, which shut its less-efficient and older saltworks. By the 1940s, many of the food manufacturing processes that required salt had been replaced by innovations such as refrigeration, and there was a gradual decline in salt production.

Today, the British government aims to cut the public's salt intake and has established voluntary guidelines for companies to follow in order to reduce the amount of salt that Britons consume. In recent years, the amount of salt in products made by members of the Food and Drink Federation (an organization representing British food and drink manufacturers) has fallen by 16 percent. Nonetheless, in 2020, a Briton's average salt intake was 8.4 g/day, thereby exceeding the recommended intake of 6 g/day. Public Health England has published new voluntary salt targets to gradually reduce the levels of salt in foods available in Britain by 2024. By this date, bread, biscuits and cakes, breakfast cereals, soups and sauces, crisps, and savory snacks will all contain less salt.

Fish

The waters in and around Britain yield an array of edible creatures from mussels, crabs, and scallops off of Shetland in Scotland; cockles from Poole and Cornish sardines, both from southwest England; herring in the North Sea; and the brown shrimps that live in the Wash (a bay on the east coast of England). There is even a sustainable cockle fishery in the River Thames that operates between Essex and Kent in southeast England. Numerous fish live in other British rivers. For instance, the River Wye in Wales is known for its trout and salmon, the River Dove in Derbyshire (central England) contains grayling, roach, bream, and pike amongst others, and the River Itchen in Hampshire (southeast England) is renowned for its trout. England's largest natural lake, Lake Windermere in the famous Lake District's area of northern England, yields pike, perch, eels, trout, and Arctic charr. Salmon and seatrout also travel through the lake.

Despite the variety of seafood available in British waters, the most commonly eaten seafood in Britain are cod, haddock, tuna, salmon, and prawns. Certainly, Britons eat more cod and haddock than any other nation, partly because these are the fish served most often in fish and chips. Most of the cod and haddock eaten in Britain are caught in the Icelandic, Norwegian, and Barents Seas.

Fishing is one of Britain's most historic means of obtaining food. For instance, the oldest fish trap in Britain was found near Newport, Wales, and dates from around 1200 BCE, while in west London, fish weirs dating from 650 to 890 CE have been found in Brentford, Isleworth, and Kew. However, archeologists note that a marine diet was unusual in Iron Age (800 BCE to 1 CE) Britain despite Britain's abundance of aquatic creatures, possibly because of social restrictions or taboos surrounding the eating of seafood.

By the sixteenth century, the eating of fish denoted a high social standing for members of the British elite would serve ostentatious feasts featuring hundreds of pike and bream as well as thousands of eels in order to display their wealth. At this time, the wealthiest Britons kept fishponds on their land to ensure they had a constant supply of fish, for to own fish was the ultimate status symbol.

Britons have long fished abroad too, for they first fished in Icelandic waters during the fourteenth century and operated the Grand Banks cod fishery off the coast of Newfoundland, Canada, since the seventeenth century. Fish from such far-off locations was preserved through salting. Following the introduction of steam trawlers in the 1870s, Britain's fishing capacity grew greatly for the trawlers allowed British fishers to trawl greater depths using larger nets that held more fish. In 1825, American entrepreneur Clarence Birdseye invented the double belt freezer that allowed cold brine to be chilled and freeze fish quickly at sea. This innovation allowed Britain's long-distance fishing fleet to catch cod that could then be frozen and sent back to Britain.

During the Industrial Revolution, working-class people living in major cities began to fish for pleasure. However, the industrialization caused pollution to such rivers as the Tyne, Mersey, Thames, and Don. In the nineteenth century, the development of the railways helped the British fishing industry grow for before the railways, the fishing industry used a network of inland transport such as boats and horse-drawn carts to carry fish from ports to markets. Railways meant fish could be carried to markets quicker than before, and the market for fish was extended to more areas.

By 1930, British demand for fish increased further while technological advances, especially the development of the steam trawler, allowed British fishing boats to operate further afield. In the 1890s, British trawlers could reach Icelandic waters, but by the 1920s, British trawlers could operate near Bear Island, in the western Barents Sea. Since the fish stocks of the North Sea (part of the Atlantic Ocean in northern Europe) were declining, the ability to fish further afield became increasingly important to Britain. Therefore, in 1929, the British government began to survey fishing grounds around Bear Island, which it believed contained unlimited fish. By the early 1930s, however, the British fishing industry faced many problems. Fish prices were declining so the fishing industry responded by catching more fish. Consequently, the supply of fish outstripped demand causing the industry to come under close government scrutiny. Ultimately, the creation of several government reports into the fishing industry resulted in the Sea Fishing Industry Act (1933) and the establishment of the Sea Fisheries Commission, which examined all aspects of the fishing industry. The act limited the number of fish British fishers could catch in distant water during the summer and also introduced regulations to protect immature fish.

Post–Second World War, the British fishing industry faced greater international competition for fish stocks. Therefore, the British government considered various ways to increase the industry's efficiency, for following the war, the British fleet was in need of large-scale refurbishment. The interruption of fishing during the Second World War had led to an increase in North Sea fish stocks, but by 1947, the number of fish in these waters had fallen again due to the uptake in fishing. Then, in November 1949, the postwar boom in fish prices collapsed, leaving the British industry facing a dire situation. The British government reacted by creating the White Fish Authority that gave financial support to British fisheries operating in near and middle-distance waters. In the 1950s, the British fishing industry revived somewhat, but a gradual decline followed, for, increasingly, British distant-water trawlers ran into disputes over territorial rights. The distant-water fishing industry depended on the idea of the freedom of the high seas together with the assumption that the sea was a resource open to exploitation by all. After the Second World War, however, this idea was challenged increasingly. For instance, in the 1930s, the Norwegian government had claimed a 4-mile territorial limit, and, after the Second World War, it enforced these limits. Subsequently, several British trawlers were apprehended by the Norwegian authorities leading the British government to take their case before the International Court of Justice. Similarly, the Icelandic government was concerned about the depletion of fish stocks along its coast. After Iceland gained independence from Denmark in 1944, Iceland annulled the Anglo-Danish Territorial Waters Agreement of 1901, which mutually restricted territorial waters to within 3 miles of the coast. Now, the Icelandic government extended the territorial limit to 4 miles. In response, British authorities banned Icelandic fishing boats from landing fish in British waters in a dispute that came before the International Court of Justice. The events led to a lengthy dispute between Britain and Iceland known commonly as the Cod Wars. In 1956, a decision by the Organisation of European Economic Co-operation forced Britain to accept the 4-mile limit. In 1958, the United Nations held the first International Conference on the Law of the Sea at which a number of countries, including Iceland, made claims for extending the limit of their territorial waters to 12 miles. Britain did not recognize Iceland's 12-mile declaration and so continued to fish within the new limit. This led to Iceland's Navy hassling British trawlers, resulting in the British Royal Navy being deployed to protect British ships. Britain agreed to the 12-mile limit following the United Nations Conference on the Law of the Sea between 1960 and 1961. Britain's inability to ship in Icelandic waters meant that British fishing vessels operating in the

Barents Sea off of northern Norway and Russia caught increasing amounts of fish, however.

In 1970, the European Economic Community (EEC, a precursor to the European Union [EU]) introduced the Common Fisheries Policy (CFP), which allowed member nations equal access to community waters after 10 years of membership. The British fishing industry considered this to be against their interests, but nevertheless, the then British prime minister Edward Heath (1916–2005) went ahead and joined the EEC. In 1972, however, Iceland declared a 50-mile territorial limit, and the ensuing dispute saw that Icelanders had sabotaged the nets of British trawlers. In 1973, Britain and Iceland agreed that for the next 2 years some British trawlers could operate within the 12-limit. In 1975, it became apparent at the third United Nations Conference of the Law on the Sea that various countries supported a 100-mile territorial limit, and so, in May 1975, Iceland declared a 200-mile limit. Britain refused to recognize this limit initially but in 1976 conceded, effectively ending Britain's ability to operate long-distance fishing.

There is massive pressure on the seafood species most popular in Britain. Cod and haddock stocks around Britain and elsewhere have been reduced because of intensive commercial fishing, though North Sea cod stocks have increased slightly in recent years. Similarly, tuna numbers have declined hugely worldwide due to demand. There are also fears that salmon and prawns in British waters are being overfished. Since cod and haddock are so dominant in the market, other edible fish species such as coalfish, whiting, and dab are not valued by consumers and so are harder to sell to the public despite the fact that they are, inevitably, caught along with the cod and haddock. Typically, these low-value fish are either returned to the sea dead or processed into fish products that are then exported. In Britain, there have been various attempts to persuade Britons to eat a wider variety of fish including campaigns headed by such celebrities as food broadcaster Hugh Fearnley-Whittingstall.

Conservation groups like the Marine Conservation Society have launched similar campaigns. For instance, in 2018, the society called for Britons to eat fish including hake, dab, and megrim in order to ease the pressure on cod and haddock. The blue Marine Stewardship Council ecolabel denoting fisheries that meet the council's standards for sustainable seafood production are a common sight in British food shops. Fish carrying the Marine Stewardship Council label are caught or produced in line with the Marine Conservation Society standards.

Despite the wealth of British seafood, Britain imports more fish than it exports. In 2020, the UK (Britain and Northern Ireland) imported £3,206 million worth of fish but exported only £1,627 million worth of fish. By quantity, tuna was the most imported fish while salmon was Britain's most exported fish. English vessels comprised 45 percent of the UK fishing fleet while Scottish vessels accounted for 37 percent of the total number of UK fishing vessels. However, the Scottish fleet had the highest capacity. The Scottish fleet caught high volume fish that sold for lower prices, such as herring and mackerel, which were caught in the North Sea and the waters west of Scotland. Contrastingly, the English fleet caught lower volume fish species that reach a higher price, such as sole and plaice.

For the entirety of Britain's membership of the EU, EU rules and regulations impacted the British fishing industry significantly. The EU's fishing policy and the principle of allowing all member states equal access to Europe's fishing waters were formalized under the CFP that came into force in 1983. The policy meant EU member states did not control their own territorial waters or set their own fishing quotas for fish were classed as a common resource. Although individual member states of the EU were responsible for policing their waters and enforcing EU regulations, all EU member states with a coastline and fishing industry had to share territorial waters with each other, and all countries had the right to fish in each other's waters. Supporters of EU membership stressed that British fishers had the right to fish elsewhere in EU waters. However, opponents of Britain's membership of the EU pointed out that Britain has some of Europe's most productive fishing grounds so while EU vessels wanted to access Britain's territorial waters, there was little incentive for British fishers to operate elsewhere in the EU. In 2015, EU vessels caught 683,000 tonnes of seafood worth £484 million in British waters, but British vessels caught only 111,000 tonnes of seafood worth £114 million in the waters of other EU member states.

Despite the fact that fishing is not hugely important to the British economy, the fishing industry is considered immensely culturally important to many British coastal communities. Many of these communities voted strongly in favor of leaving the EU as they blamed the EU for the decline of the British fishing industry in general. In particular, these communities were angered at the loss of control of British waters, which they saw as a damaging consequence of EU membership. For these reasons, in Britain, fishing has a sociopolitical importance that is far greater than its economic significance demands. Fishing played a huge role in the run-up to Brexit, for the overwhelming majority of Britain's commercial fishing industry favored Brexit in order to leave the CFP and return control of Britain's fishing grounds to British fishers. Indeed, areas of England that have a long-standing fishing industry, such as Hull in Yorkshire and Grimsby in Lincolnshire, had some of Britain's highest proportion of Leave votes. After the EU referendum, there was much speculation as to how great a role commercial fishing would play in the negotiations surrounding the UK's withdrawal from the EU, and following the referendum, there was much prolonged negotiation between Britain and the EU concerning fishing rights. In November 2020, the Fisheries Bill, which allowed the UK to control its waters out to 200 nautical miles passed into UK law. This ended the automatic right of EU vessels to fish in British waters. At the start of 2021, a new post-Brexit trade deal came into force that allowed EU member states' boats to fish in the waters off Britain if they had special licenses. At the same time, British fishing vessels need a license to fish in the waters of EU member states. Also, under the post-Brexit trade deal, over a five-year adjustment period, 25 percent of EU boats' fishing rights to UK waters will be transferred to the UK fishing fleet while the EU fishing quota (the amount of fish that EU boats can catch in UK waters) will reduce by 15 percent in the first year and 2.5 percentage each year thereafter. Consequently, it is expected that by 2026, British boats will be able to access an extra £145 million of fishing quota every year.

In early 2022, negotiations on a Free Trade Agreement between the UK and Greenland began as the two countries sought to reduce or remove tariffs on seafood.

Britain has a long history of fishing in Greenland's waters with this area being especially important to vessels from Hull, northern England. Historically, Hull-based fishing boats had fished in Greenland's waters during the autumn and winter. In 2020, the British and Greenland governments announced they would work together to develop fisheries in the North Atlantic because Britain is no longer restricted by the EU's common fisheries regulations. Like the UK, Greenland left the EU in part because of worries about the EU policy that allowed all member states open access to each other's waters. The policy is also a major reason why Norway, Iceland, and the Faroe Islands (part of Denmark) have never joined the EU.

From the Land

Sugar

The first record of sugar in Britain dates back to 1099 having been brought home by English soldiers returning from the Crusades. By the 1200s, sugar came to Britain via ports in Venice (now in Italy). At this time, sugar was a luxury good used mainly as a spice or a medicine. However, the sugar of this time was a gritty product created by drying sugar cane extract in the sun rather than a refined product.

Only in the 1500s did sugar lose its luxury status when Portuguese colonists in Brazil started to produce sugar in industrial quantities. Funded by Dutch merchants, the Portuguese began to traffic African slaves to farm the sugar, which subsequently was shipped to Europe.

Sugar was essential to the lavish banquets of the Elizabethan era for it was used both as a food and as an artistic medium as sugar was shaped into intricate works that symbolized the wealth of the hosts. Consequently, sugar became a status symbol in the feasts of the wealthy. In the mid-seventeenth century, British colonists in Barbados, Jamaica, and elsewhere adopted the same business model as the Portuguese. The resultant sugar was available in Britain in various forms and at different price points. Triple-refined white sugar was the most expensive, while brown sugar or molasses was the cheapest. Sugar was used both as a cake ingredient and as a preservative that kept foods good for longer, for instance, turning perishable fruit into jams and chutneys. By 1700, refineries known as "sugar bakers" existed across Britain. The advent of sugar refineries was important for where once sugar used to be processed in the Caribbean before being transported to Europe, sugar merchants could now import semi-processed sugar that could be refined in Britain. Refined sugar was then transported around Britain. The English authorities supported this industrial activity by putting in place protectionist taxation policies that subsidized imports of semi-processed sugar. Refining was so successful that British traders started to export their surplus sugar across Europe, as well as re-exporting brown sugar globally.

In the eighteenth century, France overtook Britain as Europe's main sugar supplier. Nevertheless, the early sugar trade provided British merchants with a financial model that was adopted and adapted for other goods including cotton. As the availability of sugar grew, so did its centrality to the British diet. Sugar was especially important because it was added to tea and coffee, which at this time were naturally bitter. Eighteenth-century Britons shifted away from using sugar that resulted from West Indian slavery and opted for sugar from southeast Asia, which was marketed as "free-gown." This was one of the first examples of how consumer purchasing power influenced British life. Sugar was one of the most profitable products to come from Caribbean plantations, so British abolitionists encouraged a boycott of Caribbean sugar so as to undermine slavery's economic foundation. The first campaign to reject Caribbean sugar occurred in 1791–2, but the campaign was reignited in the 1820s because while the 1807 Abolition of the Slave Trade Act made it illegal to engage in the slave trade throughout the British colonies, slavery continued in the West Indies. Many abolitionist societies produced objects such as sugar bowls that carried slogans criticizing the use of slaves in the production of West Indian sugar. Thus, purchasing East Indian rather than West Indian sugar became a badge of honor for many Britons. Though East Indian sugar was more expensive than sugar produced in the West Indies, British confectionery shops at this time advertised that they only used East India sugar in order to distance themselves from the slave trade.

By 1800, sugar was omnipresent in England, found in everything from desserts at the most lavish banquets to the humblest cup of tea. In the nineteenth century, cheap jam (made from one-third fruit to two-thirds sugar) started to become a working-class staple food to the extent that sugar comprised 14 percent of the average Briton's calorie intake as the working class, especially women factory workers, enjoyed the convenience of bread and jam for breakfast. The availability of sugar meant that Britain's annual sugar consumption per person was 4 lb in 1704, grew to 18 lb in 1800, and reached 90 lb in 1901. By this point, Britain had the highest sugar intake in Europe.

The nineteenth century saw the invention of machines that permitted the mass production of confectionery. Consequently, confectionary became cheaper, and British confectionary companies began to start making sweets that are still enjoyed today. As Britain's towns grew, the confectioners found they had a new customer: urban factory workers who needed a high calorie intake in order to energize their long working day. Factory workers soon found sweets were the most enjoyable way for them to obtain the necessary calories and ate them by the bagful. Sweets were also hugely popular with Victorian children, hence sweets from this time are often brightly colored to appeal to the young. Brightly hued sweets such as jelly babies, wine gums, and coconut ice looked attractive in shop windows, enticing shoppers of all social classes inside at a time when shopping was becoming a leisure activity.

During the 1920s, sugar beet farming was introduced to Britain. Today, the British sugar beet industry is responsible for roughly half of all the sugar used in Britain and is exported worldwide. The British sugar beet industry involves some 3,000 growers as well as supporting up to 9,500 jobs both on farms and in manufacturing. Additionally, the sugar beet sugar supply chain involves approximately 7,000 businesses. Most British sugar beet is grown in eastern England near Britain's four sugar beet factories. Consequently, on average, sugar beet travels only 28 miles from farm to factory meaning Britain's domestic sugar sector has some of Britain's lowest "food miles." British sugar is sold in various formats including granulated, superfine, powdered, and liquid forms. Today, the UK uses 1.7 million tonnes of sugar. The demand for sugar is driven by two sectors: the food and drink manufacturing industry and retail sales. Around 80 percent of the sugar is used by food and drink manufacturers as an ingredient in baked goods, confectionary, desserts, and drinks. The remaining 20 percent of sugar is sold to supermarkets, coffee shops, eateries, and so on.

Wheat

Wheat was introduced to Britain around 5,000 years ago with Britons first exporting surplus wheat to Europe 1,000 years before the Romans arrived. However, it was only in the twelfth century that milling wheat for flour became common. By the start of the nineteenth century, wheat was Britain's most important food crop. The wheat grown in earlier times was much taller than the wheat grown today, for over time, the pursuit of higher yielding wheat varieties means that these ancient varieties have been almost completely lost. Around the mid-1800s, British plant breeders began to grow wheat selectively, opting to grow shorter, stiffer growing wheat that produced significantly higher yields. Around this time, Britain also started to import more wheat from Canada, and millers began to use roller mills that worked well on tough wheat with a thick bran. This, combined with the rising demand for white loaves to make sandwiches to feed an increasingly industrialized workforce, meant bakers preferred to use the imported wheat that had higher protein levels. At the start of the twentieth century, it was realized that imported Canadian wheat did not produce a good crop in the British climate, but nevertheless did produce a high-protein grain. Therefore, the newly formed Plant Breeding Institute decided to cross Canadian wheat with British varieties. Until the 1970s, Britain relied on imported wheat for bread making as well as flour for general usage. However, plant breeders, farmers, millers, and bakers worked together to develop new wheat varieties that could grow abundantly in Britain. Consequently, the amount of domestically grown wheat used in Britain increased greatly—from 2 million tonnes at the start of the 1970s to over 5 million tonnes today. Traditionally, modern British farmers grow a range of different wheats to meet the demands of various markets. Hard wheats (those with high protein and gluten content) are used to make foods such as bread while soft wheats (those with low-protein levels and weak gluten) are used to make biscuits and to make flour for general usage. The lowest quality British wheats are used to make animal feed.

Today, wheat is the UK's main arable grain crop. Approximately 2 million hectares of wheat are grown in the UK with an average yield of roughly 8 tonnes per hectare. The UK's wheat harvest is worth around £1.2 billion though the price varies—in October 2022, it was valued at around £140 per tonne. A quarter of all British wheat is exported. Most wheat grown in Britain is winter wheat sown from September to November and harvested the following August or September. Winter wheat produces the highest yield because it has a longer growing season than spring wheat. Winter wheat accounts for nearly all the wheat used by British millers.

In 2021, the UK wheat harvest was expected to yield 14 million tonnes, an increase of 45 percent on the 2020 harvest. The 2020 crop was low as heavy autumn rainfall impacted seed drilling. Subsequently, the growing plants suffered during an extended dry period in spring that hit farmers in the south and east of England especially hard. In 2022, 500,000 tonnes of British wheat exports were forecast to be exported, a figure more than double that of the previous year. At the same time, imports of wheat to Britain were significantly lower as millers switched to processing more home-grown grain. Part of the reason for the fall in imported wheat may be the Russian invasion of Ukraine for Ukraine produces much of wheat used in Europe.

British farmers grow around fifty different wheat varieties that are approved through an official testing system. Plant breeders and flour producers assess new varieties for their characteristics and best usage with the assessment added to the AHDB Recommended List (RL), an independent assessment of how new varieties perform. The list is used mainly by farmers. The development of new varieties is an ongoing process as varieties are always being sought that can provide a higher yield, improved disease resistance, or better nutritional value.

The RL assesses how new wheat varieties perform and classifies them depending on their suitability for end use (see Table 1):

Barley and oats are other important British grain crops. In Britain, two crops of barley are grown—winter barley sown September to November and spring barley sown between February and May. The brewing industry is the main purchaser of British barley for it buys around 1.9 million tonnes of barley annually for use in malting. Spring barley is used chiefly for producing malt for distilling and to create lager, while winter barley is used in the production of ales and food. The total barley production of the UK increased from 8 million tonnes in 2019 to 8.1 million tonnes in 2020. Demand for barley from the brewing and distilling sector started to recover once Covid-19 lockdown restrictions on the British hospitality sector were lifted.

Table 1 The AHDB Recommended List shows how new wheat varieties perform and their suitability for end use

Classification	Qualities and uses	Number of varieties currently on the RL
UKFM Group 1	Bread-making varieties with consistent milling and baking performance	4 winter; 3 spring
UKFM Group 2	Varieties with bread-making potential but not suited to all grists because of variability in performance or some undesirable traits	4 winter; 3 spring
UKFM Group 3	Soft varieties used for biscuits, cakes, etc. They are lower in protein (11.0–11.5 percent) and have extensible but not elastic gluten	10 winter
UKFM Group 4	Hard and soft wheats used mainly for animal feed. Millers may use some varieties in general-purpose grists	7 winter (soft); 12 winter (hard); 5 spring (hard)

Source: Adapted from https://www.ukflourmillers.org/wheat

In Britain, oats are used mainly as a component in breakfast cereals though Britons also use oats in home baking, to make stuffing and crumble toppings, and to thicken soups and smoothies, with various types available to buy including jumbo oats, instant oats, and rolled oats. The high nutritional content of oats means they are considered something of a superfood and are championed by such organizations as the cholesterol charity Heart UK. In 2021, the UK oat harvest increased by 4.2 percent to 1.1 million tonnes, the highest since 1973. The rise came despite the fact that 5 percent less land was given over to oat farming.

Rape

Rape (also called rapeseed or oilseed rape) is part of the Brassicaceae family and is grown primarily for the high-quality edible oil it produces. The first record of rape being grown in Britain came in the fourteenth century, but it was only in the 1970s that commercial British rape production developed. Today, almost 1 million acres of rape are grown in Britain, their bright yellow flowers providing an arresting sight each summer. In 2021, rape yields returned to an average rate at 3.2 tonnes per hectare after experiencing a historically low harvest in 2020. The increase came despite the area planted with rape decreasing by 19 percent to 307,000 hectares. The increase in yield occurred mainly because damage by the cabbage stem flea beetle reduced, and farmers experienced favorable soil conditions. The British rape industry is worth about £700 million per year.

Rape is important to British grain production as it is grown as a "break crop," naturally adding nitrogen to the soil in which it grows. This nitrogen helps to improve the yield of the crops such as wheat that are grown on the soil subsequently. As a break crop, rape also suppressed weeds, which is beneficial to the growing of cereals such as barley. However, growing rape may be one of the reasons for Britain's diminishing honeybee population. As rape is high in pollen, it is especially attractive to honeybees, which are one of rape's main pollinators. However, it is thought that the pesticides used in rape cultivation may be dangerous to the bees. In addition, rape's pungent smell taints the taste of the honey produced by bees that have visited rape plants.

In Britain, rapeseed oil is found in mayonnaise, margarine, and salads. Since about 2008, rapeseed oil has become increasingly popular in Britain as it is tasty and prized for its health benefits (rapeseed oil contains omegas 3, 6, and 9, which can help reduce cholesterol and maintain healthy joints, brain, and heart functions). Also, as rapeseed is high in monounsaturated fats, it can be heated to a high frying temperature without spoiling its antioxidant content or flavor.

Milk and Cheese

In Britain, milk obtained from various animals has been drunk, or eaten as an ingredient in butter and cheese, for millennia. Indeed, milk fats preserved in pots have been found that date from about 4000 BCE. During the Neolithic period, milk and cheese were likely considered special foods rather than part of everyday diets.

By medieval times, cows' milk had come to supersede milk from sheep, donkeys, and goats. By the Tudor period (1485–1603), dairy products together with eggs, bread, and pottage were enjoyed mainly by the poor. While cattle were kept throughout Britain, they were found particularly in Cheshire in northern England and in Scotland. By the seventeenth century, these areas had become recognized as centers of commercial dairy farming. Peasant farmers in these areas prized their cattle for not only providing an income, but also because dairy products fed cattle-owning families. The enclosure system of land division impacted farmers' ability to keep cattle, however, and from the late seventeenth century, only peasant farmers in northern England could find enough unenclosed land to graze cattle. Contrastingly, cattle in southern England tended to be kept on large farms that used the cattle's milk to make butter and cheese. Large farms overcame the problem of how to feed cattle in winter by growing fields of plants that could be fed to animals. The ability to feed cattle all through winter meant Britons could enjoy dairy products year-round. Urban markets soon began to thrive and so dairy farms appeared around towns, especially London. It also became normal for people to keep cows in towns with cattle owners serving as both dairy producers and retailers of dairy products. In London, cattle kept in locations including Lincoln's Inn Fields and Islington were milked by milkmaids early in the morning. The milkmaids then took the milk to shops or hawked it around city streets. Whey became a fashionable London drink, and junkets and syllabubs were widely popular.

By the start of the eighteenth century, milk was being added to tea, coffee, and hot chocolate too. This era also saw farmers seek to improve their dairy cattle and engage in scientific breeding of cows belonging to breeds such as Channel Islands, Durham Shorthorns, and Flanders. Large dairy herds became common in the southeast English counties of Middlesex, Surrey, Buckinghamshire, and Oxfordshire. The growth of dairy farming in these counties reflects that the appetite for milk in urban areas was growing rapidly, especially in nearby London. Meanwhile, buttermilk became a popular drink among the poor living in Edinburgh and Bristol.

Between 1761 and 1801, however, more than 3 million acres of land that were previously available for dairy farming were enclosed, particularly in the English Midlands and southern counties, bringing much hardship to local cattle farmers for they were no longer able to keep as many cattle as grazing land was reduced in area. By the start of the nineteenth century, the poor in northern England, Scotland, and Wales enjoyed dairy products alongside oats, barley, and potatoes, whereas those in southern England did not include dairy in their diets. Indeed, estimates suggest that 90 percent of people in southern England consumed so little dairy that they suffered from calcium deficiency. Between 1801 and 1911, the population of England and Wales expanded rapidly while simultaneously the population distribution changed so that most people lived in cities whereas previously, most people had lived in rural areas. During this time, milk became a mainstay of the farming economy as it became an important traded commodity, but because milk was highly perishable, it could not be transported far. For this reason, rural dairy farmers used their milk to make cheese and butter as these lasted longer during transportation and so could reach people living in towns.

This situation changed in the mid-1840s for the coming of the railways meant milk could be transported faster and farther.

Before the First World War, sweetened condensed milk became a popular substitute for fresh milk (poor families also substituted it for breastmilk). By this time, Britons had become suspicious of fresh milk as it was often adulterated with chalk or flour or diluted with water. Also, in London especially, cows were often kept in unsanitary conditions with milk produced unhygienically. Such was the concern raised by scientists about the state of British milk that in 1872, the government passed the Adulteration of Food, Drink and Drugs Act, which made it illegal to sell products containing undisclosed substances. By the start of the twentieth century, the quality of British milk had improved greatly for the most part. Advancements in microbiology also meant that some scientists started to theorize bovine tuberculosis was causing milk-drinkers to become ill with the human form of the disease. In 1913, it was concluded that there was a link between the two illnesses. Consequently, in the 1920s, steps were taken to prevent milk carrying tuberculosis. Tuberculosis was not the only disease present in British milk, however, for in 1904, medics reported that outbreaks of typhoid fever, scarlet fever, diphtheria, and diarrhea linked to milk had caused the deaths of 30,000 British children. This prompted large dairies to pasteurize or sterilize their milk though some public figures argued that these processes reduced milk's nutrient content. By 1906, milk had become politicized as some local councils started to provide needy children with free school meals. It was argued that all children should be given a pint of milk per day as part of their meals, but this led to discussions about whether this was a step toward public ownership of milk supplies. By 1936, 83 percent of British children received milk in school, while local councils also gave or subsidized milk to poor mothers and children under 5 years.

During the First World War, milk was unrationed. Even though the price of milk was controlled, it became more expensive during the war as supply started to dwindle due to labor shortages and a lack of food for dairy animals. Nursing mothers and children were prioritized for milk supplies, and poor mothers were given free milk. At the same time, United Dairies was formed by the merger of two dairy companies and came to control much of Britain's wholesale milk trade. Although disliked by some Britons as a semi-monopoly on milk, United Dairies developed a tuberculosis-free milk (available at a premium price) as well as extensive pasteurization and bottling improvements.

In 1919, British agriculture fell into a depression and over the next 20 years, 3 million acres of land used for dairy reverted to pasture. At the same time, milk was drunk mostly in tea or eaten in puddings or with breakfast cereals. In 1935, youth-orientated milk bars serving milkshakes began to open in British seaside resorts but consumer confidence in milk remained low still. The Second World War changed the public's perception of milk, however, as Britons came to believe milk was essential to children's health. Consequently, milk supplies rose during the war (milk was again unrationed), and milk provision became central to various postwar welfare schemes. The most significant of these schemes was the extension of the milk school scheme, which was praised for improving the health of the nation. Up until the 1970s, British milk consumption remained at around 5 pints per person per week. In the 1970s, however, Britons began to drink less tea and, therefore, less milk too. Less milk was also being used within households as families made fewer cakes and milk-based desserts. In the 1980s, milk consumption fell further when public health bodies recommended Britons reduce their fat intake to lessen the chance of coronary disease. At this time, milk accounted for 17 percent of the saturated fat in British diets. When the Chernobyl nuclear disaster occurred in 1986, demand for milk fell again as Britons feared milk produced in Britain might contain radiation.

Following the warnings regarding the link between coronary disease and milk, many Britons who continued to drink milk switched from using full-fat milk to skimmed and semi-skimmed milk. This change was especially true among wealthy consumers for the lowest paid and elderly still tended to opt for full-fat milk. According to the British government's Department for Environment, Food and Rural Affairs, in 1974, a Briton's average per capita milk consumption was 2.7 liters per week. However, in 2018, this had almost halved, though 98.5 percent of households did still buy milk. The decline was due to a reduced consumption of foods associated with milk such as tea, coffee, and breakfast cereals, and the rise in plant-based alternatives to milk. Nonetheless, today, cows' milk is readily available throughout Britain though goats' milk can also be found in many shops. Typically, shops and eateries also stock plant-based milks such as soy and almond milks. This reflects that recently, plant-based milks have entered the mainstream with 32 percent of Britons opting for plant-based milk. The increased demand for plant-based milks is in line with Britons' growing interest in environmental issues and veganism. A 2021 poll found that oat milk was Britons' favorite plant-based milk, for in 2020, Britons spent £146 million on oat milk, up from £74 million the previous year. Nevertheless, cows' milk remains Britons' preferred milk with the British cows' milk market worth over £3 billion.

While the consumption of cows' milk is falling, Britain's cheese industry continues to grow. In Britain, cheese is not only eaten as is, but is also an ingredient in sandwiches, soups, salads, traditional ploughman's lunches, soufflés, and more. While cheese has been made in Britain for around 2,000 years, the British cheese-making industry truly emerged in Roman England—cheese making was a high priority for the Romans as cheese was needed to feed its army of around 45,000 men. Every Roman legionary (elite soldier) in England was awarded an ounce of cheese in his daily rations, and Roman-era cheese molds have been discovered at both Corbridge Roman Town on Hadrian's Wall in Northumberland and Wroxeter Roman City in Shropshire. The earliest cheeses made in Britain evolved into Cheshire and Lancashire cheeses and were made in very localized areas by peasant farmers. Later, medieval monks proved voracious consumers of cheese, and many monasteries operated their own dairies. Most of the cheeses made by the monasteries produced hard cheese that was low fat for the cream was skimmed off to turn into butter.

In the 1530s, the Dissolution of the Monasteries caused the British cheese-making industry to enter into a serious decline. The decline lasted until the seventeenth century when modern cheese-making practices started to evolve as dairies began to cater to growing urban populations. However, the mass production of cheeses by large dairies meant small-scale British artisan cheese making declined. By the twentieth century, the number of British artisan cheese-makers had fallen alarmingly.

In the 1870s, British factories began to mass produce cheese, and, increasingly, British cheese-makers could not compete with cheap cheese imported from Australia, New Zealand, and the Netherlands. Indeed by 1929, New Zealand Cheddar was 4p per pound cheaper than farmhouse British Cheddar. As they could not compete with the foreign imports, in the 1930s, most British dairies switched from making cheese to producing milk, which was more profitable than cheese or butter. British artisan cheese making all but died as a result of the Second World War for during the war, milk that would normally be used to make a variety of British cheeses was redirected to factories to make so-called Government Cheddar. This cheese was part of the rationing scheme to help Britain feed itself during times of food shortages. Rationing had a disastrous impact on British cheese for the cheese ration allowed civilians only 1 ounce of cheese per person (with an extra 3 oz for vegetarians). In this way, rationing favored hard, block cheeses that were easy to cut into cubes. Creamy or crumbly cheeses were unsuitable for rationing as they could not be divided precisely.

The decline in British cheese making continued in the 1960s for many cheesemakers retired or went into milk production. Supermarkets also tended to stock cheap, easy-to-display, factory-made block cheeses rather than artisan-produced cheeses. By the early 1970s, only around sixty cheese-making farms existed in England. Frustrated by the proliferation of bland, mass-produced cheese, in the late 1970s, cheese enthusiasts began to revive British artisan cheeses—a movement now known as the Great Cheese Renaissance. The enthusiasts researched traditional British cheese-making methods which they combined with Continental European cheese-making recipes and techniques. This combination resulted in new British cheese such as the sheep's milk cheese Beenleigh Blue from Devon, southwest England, which is inspired by the French blue cheese, Roquefort.

Today, there are around 700 varieties of British cheese. Classic British cheeses include Cheddar, Caerphilly, Double Gloucester, Lancashire, and Stilton. Cheddar is a hard, cows' milk cheese that originated from the village of Cheddar in the southwest English county of Somerset and has been made since at least the twelfth century. "Cheddar" cheese is made globally, but in 2007, the Protected Designation of Origin name "West Country Farmhouse Cheddar" was registered in the EU. Following Brexit, the name was also registered in the UK as Cheddar made in Somerset, Dorset, Devon, and Cornwall from local milk using traditional methods. In 2013, Protected Geographical Indication was registered for Orkney Scottish Island Cheddar. Another hard, cows' milk cheese, Caerphilly originates from the town of Caerphilly in southern Wales where it was first made circa 1830. Originally, Caerphilly was made to use up surplus milk and soon became a favorite with local coal miners who liked Caerphilly because its thick rind meant it traveled well, and its salt content helped the miners replace the electrolytes they lost while toiling down the mines. As British cheese making declined in the twentieth century, many artisan Caerphilly producers were lost, a situation that worsened after the Second World War, when government Cheddar was introduced. By the 1950s, only Duckett's Caerphilly, which is still produced today, remained. Today, much of the cheese sold as Caerphilly is made in England.

Double Gloucester is a smooth, hard cheese that originated in 1498 in Gloucester, southwest England. The cheese is made from the milk of Old Gloucester cows, one of Britain's oldest native cattle breeds that were once common throughout the west of England but which in 1972 were classified as endangered. Double Gloucester has a straw-like color from the addition of the plant extract annatto, which is a natural colorant.

> ### Cooper's Hill Cheese Rolling
>
> The Cooper's Hill Cheese Rolling annual extreme sport event sees competitors from around the world chase a large Double Gloucester cheese decorated with ribbons down Cooper's Hill in the southwest English county of Gloucestershire. As the cheese rolls, it can reach speeds of up to 70 mph as it hurtles down the near vertical hill over a 200-yard long course. The winner of the competition is the first runner to reach the bottom of the hill in the cheese's wake and takes home the cheese as a prize. The Cheese Rolling's origins are unknown, but the event may date back at least 600 years.

Annatto is also used to color the British cheese Red Leicester, which contains higher levels of annatto hence its redder hue. Lancashire is a semi-hard, cows' milk cheese originating from the northern English county of Lancashire. Lancashire cheese is available as three distinct varieties: Creamy Lancashire, mature Tasty Lancashire, and Crumbly Lancashire, which is a recent innovation suitable for factory production. Lancashire cheese making dates back from 1199 when King John allowed the city of Preston to host a cheese festival. By the 1300s, Lancashire cheese was being shipped to London from Liverpool. From around the 1790s, the method used to make Lancashire cheese changed, meaning the cheese started to look like the modern Tasty Lancashire and Creamy Lancashire. To make the cheese, whey was drained and placed in a vat in which it was pressed by a stone. Consequently, early Lancashire cheeses were flat in shape. This production technique meant the cheese lacked consistency, however, and in 1892, the production was standardized using a recipe and methods that are still used today. By the early twentieth century, there were over 200 artisan Lancashire cheese-makers, but the Second World War saw Lancashire cheese production fall, for not being a hard cheese meant Lancashire was unsuitable for rationing. Once cheese production resumed in the 1950s, there were only twenty-two artisan Lancashire cheese producers who remained. Lancashire cheese was reinvigorated in the 1960s, however, when Lancashire Crumbly was invented in order to compete with other white, crumbly British cheeses such as Cheshire and Wensleydale. Today, Lancashire cheese is undergoing another resurgence of interest as it is made using locally sourced milk and so chimes with the demand for locally produced foods. Stilton, which is Britain's most famous blue cheese, has its roots in the early eighteenth century. Since 1996, stilton has enjoyed European Protected Designation of Origin status, meaning it can only be made in the English counties of Derbyshire, Nottinghamshire, and Leicestershire, by producers who follow traditional recipes.

Fruit and Vegetables

No one fruit or vegetable prevails in Britain. Common vegetables include potatoes, onions, carrots, and cabbage while fruits include apples, pears, bananas, and berries. Exotic fruits and vegetables are also widely available, especially in areas with large ethnic communities. Various parts of Britain are associated with different produce, however.

Rhubarb

Rhubarb, which is prized for its edible stalks, is available in Britain in two main types—natural, outdoor rhubarb and forced rhubarb. Forced rhubarb is grown in darkness to create bright pink, tender stems and is available from January to March. Forced rhubarb is grown throughout Britain but is most associated with the northern English county of Yorkshire, where it is produced in the so-called Rhubarb Triangle (between the towns of Morley and Rothwell and the city of Wakefield), where rhubarb thrives in the cold winters. Initially, forced rhubarb is grown outside for 2 years for exposure to frosts toughens the plants' roots. Next, the rhubarb is lifted from the ground and placed in dark sheds where the rhubarb is heated in order to make the rhubarb grow quickly in search of light. Forced rhubarb is harvested by candlelight as this maintains the rhubarb sticks' tenderness and ensures that the rhubarb roots continue to grow. If the rhubarb crowns are exposed to light, they stop growing and photosynthesis occur, resulting in bitter-tasting sticks. The rhubarb sticks are hand-harvested to prevent the crowns from developing botrytis (a type of fungus), which would rot the plant. Once the rhubarb is harvested, the crowns are composted. The forcing process produces rhubarb that is sweeter, pinker, and more flavorsome than unforced rhubarb, which is available from spring.

Rhubarb first came to Britain in the 1620s when it was brought to England by Sir Matthew Lister, physician to Kings James I and Charles I, and used as a purgative. By 1657, rhubarb's medicinal properties meant that in England, it commanded a price three times that of opium. In 1817, gardeners working at the Chelsea Physic Garden in London discovered the forcing process when they covered a leftover rhubarb crown with soil only for it to re-emerge resplendent with sweet pink stalks a few weeks later. Gradually, forced rhubarb became a staple crop of northern England, especially west Yorkshire, which became the first place in the world to construct rhubarb-forcing sheds heated using cheap coal from local mines. In 1877, the first forced rhubarb was cultivated to fill a gap in the area's market-garden economy. Soon, forced rhubarb exploded in popularity and daily Rhubarb Express trains transported tons of rhubarb from Yorkshire to London's Covent Garden Market.

Historically, 90 percent of the world's forced rhubarb was grown in the Rhubarb Triangle. However, in the 1960s and 1970s, many rhubarb fields had houses built upon them because they were located near expanding urban areas. Whereas there were once 200 forced rhubarb producers, there are now only around a dozen growers. Nevertheless, forced rhubarb, indeed rhubarb in general, is undergoing a renaissance in Britain. While traditionally rhubarb was used to make sweet dishes such as crumbles, pies, fools, trifles, and tarts, increasingly in Britain, rhubarb is also found in savory foods like chutneys, used to flavor gin, or paired with oily fish and rich meats.

Apples

Commercial British apple growing is associated with southern England for large apple orchards are found in the counties of Kent, Worcestershire, Herefordshire, and Essex. There are also small-scale apple farms elsewhere in Britain. Today, over 2,500 apple varieties grow in Britain. The British apple season sees trees flower from early May to mid-June with the ripening period occurring between August and October. In Britain, apples are commonly eaten raw, juiced, or used in sweet dishes such as crumbles, pies, and tarts. They are also a popular ingredient in chutneys and a traditional accompaniment to roast pork.

While wild apples could be found growing across Britain during the Neolithic period, many apple varieties were introduced to Britain by the Romans. The first recorded mention of apples came in 885 when King Alfred referred to the fruit. During the eleventh century, French apple varieties such as the Costard arrived in England as a result of the Norman invasion. It was during this period that monasteries developed apple orchards on their grounds, and monks began to experiment with cross-pollination to create new apple varieties. By the thirteenth century, the Costard was grown throughout England.

In the eighteenth century, British botanist Thomas Andrew Knight undertook numerous cross-pollination experiments in order to develop improved apple varieties. Knight's experiments inspired many British gardeners, including Thomas Laxton who developed several apple varieties including the eating apple, Laxton's Superb. The world's first cooking apple, the Bramley, was introduced in 1809. It was during Victorian times, however, that Britain became home to over 2,000 types of apples including the eating apple varieties Pitmaston Pineapples, Ribston Pippins, the cooking apple varieties such as Bramley and Howgate Wonder, and Alfriston, which is good for juicing. Later in the era, the introduction of new English apple varieties peaked as gardeners strove to improve on existing varieties. To this end, the Ribston Pippin apple, created at the start of the Victorian era, was superseded in 1850 by the Cox's Orange Pippin. After the Second World War, much research went into developing smaller apple trees that allowed apples to be harvested nearer the ground, thereby making it quicker and cheaper to gather fruit. Smaller trees also allowed more sunlight to reach developing fruit on the branches, something that improved the density of the fruit on the trees. Another benefit of smaller trees was that they could be planted closer together, which resulted in greater orchard productivity.

When Britain joined the EEC in 1973, an unlimited number of apples were imported into Britain. Consequently, British apple growers faced stiff competition from high-yielding apple varieties, such as Granny Smith and Golden Delicious, which could not grow well in Britain. Moreover, the imported apple varieties were heavily advertised, leading to their popularity among British shoppers. Contrastingly, British apple growers grew varieties that had been bred for taste rather than high yields and were unable to compete with the low-cost imports. Resultantly, many British apple orchards became unprofitable and either closed down or were replanted with other crops. In the 1990s, British apple growers faced further competition when Gala and Braeburn apple varieties were introduced to Britain from New Zealand. The new varieties proved hugely popular with Britons, and so British growers started to grow them too at the expense of native varieties. Over subsequent decades, British apple growers began to grow other new varieties including Jazz, Rubens, and Cameo, all of which grow well in British orchards.

Despite the thousands of apple varieties grown in Britain, in 2018, only 40 percent of the apples consumed by Britons were homegrown; today, Britain imports over 70 percent of its apples. Moreover, in 2022, a study by the National Trust heritage organization reported that 81 percent of English and Welsh orchards had vanished since the early 1900s because of growing urbanization and changing land use. Nonetheless, currently the British apple is enjoying a resurgence as hundreds of community orchards revive heritage apple varieties and small-scale growers sell at farmers' markets. The Common Ground environment group pioneered the British apple renaissance, for 30 years ago, the group began a campaign to save Britain's traditional orchards. The group also initiated an annual Apple Day to celebrate British apples and orchards. The first Apple Day was held on 21 October 1990 and has been marked annually ever since through a growing number of events held across Britain.

Watercress

Watercress grows in shallow, fast-flowing streams across Britain though less so in northern Scotland. Traditionally, peppery-tasting watercress is hand-picked from the wild and used as an ingredient in salads, soups, and sandwiches, and more commonly to garnish dishes. The vast majority of British watercress comes from the southern English counties of Hampshire and Dorset. The British watercress season start in May and ends in November.

Watercress is known for its nutritional content for it is rich in vitamins A, C, E, and K and is a source of calcium, folic acid, and iron. The plant's nutritiousness was recognized by the ancient Greeks and Romans, and today it is deemed a "superfood." As an indigenous plant, watercress has long been eaten in Britain, and by the 1800s, watercress sandwiches were a dietary staple of the working class living in Hampshire and Dorset because it was free to pick from local waterways. Since 1808, however, watercress has also been grown as a commercial crop. In the 1860s, the Hampshire town of Arlesford, which is surrounded by chalk streams perfect for watercress-growing, became the center of the watercress industry. However, watercress does not keep well so it was not possible to transport harvested watercress by horse and cart. Therefore in 1865, the Mid-Hants railway that connected Alresford to London's Covent Garden Market opened, and soon, Hampshire watercress was in such demand that numerous commercial watercress farms became established throughout the county. The Mid-Hants railway allowed watercress to be transported to London and beyond, and although the railway carried all sorts of things, it transported such huge quantities of watercress that it soon became known as the *Watercress Line*. In Victorian London, street sellers sold bunches of the watercress in paper cones for snacking, and in spring and summer, poor households ate raw watercress as a breakfast food, something that earned watercress the nickname "poor man's bread." During the First and Second World Wars, watercress sandwiches became a staple food at high tea as people relied on homegrown foods in the face of food shortages. The British watercress industry began to decline once import restrictions were lifted and foreign salad ingredients became available again postwar. Gradually, watercress gained a reputation for being useful only as a garnish, leading to a fall in demand. Indeed, while in the 1940s there were more than 1,000 acres of watercress under cultivation, by the end of the twentieth century, this figure had fallen to 150 acres. The *Watercress Line* closed in 1973 meaning that Hampshire watercress had to be transported by road (in 1985, the *Watercress Line* reopened as a heritage railway). By the 1980s, watercress was deemed unfashionable leading to far lower demand. Consequently, 90 percent of Hampshire growers left the watercress industry.

In 2003, in an effort to get Britons to eat more green vegetables, the "Not Just a Bit on the Side" campaign was initiated by British watercress farmers to stimulate demand for their product. Despite the efforts of the British growers, much of the watercress sold by British supermarkets comes from Spain, meaning it is at least 5 days old by the time it is bought by consumers. Britain's largest watercress producer to still cut watercress by hand is Hairspring Watercress based in the southern English county of Sussex for recently, mechanized watercress harvesting has become the most common method of gathering watercress.

Since 2006, the Alresford Watercress Festival has taken place in May, featuring local artisan food stalls and presided over by the Watercress King and Queen who parade holding newly harvested watercress. The festival also features a Watercress Eating Championship.

Raspberries

Raspberries were first cultivated by the Romans, who introduced the fruit throughout their empire. Raspberries only became popular in Britain during the Middle Ages, however, once they had been hybridized by British growers. Over the centuries, it became evident that raspberries grown in the eastern Highlands of Scotland, especially in Perthshire, were superior to those from elsewhere in Britain. The deliciousness of Scottish raspberries is due partly to Perthshire's loam soil, which warms up quickly and drains well, and the weather as Perthshire is drier than much of Scotland, yet also receives regular rainfall. Perthshire also enjoys moderately warm summers and, like the rest of Scotland, benefits from long daylight hours in the summer that boosts raspberry canes' growth.

It was only in the Victorian period, however, that Scottish raspberries were grown commercially and became widely available outside of Scotland. In 1890, J. M. Hodge, a raspberry grower from the Perthshire town of Blairgowrie, rented land to cultivate raspberries on a larger scale. Hodge then established the Blairgowrie & Rattray Fruit Growers Association to unite local fruit producers and to start industrial fruit production. Hodge also linked up with Sir William

Hartley, the English philanthropist who founded the Hartley's jam company, which enabled Scottish raspberries to become known throughout Britain. Soon, Blairgowrie was nicknamed Berry Town. As well as Perthshire, Scottish raspberries are also grown in Aberdeenshire, Fife, Ayrshire, and the Scottish Borders.

In the 1950s, demand for Scottish raspberries grew to such an extent that a dedicated steam railway, The Raspberry Special, was used to transport them to London shops and jam manufacturers in southern England. In the 1980s, however, the Scottish raspberry industry fell into decline as growers faced fierce competition from Eastern Europe. Scottish growers also became victim to the raspberry root rot fungal disease. Nevertheless, in recent years, the British fresh fruit market has grown rapidly with consumption expected to continue to increase. While some Scottish raspberries are still grown for jam making and other raspberry processing uses, now most Scottish raspberries are grown for the fresh market. Raspberry farming is so important to many Scottish farmers that they have invested in the newest technology to ensure the best possible harvest, and experiment to create improved raspberry species.

In recent years, British raspberry consumption has risen year-on-year thanks to more consistent supplies of both native and imported fruits, improved varieties, and Britons' growing love of berries. In the year up to May 16, 2021, raspberry consumption rose 7.5 percent in value and 5.7 percent in volume. During this period, Britons bought more raspberries than ever before, with sales worth £371 million. By developing new varieties, British growers have managed to extend the British raspberry growing season, which now runs from June to October, with some varieties fruiting for up to 5 months of the year.

Further Reading

BBC. "1953: Sweet rationing ends in Britain." *BBC: On This Day* (2008). http://news.bbc.co.uk/onthisday/hi/dates/stories/february/5/newsid_2737000/2737731.stm (accessed September 27, 2022).

BBC: Bitesize. "The bittersweet history of confectionery" (2022). https://www.bbc.co.uk/bitesize/articles/zm2q4xs (accessed August 17, 2023).

British Sea Fishing. "The big five fish species." https://britishseafishing.co.uk/the-big-five-fish-species/ (accessed September 27, 2022).

British Sea Fishing. "Brexit and Britain's fisheries." https://britishseafishing.co.uk/brexit-and-britains-fisheries/.

British Sugar. "Back British sugar." https://www.britishsugar.co.uk/back-british-sugar (accessed October 3, 2022).

Broomfield, Andrea. *Food and Cooking in Victorian England: A History*. Westport, CT: Praeger, 2007

Burnett, John. *Liquid Pleasures: A Social History of Drinks in Modern Britain*. London: Routledge, 1999.

Countryside Online. "British sugar: All you need to know" (January 13, 2021). https://www.countrysideonline.co.uk/food-and-farming/feeding-the-nation/sugar/ (accessed September 26, 2022).

Crown. "National Statistics: Chapter 7: Crops." Department for Environment, Food & Rural Affairs (July 27, 2022). https://www.gov.uk/government/statistics/agriculture-in-the-united-kingdom-2021/ (accessed October 6, 2022).

Department for Environment, Food and Rural Affairs. "Farming statistics—final crop areas, yields, livestock populations and agricultural workforce at 1 June 2020 United Kingdom" (December 22, 2020). https://assets.publishing.service.gov.uk/government/uploads/system/uploads/attachment_data/file/946161/structure-jun2020final-uk-22dec20.pdf (accessed October 4, 2022).

Fort, Tom. *Casting Shadows: Fish and Fishing in Britain*. London: William Collins, 2020.

Gooding, Mike J., and Peter R. Shewry. *Wheat: Environment, Food and Health*. Chichester, UK: John Wiley & Sons, 2022.

Harkness, Caroline Caroline, Mikhail A Semenov, Francisco Areal, Nimai Senapati, Miroslav Trnka, Jan Balek, and Jacob Bishop. "Adverse weather conditions for UK wheat production under climate change." *Agricultural and Forest Meteorology* 282–283 (March 15, 2020): 107862. https://www.sciencedirect.com/science/article/pii/S0168192319304782 (accessed October 4, 2022).

Lloyd, Chris. "'Spectacular' 6,000 year old salt-making site found on Teesside." *The Northern Echo: News* (March 31, 2021). https://www.thenorthernecho.co.uk/news/19200577.spectacular-6-000-year-old-salt-making-site-found-teesside/ (accessed September 25, 2022).

Marine Management Organization. "UK sea fisheries statistics 2020." https://assets.publishing.service.gov.uk/government/uploads/system/uploads/attachment_data/file/1020837/UK_Sea_Fisheries_Statistics_2020_-_AC_checked.pdf (accessed September 27, 2022).

Marine Stewardship Council. "UK and Irish fisheries spotlight." UK & Irish Fisheries. https://www.msc.org/uk/what-we-are-doing/uk-irish-fisheries (accessed October 3, 2022).

Miller, Norman. "The UK's heritage apple renaissance." *BBC Travel: Forgotten Foods* (July 6, 2022). https://www.bbc.com/travel/article/20220705-the-uks-heritage-apple-renaissance (accessed October 6, 2022).

Palmer, Ned. *A Cheesemonger's History of the British Isles*. London: Profile Books, 2019.

Public Health England. "Salt reduction targets for 2024" (September 2020). https://assets.publishing.service.gov.uk/government/uploads/system/uploads/attachment_ data/file/915406/2024_salt_reduction_targets_070920-FINAL-1.pdf (accessed September 26, 2022).

Robinson, Robb. "The evolution of railway fish traffic policies, 1840–66." *Journal of Transport History* 7, no. 1 (1986): 32–44. https://doi.org/10.1177/002252668600700103 (accessed October 2, 2022).

Salt Association. "The history of salt." https://saltassociation.co.uk/education/salt-history/ (accessed September 23, 2022).

The Scotsman. "When sea salt was Scotland's white gold" (March 10, 2017). https://www.scotsman.com/sport/football/when-sea-salt-was-scotlands-white-gold-601568 (accessed September 25, 2022).

Seafish Industry Authority. "The economic impacts of the UK sea fishing and fish processing sectors: An input–output analysis." https://www.sff.co.uk/wp-content/uploads/2017/03/Seafish-2006_I-O_Key_Features_Final_090108.pdf (accessed August 17, 2023).

Searl, Fred. "Raspberry volumes set for big rise as season begins." *Fresh Produce Journal* (June 23, 2021). https://www.fruitnet.com/fresh-produce-journal/raspberry-volumes-set-for-big-rise-as-season-begins/185604.article (accessed October 10, 2022).

UK Fisheries Ltd. "UK's distant waters fishing fleet" (2022). https://ukfisheries.net/uk-fish-consumption (accessed September 23, 2022).

Wood, Zoe. "One in three Britons drink plant-based milk as demand soars." *The Guardian: Food & Drink Industry* (September 17, 2021). https://www.theguardian.com/business/2021/sep/17/britons-drink-plant-based-milk-demand (accessed October 9, 2022).

3

Appetizers and Side Dishes

Britain does not have a strong tradition of serving appetizers with drinks. The most common nibbles eaten whilst enjoying drinks, whether with friends at home, at the pub, in a hotel bar, or at a restaurant, are roasted nuts, olives, crisps (chips), or crudités (raw vegetables such as celery, radish, and cucumber) presented in small bowls. Sometimes, wasabi peas or Japanese rice crackers are served too. Generally speaking, the grander the occasion, the more luxurious the nuts or crisps—for example, if drinking in a basic pub, the appetizers may be a packet of peanuts and an unexciting packet of branded crisps or pork scratchings (deep-fried, salted pig skin). At a more refined pub or gastropub, so-called bar snacks may be served. These can take the form of fancier nuts such as smoked almonds poured from glass jars into little bowls or a more luxurious brand of crisps. Alternatively, small tins of fish (e.g., sardines or whiting) may be available to snack on whilst drinking. At upscale hotels and restaurants, drinks may be served alongside small bowls of unusual crisps such as those made from blue-skinned potatoes, stuffed olives, Japanese crackers, and fried broad beans. Some high-end restaurants may offer raw radishes served with sea salt.

At events such as wedding receptions, mini versions of dishes such as fish and chips, shepherd's pie, or burgers may be served to guests as they mingle. Squares of smoked salmon on blinis (Russian-style buckwheat pancakes) or toast are also popular at weddings. At Christmas, supermarkets launch numerous canape ranges that usually include foods such as mini quiches, small sausage rolls, vol-au-vents, and beef wellingtons. Appetizers inspired by global cuisines most especially Indian, Thai, and Chinese, for example, mini samosas (Indian spiced pastries), mini satay chicken kebabs, and mini dim sum, are also usually included in shops' Christmas party food ranges. Christmas also sees British magazines become awash with recipes for appetizers.

Perhaps the most notorious British appetizer is the cheese and pineapple hedgehog, which is cubes of Cheddar cheese and tinned pineapple skewered on to cocktail sticks and stuck randomly into a grapefruit half so as to resemble the spikes of a hedgehog. During the 1970s and 1980s, a cheese and pineapple hedgehog would be the centerpiece of any British buffet table, but today it is only really served as an ironic nod to past food fashions. On a similar theme, in Britain, mini sausages may also be served on cocktail sticks alongside predinner drinks. However, mini sausages on sticks are merely placed on a platter rather than arranged to resemble a hedgehog. The sausages may be accompanied by a dipping sauce such as honey and wholegrain mustard.

While there are few traditional British appetizers, there are a few ingredients such as smoked salmon that are often used when making canapes in Britain. Smokehouses existed across medieval England but whereas pork was smoked inland, British coastal communities smoked fish. Due to the lack of refrigeration at this time, smoking fish was the best way to preserve it. In England, the first commercial smoking of fish likely occurred in the seventeenth century, but in London, salmon smoking began at the end of the nineteenth century when Jewish Eastern European migrants who had settled in London's East End smoked fish as a method of fish preservation. The Jewish migrants brought with them their own cuisine, and their desire for traditional Jewish food products meant that soon smokehouses were introduced to the East End (a loosely defined area located east of the Roman and medieval walls of the City of London north of the River Thames that includes the includes the boroughs of Hackney, Newham, and Tower Hamlets). To begin with, Jewish people in East London imported salmon from the Baltic area of Europe as they did not realize that Scotland had a tradition of producing high-quality wild salmon. Once the east Londoners learnt of Scotland's salmon tradition, however, they started to smoke Scottish salmon that they purchased at Billingsgate fish market. Much to the east Londoners' delight, the Scottish salmon produced a finer tasting smoked salmon than the imported fish. The light smoke used by fish smokers in London created the so-called London Cure, which ultimately became popular globally. London Cure smoked salmon is popular as the smoke used to preserve the fish does not have a heavily smoked flavor. The light smoke allows the flavor of the fish to shine through unlike cheaper, mass-produced salmon, which often uses lower quality salmon and high levels of salt or liquid smoke that creates a lingering, excessively smoky taste. In time, London Cure smoked salmon became a gourmet delicacy with dozens of smokehouses located in the East End—indeed an area of Bow in east London became known as Fish Island. By the 1920s, smoked salmon became a gourmet food and as late as the mid-1970s, there was still around twelve salmon smokers operating in the East End. In the 1980s, however, the industrialization of smoked salmon meant all but the H. Forman & Son London smokehouses closed.

Today, London Cure smoked salmon is a protected food enjoying Protected Geographical Indicator status. To qualify as London Cure smoked salmon, the salmon has to originate in Scotland and be cured in the Hackney, Tower Hamlets, or Newham areas of east London using only salt and oak smoke. Using traditional techniques, only the outside of the salmon should come into contact with smoke. Eventually, the outside of the salmon is removed so that the salmon flesh beneath is dried but does not taste of smoke. Today, smoked salmon is often served as an appetizer on toast, on blinis, or on squares of brown bread and butter. Alternatively, smoked salmon may be incorporated into canapes such as smoked salmon mousse, or the filling of mini quiches and vol-au-vents.

Another fish product, Gentleman's Relish also known as Patum Peperium, is also used in appetizers occasionally, usually by being spread on toast. Gentleman's Relish is a salty, slightly fishy-tasting paste made predominantly from salted anchovies. Gentleman's Relish was invented in 1828 by John Osborn, an English merchant living in Paris, who gave his creation a deliberately grand name combining elements of Latin and Greek to suggest the spread's peppery paste in order to tempt fashion-conscious customers to buy the product. When Osborn's son brought his father's business to London, Gentleman's Relish became known as Patum Peperium. According to the current manufacturers of Gentleman's Relish, Elsenham, the spread is still made to the original recipe, which uses best-quality Spanish anchovy fillets that are left to mature in barrels of salt for 18 months before being rinsed in brine, cooked, cooled, and blended with butter, rusk, and a secret blend of herbs and spices.

Traditionally, Gentleman's Relish is eaten spread very thinly on hot buttered toast, either on its own or topped with sliced cucumber or sprouts of mustard cress. According to famous nineteenth-century British food writer Isabella Beeton, Gentleman's Relish should be spread on toast as an appetizer and served to gentlemen to enjoy with port. Gentleman's Relish is also an ingredient in the British dish Scotch woodcock, which consists of scrambled eggs served on toast that has been spread with Gentleman's Relish. The makers of Gentleman's Relish also make a smoked salmon version of the spread called Poacher's Relish.

Slices of smoked salmon accompanied by wholemeal bread, toast, a lemon wedge, and sometimes crème fraiche are often served as a starter in British restaurants. Starters (sometimes called entrées) are small dishes prepared in individual portions that are served to diners in restaurants, at special meals and, occasionally, private dinner parties, before the main course. Fish and seafood are popular ingredients for British starters as they are lighter than meat ingredients and therefore unlikely to make diners full before the main course. As well as smoked salmon, other popular fish and seafood starters include some variation on the prawn cocktail, which typically comprises shelled, cooked prawns dressed in Marie Rose sauce (a blend of tomatoes or tomato ketchup mayonnaise or salad cream, Worcestershire sauce, and lemon juice), lettuce, and then sprinkled with cayenne pepper; scallops, smoked eel, oysters, or a dish featuring crab or lobster are also popular. Vegetarian starters often feature goats' cheese or heritage varieties of vegetables such as beetroot or wild mushrooms. Vegetable soups are also popular starters in Britain. Traditional British soups include leek and potato (called *Cawl cennin* in Wales where the leek is a national emblem), asparagus, broccoli and Stilton cheese, cream of watercress, cock-a-leekie (leek and chicken soup often thickened with rice with added prunes) and Cullen Skink (made from smoked haddock, potatoes, and onions). *Partan Bree* from northeast Scotland is another Scottish soup that makes use of fish and seafood for it is essentially Scottish crab bisque. The name Partan bree derives from the Scots Gaelic word *partan* meaning "crab" and *bree* meaning "to brew" but used to refer to soup. Mulligatawny is a classic British soup that originated in eighteenth-century British colonial India. The soup takes its name from the Tamil *miḻaku-taṇṇīr* meaning "black pepper water," a name that reflects the soup's curried flavor. Early versions of the soup used only vegetables, spices, and rice, but later versions added such meats as chicken or veal. Modern mulligatawny recipes tend to also include lentils, mango, and coconut milk, and when eaten with boiled rice, the soup represents a substantial meal.

Mock Turtle Soup

Mock turtle soup is an eighteenth-century English consommé imitating green turtle soup. In the 1750s, turtle soup was hugely popular in Britain after sailors returning home from the West Indies brought with them turtles. Any turtles that were not eaten onboard ship were sold for a high price, and turtle soup became a luxury. At one point, 15,000 live turtles were shipped from the West Indies to Britain annually, but this situation was unsustainable, and green turtles almost became extinct. Consequently, the so-called mock turtle soup was invented that used calf's head to replicate the taste and texture of turtle meat.

> ## Brown Windsor Soup
>
> In Victorian times, Britain was home to many soups using "Windsor" in their names, but these were white soups created by chefs working for British royalty. Around this time, many brown meat broths were also eaten in Britain. Sometime in the early twentieth century, the words Windsor and brown became fused together to create the name for a cheap brown meaty soup served in cafés and hotels. Consequently, the name brown Windsor soup became synonymous with a kind of dreary British cuisine and was the butt of numerous British comedy shows such as *The Goon Show*, as well as *Carry On* films.

Another British soup, oxtail, is made using fried beef tails to create a rich, clear broth. Like mulligatawny, cock-a-leekie, and Cullen Skink, oxtail soup can be served as either a starter or the main course.

What Britain lacks in appetizers it makes up for in side dishes, several of which accompany roast dinners. Perhaps the most famous British side dish is the Yorkshire pudding, which is the typical accompaniment to roast beef. Other British vegetable side dishes include mushy peas, Welsh onion cake (known as *teisien winwns* or *teisen nionod* in Wales), Scottish clapshot (or *clapshaw*), cauliflower cheese, and pickled onions. Britain is also home to many sauces including bread sauce, horseradish sauce, Cumberland sauce, redcurrant sauce, and mint sauce. Mint jelly and redcurrant jelly are also traditional accompaniments to roast lamb. Gooseberries, whether made into a sauce, pickled, or transformed into a jelly, are the traditional British accompaniment to mackerel dishes for the tartness of the fruit cuts through the richness of the fish.

When dining out, side orders can range from simple green or mixed side salads that tend to sport a selection of lettuce leaves, tomato, and red onion, to truffled mash potato (mash potato combined with truffle oil), or simple steamed vegetables such as spinach, sprouting broccoli, turnip leaves, or (when in season) Jersey Royal potatoes. Jersey Royals are a type of firm-textured potato grown on the island of Jersey, a British Crown Dependency located off the coast of northwest France. Jersey Royals are the only British potato variety to boast an EU Protected Designation of Origin status, a designation the potato has held since 1996. Moreover, Jersey Royals are the only fresh British fruit or vegetable to enjoy the Protected Designation of Origin status.

Chips (French fries) made from potato, sweet potato, halloumi (a salty Cypriot cheese), or polenta are an extremely popular side dish in Britain. Sometimes, the chips are dusted in truffle oil and grated Parmesan cheese (Parmesan truffle fries) or described as triple-cooked chips. Triple-cooked chips were invented by chef/restauranteur Heston Blumenthal and were first served at Blumenthal's restaurant *The Fat Duck* in 1995. To make triple-cooked chips, potato is simmered initially, then cooled, drained, and frozen, then deep-fried, cooled, then deep-fried again. The resulting chips have a crunchy crust yet a soft, fluffy inside. Today, triple-cooked chips are a standard side dish in many British pubs and restaurants.

Yorkshire Pudding

Yorkshire pudding (often abbreviated to Yorkshire pud) is perhaps the quintessential British side dish to accompany roast Sunday lunch, most particularly roast beef. In the past, beef tended to be cooked on a spit in the fireplace of a house and below the meat was placed a metal tray in which the meat's fat and dripping (tallow) could be collected as the meat cooked. When the roast had finished roasting, a batter comprising egg, flour, and milk was added to the tray of hot fat. The dripping contained essential nutrients such as vitamin D, so by catching the dripping in the pan, the nutrients were utilized rather than wasted in the fire. In earlier times, sources of these nutrients were hard to find, especially in northern England, because meat was expensive and working-class northerners did not earn a lot. Therefore, it was important that no food or nutrient was wasted. The batter would cook in the hot fat and dripping and rise in the manner of a soufflé while forming a crunchy base where the batter came into contact with the hot fat and dripping mix. The resulting pudding would then be cut into squares. Today, some Britons omit the meat fat and dripping and cook their Yorkshire pudding in hot sunflower or vegetable oil.

In most parts of Britain, Yorkshire pudding is served as an accompaniment to roast dinner, but it is traditional in Yorkshire to eat Yorkshire pudding as a separate course before the roast meat. The reason for this is that in Yorkshire, the rich gravy from the meat drippings was served up with the Yorkshire pudding course, while the roast meat itself, together with vegetables, was typically served with a sauce made from parsley. By serving the pudding and dripping separately, diners could become full quickly, which since meat was expensive meant families could save money by allowing the meat to stretch further. Also, in Yorkshire, some locals like to fill a Yorkshire pudding with jelly, and thus serve the pudding as dessert with ice cream.

The northern English county of Yorkshire prides itself on being the birthplace of Yorkshire pudding for traditionally, savory puddings common in southern England were not typically cooked in hot fat and so were usually softer and more pudding-like in texture than Yorkshire pudding. A recipe for the so-called dripping pudding first appeared in print in 1737 in *The Whole Duty of a Woman*, an anonymous guide to women's conduct that included several recipes. Then, in 1747, Hannah Glasse published a recipe for a dripping pudding in her book *The Art of Cookery Made Plain and Simple* that she called the Yorkshire pudding.

Today, Yorkshire puddings are made either as one large pudding that is then cut into portions or as individual little puddings. It is also possible to buy ready cooked, frozen Yorkshire puddings that just need reheating in a home oven. Such is the popularity of Yorkshire puddings that the first Sunday of February each year is designated the National Yorkshire Pudding Day in Britain, which is intended as a celebration of all things Yorkshire pudding–related.

Vegetable Side Dishes

Britain is home to numerous vegetable side dishes that include mushy peas, onion cake, and clapshot. Perhaps the most iconic British vegetable side dish is the mushy peas for they are the traditional accompaniment to the beloved British meal of fish and chips. Mushy peas are dried marrowfat peas that are soaked overnight in water and baking soda, before being rinsed in fresh water, placed in a saucepan of clean water, brought to the boil, and then simmered until soft. In northern England, often mushy peas are also served alongside meat pies as a dish called pie and peas.

Additionally, in the counties of Yorkshire, Nottinghamshire, Derbyshire, and Lincolnshire, mushy peas are eaten as a snack on their own, while in Nottinghamshire, it is traditional to eat mushy peas accompanied by mint sauce. A similar dish, parched peas (also called black peas) are field peas (or cowpeas) that have been left to dry on the plant and then boiled slowly until extra thick and mushy, before being sprinkled with malt vinegar. Traditionally, parched peas are eaten as a Bonfire Night treat in parts of Greater Manchester and Lancashire. Meanwhile, in the northeast of England and the northwest English county of Cumbria, Carlin peas are eaten on Carlin Sunday (the Sunday before Palm Sunday). Carlin peas take the form of purple podded peas boiled until tender, then fried in butter or dripping before being seasoned with vinegar, black pepper, brown sugar, and occasionally rum. Carlin peas can be eaten hot or cold. While some Britons maintain that mushy peas are most closely associated with northern England—hence mushy peas are sometimes referred to jokingly as Yorkshire caviar—mushy peas are eaten across Britain and can even be bought canned from supermarkets.

Welsh onion cake, called *teisen winwns, teisen nionod,* or *cacon nionod* in Wales, is a comforting, hearty side dish. The dish is both cheap and easy to make as it consists of layered potatoes and onions topped with butter, then baked in a cake tin or pie dish until soft and golden. There is no set recipe for a Welsh onion cake so sometimes herbs such as rosemary, parsley, or sage are added to the dish or pieces of cheese, such as the Welsh cheese Caerphilly, are placed among the layers of potatoes and onions. Typically, the Welsh onion cake is served alongside sausages, roast meat, or roast chicken, but the dish can also be served as a vegetarian main course.

Cauliflower cheese is another comforting, filling British side dish that is usually served with roast dinners. Like the Welsh onion cake, the cauliflower cheese can also be served as a vegetarian main meal. The cauliflower cheese is also popular a jarred baby food. It comprises pieces of boiled cauliflower covered in a cheese sauce (typically Cheddar cheese is used for the sauce, but this can vary with some Britons using Stilton cheese or Swiss cheese). More luxurious versions of the cauliflower cheese incorporate English mustard and nutmeg into the cheese sauce. The cauliflower cheese is often topped with grated cheese and sometimes breadcrumbs before being baked in the oven until golden. The origins of the cauliflower cheese are unknown, but cauliflowers were introduced to Britain in the seventeenth century, so cauliflower cheese likely originated at around that time. Isabella Beeton included a recipe for Cauliflowers with Parmesan Cheese side dish in her book *Mrs Beeton's Book of Household Management* (first published in 1861).

Another hot British vegetable side dish is clapshot, a traditional recipe for neeps (swede) and tatties (potatoes) from Scotland's Orkney Islands. Traditionally, the dish is served with haggis but is also served alongside lamb chops, meaty stews, or bere bannocks (a bread from the Orkney Islands that is made using beremeal, an ancient kind of barley grown and milled in Birsay, Orkney). Clapshot is similar to the Irish potato side dishes champ and colcannon, but clapshot differs by combining swede with potatoes instead of cabbage or spring onions. Sometimes, onions, butter, dripping, and chives are added to the swede and potato mix.

Pickled onions are served cold on the side of dishes rather than warm. Pickled onions are made of onions steeped in a solution of vinegar and salt, usually with other preservatives and flavorings such as spices and peppercorns. Typically, small white onions known as silverskins are pickled whole to make pickled onions, though red onions or shallots can also be used instead. Sliced Spanish onions are also sometimes pickled. The vinegar used to pickle onions can range from malt vinegar to white distilled vinegar, apple cider vinegar, or balsamic vinegar.

While pickling has existed as a method of food preservation since antiquity, pickling became commonplace in Britain during the eighteenth century when the growth of the printing industry meant cookery books and guides to household management became hugely popular including Sarah Harrison's cookbook *The House-Keeper's Pocket-Book* (1739), which contains a recipe for pickled onions. The popularity of such books meant food preservation became trendy, and pickling vegetables in vinegary liquids became *de rigueur*. Over time, onions became one of the most popular vegetables to preserve. Today, pickled onions are often served to accompany fish and chips and ploughman's lunches. The onions are also used to garnish the gin and dry vermouth cocktail known as a Gibson. While some Britons pickle onions at home, jars of pickled onions are widely available in British shops.

Sauces

As well as side dishes, Britain also boasts many traditional sauces, most of which are made from vegetables or fruit and are served on the side of dishes. Such British condiments as English mustard and jellies made from mint or redcurrants are also served alongside dishes.

One British sauce that is made from neither vegetables nor fruit is bread sauce, which is a milk-based sauce thickened by stale breadcrumbs and flavored with onion, herbs such as bay leaf and rosemary, spices such as nutmeg, clove, and black pepper. Sometimes, bread sauce is enriched with butter or juices from roasted meat. The origins of bread sauce stretch back to medieval times when thickening sauces with breadcrumbs became a popular way to use up stale bread. Typically, bread sauce is served alongside roast birds such as chicken and turkey and as such is often part of Christmas dinner in Britain. Bread sauce can also accompany roast gamebirds, such as pheasant, grouse, partridge, and quail. These birds are usually served not just with bread sauce but also alongside thinly sliced, deep-fried slices of potato known as game chips.

In Britain, a pungent sauce made from horseradish (a perennial root vegetable of the Brassicaceae family that also includes mustard and wasabi) is the traditional sauce to serve with roast beef. Horseradish sauce has a strong flavor because it comprises grated fresh horseradish root mixed with white vinegar, and a creamy substance such as cream, sour cream, yogurt, whipped cream, or crème fraîche. Horseradish sauce is also sometimes paired with salmon. A variation on the horseradish sauce is Tewkesbury mustard, which is a blend of mustard and grated horseradish originally sold in the form of balls of mustard. According to legend, Tewkesbury mustard balls enrobed in gold leaf were presented to British king Henry VIII in 1535 when he visited the town of Tewkesbury in the southwest English county of Gloucester. Horseradish grew prolifically as a weed around Tewkesbury, and so locals added it to their local mustard to make the mustard spicier. The resultant horseradish and mustard mix was especially thick and pungent, meaning Tewkesbury mustard became famous throughout England and is even mentioned in William Shakespeare's play *Henry IV*. At the start of the nineteenth century, however, the manufacture of Tewkesbury mustard died out as other mustards began to be manufactured using mustard flour. Today, production of the traditional Tewkesbury mustard balls has restarted with the balls featured in the annual re-enactment of the Battle of Tewkesbury (one of the most important battles of England's Wars of the Roses when the forces of King Edward IV and the House of York trounced the rival House of Lancaster).

Mustard is a hugely popular condiment in Britain with English mustard being eaten on foods including sandwiches, burgers, served alongside roast dinners as well as being added to stews and sauces, included in marinades, or used to coat ham. Other ready-made mustards available in Britain include French mustard, Dijon mustard, American mustard, Polish mustard, wholegrain mustard, and more artisan products such as mustard mixed with honey, wasabi, or yuzu (an East Asian citrus fruit). Mustard mayonnaise is also common in Britain being used in sandwiches, burgers, or on the side of dishes.

English mustard is available both as a powder from which people can prepare their own mustard or as a jarred ready-made product that has a thick consistency. Both the English mustard powder and jarred product are bright yellow in color because English mustard is made using both yellow and brown mustard seeds. The use of both seeds gives the mustard a strong, hot flavor and a low acid content. The most famous brand of English mustard is Colman's of Norwich, which in 1814 started to sell mustard powder in the company's famously mustard-yellow colored tin. English mustard is an essential ingredient in the hugely popular

British condiment piccalilli (also sometimes called mustard pickle), which is a relish comprising chopped pickled vegetables, mustard powder, and spices, most importantly turmeric, which gives piccalilli its bright yellow color. Piccalilli is served on the side of salads, in sandwiches, and so on.

The name piccalilli likely dates back to the mid-eighteenth century when a recipe for "Paco-Lilla, or India Pickle" was published in Hanna Glasse's *The Art of Cookery Made Plain and Easy* (1747), while in 1769, Elizabeth Raffald's cookbook *The Experienced English Housekeeper* provided a recipe "to make Indian pickle, or Piccalillo," and Richard Briggs's 1788 cookery book *The English Art of Cookery* describes how to make "Picca Lillo." By 1799, the spelling of piccalilli had become standardized with advertisements for the condiment appearing in an edition of *The Times* newspaper. If piccalilli has its roots in India, which is suggested by the alternative name given by the eighteenth-century food writers, then early versions of the condiment was likely made more along the lines of Indian pickles and therefore would have included such ingredients as mangoes, which were not available in eighteenth-century Britain. Instead, in modern Britain, piccalilli tends to be made with vegetables such as cauliflowers, gherkins, onions, French beans, and carrots.

Another of Britain's most well-known sauces is Cumberland sauce, a piquant sauce comprising redcurrant jelly, mustard, orange juice and peel, and port. Traditionally, Cumberland sauce was served with cold meats. There is some dispute as to the origins of Cumberland sauce with some historians suggesting the sauce stretches back to 1726 when John Nott, the chef to the dukes of Somerset, Ormond, and Bolton, included thirteen redcurrant recipes in his 1726 book *Cook's and Confectioner's Dictionary*. Piquant fruity sauces with the addition of a sour liquid such as verjuice or vinegar were popular in medieval British cuisine, and it may be that Nott's redcurrant recipes were inspired by these. However, other food writers claim the sauce is likely of nineteenth-century origin and named either in honor of the duke of Cumberland or the English county of its origin (Cumberland being a historic county of northwest England).

The earliest dictionary entry for Cumberland sauce dates from 1878, but the sauce is referred to in *The Times* newspaper report of a banquet in Berlin in 1872, attended by the European rulers Wilhelm I, Franz Joseph, and Alexander II, at which boar's head was served with the so-called sauce Cumberland. A European origin of Cumberland sauce is possible, for in 1853, the French chef and food writer Alexis Soyer described his recipe for a Cumberland-type sauce as being akin to the German sauce to accompany boar's head. This would be apt for the Hanovarian king Ernest Augustus (1771–1851), also held the title of duke of

Cumberland and Teviotdale. Meanwhile, *The Cook's Oracle* (1817), a cookbook by the immensely popular English cook and writer William Kitchiner, mentions a "Wine sauce for Venison or Hare" that sees port or claret mixed with redcurrant jelly. In 1817, Kitchiner also published the first recorded recipe for another port sauce, wow-wow sauce, in which port is combined with wine vinegar, parsley, pickled cucumbers, pickled walnuts, English mustard, and mushroom ketchup together with beef stock, flour, and butter. The sauce is intended to be served over boiled beef. In times past, ketchup (catsup) in Britain was made with mushrooms as the main ingredient rather than tomatoes. Typically, mushroom ketchup is prepared by packing whole mushrooms in a container of salt until the liquid from the mushrooms fills the container. The mushrooms and liquid are then cooked in an oven before spices such as mace, nutmeg, and black pepper are added. The liquid is then separated from the mushrooms by straining. The end product has a dark color derived from the spores of the mushrooms. Mushroom ketchup is used both as a condiment and as an ingredient in other sauces. While tomato ketchup is far more common in Britain today, bottled mushroom ketchup can still be found in British shops.

Mint has long been used in Britain to make sauces and jellies to serve with meat, particularly roast lamb and mutton. Mint sauce is a British sauce consisting of finely chopped mint leaves combined with water, vinegar, together with a small quantity of sugar. The resulting sauce is bright green in color.

The history of mint sauce is linked to the history of lamb consumption in England. For example, in the 1500s, British queen Elizabeth I ordered that lamb and mutton must be eaten with bitter herbs in order to discourage the consumption of sheep and thus boost Britain's wool trade. This rule backfired, however, as the use of mint in the sauce to serve with lamb and more particularly, the gamier-tasting older sheep eaten as mutton, actually made eating the meat a more pleasurable experience. The reason for this improved taste is that mint is rich in branched-chain ketone molecules, which are related to the branched-chain fatty acids released when lamb or mutton is cooked. Therefore, since the mint and lamb/mutton share similar chemical structures, they taste better together. The link between mint and lamb was strengthened further by the fact that in the past, lambs were slaughtered in springtime, which is when mint proliferates in Britain. Thus, in Britain, mint became associated inextricably with lamb. In modern Britain, jarred ready-made mint sauce is widely available in shops. A popular alternative to mint sauce is mint jelly, which has a thicker, jelly-like consistency and sweeter taste than mint sauce. Like mint sauce, jarred mint jelly is readily available in Britain.

Redcurrant jelly is another condiment that traditionally accompanies roast lamb. The jelly comprises redcurrants (*Ribes rubrum*), which are rich in both natural pectin and acid, together with sugar. Some redcurrant jelly recipes include additional ingredients such as red or white wine, port, rosemary, mustard, or orange zest. Redcurrant jelly is widely available as a jarred food. Redcurrant jelly is a traditional accompaniment to roast lamb because the redcurrants' acidity balances the richness of the lamb. Although redcurrant jelly is intrinsically associated with roast lamb, the jelly is also used to accompany roast poultry and sausages. Alternatively, redcurrant jelly is added to caramelized onions to make a gravy to serve with roast meat or sausages. Melted redcurrant jelly can also be brushed over the top of red fruit tarts for the jelly makes the fruits glisten like jewels while also imparting a tangy sweetness.

Sometimes in Britain, redcurrant jelly or sauce is served to accompany oily fish such as mackerel. Similarly, gooseberries are a traditional accompaniment to mackerel in Britain. Gooseberry sauce, made from gooseberries, mint, and sugar, originated in medieval England when England was under Norman French rule. Consequently, the French word for gooseberry is *groseille à maquereau* (mackerel berry). Gooseberry sauce, gooseberry jelly, and pickled gooseberries are also the traditional British accompaniment to roast duck or pork, though in Britain, roast pork is more usually served with a sauce made from cooking apples.

Further Reading

Grigson, Jane. *Jane Grigson's Fruit Book*. New York: Atheneum, 1982.

Guzey, Demet. *Mustard: A Global History*. London: Reaktion Books, 2019.

Janovich, Adriana. "Lamb & mint: A classic pairing." *Washington State Magazine* (Spring 2021). https://magazine.wsu.edu/2021/02/17/lamb-mint-a-classic-pairing/ (accessed June 1, 2023).

Jeffreys, Henry. "Smoked salmon." *The Spectator* (December 16, 2017). https://www.spectator.co.uk/article/smoked-salmon/ (accessed May 25, 2023).

Secret Smokehouse. "London cure smoked salmon" (2023).

The Tewkesbury Mustard Company. "History of Tewkesbury mustard" (2014). https://www.tewkesburymustard.co.uk/history-of-tewkesbury-mustard/ (accessed May 30, 2023).

Wright, Fraser. "A history of Clapshot, including a recipe for making your own." *The Scotsman: Food & Drink* (December 21, 2015). https://foodanddrink.scotsman.com/

food/a-history-of-clapshot-including-a-recipe-for-making-your-own/ (accessed May 30, 2023).

Yorkshire Pudd. "The Yorkshire pudding—where did it all begin?" Yorkshire.Pudd: The Yorkshire Pudding (2023).

4

Main Dishes

In Britain, the main meals of the day are breakfast, lunch, and dinner though the constituent parts of each meal vary greatly between individuals. Typically, breakfast consists of cereal, toast, or a hot dish such as a porridge or a so-called full English breakfast (also sometimes called simply a "full English" or a "fry-up"). Often, lunch is a light meal that consists of a sandwich, hot food such as soup, or maybe a salad. More substantial lunches do exist, however, such as the traditional ploughman's lunch. Dinners vary greatly, depending on factors ranging from individuals' ethnicity, heritage, or religion. History also plays a part for traditionally fish is associated with Fridays, while Sundays are set aside as the day of the roast dinner, though somewhat contradictorily, roast dinners tend to be eaten at lunchtime. Although Britain is surrounded by sea, British main courses tend to be meat-based, and there are many meaty main courses associated with the different regions of Britain, for example Lancashire hotpot, Welsh cawl, and Liverpudlian scouse. There are, however, a few traditional fish dishes, most notably fish and chips, but also Cullen skink.

Vegetarian and vegan meals are increasingly popular at both lunch and dinner including nut roasts, and plant-based curries, pizzas, stews, and soups. British society is highly multicultural meaning Britons are just as likely to have curry for dinner as they are a traditionally British dish such as hotpot.

Breakfast

In Britain, the tradition of eating breakfast dates back to medieval times. During this period, it was typical for Britons to eat only two meals per day—breakfast and dinner. Breakfast was eaten during mid- or late morning and tended to consist of bread washed down with ale. Sometimes the bread would be accompanied by cheese, cold meat, or dripping. At this time, only the very wealthy could afford lavish breakfasts with these held to mark important occasions such as weddings. For this reason, in Britain, a wedding reception that includes a sit-down meal is sometimes called the "wedding breakfast." By the Georgian era, breakfast had become an intrinsic part of shooting parties, weekend house parties, or hunts, for the social elite loved to entertain in an elaborate fashion, which included the holding of lavish breakfasts for guests. Georgian breakfasts were leisurely affairs with food provided by the host's estate and served from silver dining services that allowed hosts to impress their guests. It became socially acceptable to read newspapers during these breakfasts, and today, in Britain, it is still considered socially acceptable to read newspapers at the breakfast table—the British feel it is rude to read at the table at any other mealtime.

Georgian breakfasts consisted of eggs and bacon (bacon first being cured at the start of the eighteenth century), as well as offal dishes such as broiled kidneys, cold meats including tongue, and such fish dishes as kippers. In the Victorian era, affluent middle-class Britons began to ape the food customs of the gentry, including the custom of eating a hearty breakfast. It was during this era that the full English breakfast became a mainstay of British breakfast time, and breakfast dishes such as devilled kidneys came to the fore. Devilled kidneys originated during the eighteenth century, but it was not until the nineteenth century that the dish became popular as a breakfast dish. By the Edwardian era, devilled kidneys were particularly popular with the members of gentlemen's clubs.

Unlike the gentry, however, the British middle classes had to go out to work meaning middle-class Britons had to eat breakfast earlier than the gentry, usually before 9 a.m. Nowadays, cereal and toast are probably the breakfasts most widely consumed by time-poor Britons rushing to get to work and school. However, when time allows, a full English breakfast or porridge is a popular alternative. Some British eateries even offer full English breakfasts throughout the day. Outside of Britain, the full English has become such a recognizable part of British cuisine that eateries in areas popular with British tourists will often serve full English breakfasts in the hope of enticing British visitors inside.

The Full English Breakfast

The full English breakfast originated in the country estates of the English gentry. The stately homes of England served as important social hubs for the wealthy and the pre-hunt hearty breakfast became an important social occasion that allowed hosts to display their hospitality and guests to swap news and gossip. As a large, filling breakfast, the full English was served not just before guests went on a hunt, but also before setting out on long journeys or as a way of welcoming new guests. As well as demonstrating a host's hospitality, serving a full English consisting of ingredients produced on their estate allowed hosts to display their wealth for not only did the host employ a chef able to cook such a fine meal, but the host must also have substantial lands to be able to produce ingredients as varied as meat and vegetables used to produce the breakfast. Unlike the full English breakfasts of today, which typically is served as eggs, bacon, sausage, and some combination of tomatoes, mushrooms, toast, and so on, early English breakfasts saw components laid out as a buffet-type arrangement with bacon, sausages, and such like served alongside dishes such as fried whiting, stewed figs, pheasant legs, potted pigeon, and blood sausage though these dishes varied regionally.

By the beginning of the Victorian era, a new class of merchants, industrialists, and businessmen, made wealthy by the Industrial Revolution, had started to emerge. The members of this social class aspired to join the upper echelons of society and so copied as best they could the customs of the gentry, including the eating of full English breakfasts. The aspirational Victorians viewed breakfast as an opportunity to demonstrate their wealth, good taste, and social standing, and in so doing, they turned the full English into an iconic breakfast dish.

During the Edwardian era, a standardized version of the English breakfast began to emerge as the dish started to be served in hotels, guest houses, and on trains across Britain. The standardized components of the breakfast included bacon, eggs, sausage, blood sausage, baked beans, half a grilled tomato, fried bread, or toast served with a jam or marmalade, tea or coffee, and orange juice. By this time, the English breakfast was enjoyed regularly by all classes of society and had come to be seen as a family meal necessary to provide energy needed to see people through long working days. This was true not just for the upper and middle classes, but also for the working class who saw the full English breakfast as important fuel that would allow them to perform long hours of physically demanding labor in factories. Indeed, as late as the 1950s, almost half of all adult Britons started the day with a full English breakfast. Thus, a breakfast that began as a meal enjoyed by the gentry to display their wealth became a mainstay of both middle- and working-class Britons. Often, the full English breakfast was served in so-called greasy spoons, basic eateries specializing in cheap, particularly fried foods. Greasy spoons emerged soon after the Second World War as alternative dining experiences to more upmarket eateries such as Lyons Corner Houses. Greasy spoons were often opened as family businesses, particularly by foreign families displaced by the war, and soon became an iconic part of British cuisine. Today, greasy spoons still exist though in smaller numbers and continue to specialize in no-nonsense, filling food sold at low prices. While greasy spoons may seem basic compared to some other cafés, they are egalitarian establishments attracting a clientele from all walks of life and as such are a beloved British institution. Moreover, greasy spoons have long been regarded as the best place to find a traditional full English breakfast though the breakfasts are also a staple of British hotels, bed and breakfasts (often abbreviated to B&Bs, these are small British lodging houses that offer overnight accommodation with breakfast), and pubs.

While the full English breakfast was standardized during Edwardian times, the dish continues to evolve and can now include not just bacon, egg, sausage, tomato, toast, and baked beans, but also mushrooms, hash browns, and French fries. Hash browns and chips are particularly controversial, with many Britons arguing that to add either to a full English is sacrilegious. It is also possible to find eateries that offer vegetarian variations on the full English that swap the bacon for, say, avocado mash. Regional variations of the full English also exist. For example, a full Scottish breakfast may include a slice of haggis, a tattie scone (scone made from potato), or a Lorne sausage (a square sausage made from minced meat, rusk, and spices that is not formed in a casing but rather is sliced from a formed block).

Meanwhile, a Welsh breakfast might feature laverbread (*barra lawr*, a Welsh delicacy made from seaweed). Additionally, some parts of England have a regional specialty sausage that they include in their breakfasts. These include the Lincolnshire sausage, which is associated with the eastern county of Lincolnshire and has a flavor dominated by sage; the Cumberland sausage, a very long, coiled sausage from the northwest county of Cumbria that is strongly flavored by black and white pepper; and hog's pudding, a type of sausage made in the southwest counties of Cornwall and Devon that consist of pork, suet, bread, and oatmeal or pearl barley.

While the full English breakfast has a reputation as being unhealthily fatty, some Britons make the dish healthier by poaching rather than frying their eggs, boiling or grilling rather than frying their tomatoes or mushrooms, and including wholemeal toast. Moreover, some nutritionists suggest that eating a full English breakfast in the morning boosts the eater's metabolism.

Porridge

Britons have eaten porridge (oats simmered in milk or water) for millennia. This is evinced by the analysis of pottery fragments by the University of Bristol that show porridge has been enjoyed in Scotland's Outer Hebrides for 5,500 years when early Hebridean farmers ate a gruel of wheat softened in warm milk. However, oats were not widely cultivated in Britain until much later when Roman invaders, in need of a weather-resistant, prolific crop to grow as animal feed, cultivated oats to feed to their horses, mules, and cattle. As oats were easier to peel than spelt and disease-resistant, oats remained a popular animal fodder in Britain for centuries after the Romans left the realm, though oats were less commonly eaten by British humans.

During the Middle Ages, oats became a major constituent of people's diets in Scotland for Scotland's lack of sunlight and humid climate allowed only hardy cereals such as oats to grow well. Being far more reliable to cultivate than wheat or maize in Scotland's harsh climate, oatmeal (oats that have had their husks removed and have been steamed and flattened) became the staple food of the Scottish lower classes. Soon numerous regional Scottish oat dishes appeared and became prominent in Scottish diets, including gruel (a thinner version of porridge), sowans (a thick drink made of fermented oats), and hasty pudding (a very thick, sweet porridge).

Today, porridge is an iconic symbol of Scotland though it is eaten across Britain.

Porridge is a highly nutritious breakfast for it is high in fiber, vitamin B, and minerals such as calcium, potassium, and iron, as well as beta-glucans, which is rich in naturally occurring polysaccharides that can lower cholesterol and blood sugar levels.

Kippers

Kippers are an iconic British breakfast dish consisting of a whole herring that has been split in butterfly fashion from its tail to its head, gutted, salted, and smoked over wood chips that are typically made of oak. Kippers are usually served grilled, boiled in a plastic bag in water, or pan fried. Often, kippers are accompanied by bread and butter with which the diner can mop up the fishy juices left on the plate once the kipper has been eaten. Occasionally, a poached egg is served on top of the kipper with this dish eaten as either breakfast or dinner. The best British kippers are reputed to come from northern England, the Isle of Man, and Scotland, and are a pale coppery color rather than a dark tone for a dark-colored kipper is often the result of the fish being dyed. Kippers are considered a nutritious breakfast as they are low in calories and high in both protein and omega-3 fatty acids that can help promote brain and heart health. Kippers are also a good source of vitamin D.

The history of kippers is uncertain, but it is known that fish in Britain have long been smoke-cured. It has been suggested that herrings originated in the Great Yarmouth area of Norfolk, eastern England, when fishermen smoked a herring accidentally. An alternative theory as to the invention of kippers is that of fish intended for processing that was left overnight by local fish processor John Woodger in a room with a smoking stove in Seahouses in the northeast English county of Northumberland in 1843. Whatever the true history of kippers, by the Edwardian era, the smoked fish were firmly enshrined as a quintessentially British breakfast food. Indeed, kippers have featured on the breakfast menu of London's high-end Savoy hotel since 1889. As well as being a breakfast food, up until the Second World War, kippers were also eaten as dinner, especially by working-class populations in inland and urban areas that lacked access to freshly caught fish. Kippers remained popular in Britain until the 1970s when people started to consider kippers an unfashionable food and sought breakfasts that were quicker to prepare.

In the 2010s, however, kippers experienced a revival as Britons turned to kippers as a healthy, cheap breakfast. The revival chimed with a trend for vintage shopping as well as the resurrection of heritage British foods and was boosted when celebrity chefs and food writers such as Nigella Lawson, Jamie Oliver, Gordon Ramsey, and Delia Smith recommended kippers. Additionally, the fact that the herring from which kippers are made were deemed a sustainable fish by the Marine Conservation Society also meant that Britons could buy kippers without feeling guilty. Consequently, in 2012, the Sainsbury's supermarket chain announced that the sales of kippers from its fresh fish counters had increased by 79 percent in the past year, while Sainsbury's rival supermarket chain Tesco claimed that its sales of fresh kippers had risen by 28 percent year-on-year, a figure that represented an extra 150,000 kippers being sold in a year. Kippers remain a popular breakfast food today.

Lunch

While British lunches often consist of a sandwich bought from a shop and eaten hastily at work, when time allows, Britons do enjoy more leisurely traditional lunchtime meals. These lunch dishes include the ploughman's lunch, which is synonymous with summer days spent in relaxing pub beer gardens, and the hearty Sunday roast, which acts as both lunch and dinner.

Ploughman's Lunch

A ploughman's lunch is a rustic English dish comprising chunky bread (often the midsection of a baguette) and butter, an English cheese (usually Cheddar or Stilton), and various accompaniments such as an apple, pickle (usually Branston—the brand name of a jarred, sweet-spicy vegetable chutney), some salad leaves, and a pickled onion. Typically, a ploughman's lunch is eaten at a pub and served on a wooden platter to be consumed with beer or sometimes cider. Although cheese is the traditional focus of the ploughman's lunch, some pubs offer variations on the ploughman's lunch by swapping the cheese for thick-cut ham, a non-British cheese such as French brie, a pork pie, meaty pâté, boiled eggs, or even tinned tuna mixed with mayonnaise.

Although the main constituents of a ploughman's lunch—bread, cheese, and beer—have been consumed in England for centuries, the term "ploughman's lunch" first appeared in print in John Lockhart's book *Memoirs of the Life of Sir Walter Scott* (1837). However, the name "ploughman's lunch" only entered common usage in the 1950s when the Cheese Bureau marketing board started to advertise the meal in pubs as a way to increase cheese sales in England, following the end of wartime cheese rationing. The popularity of the ploughman's lunch grew further in the 1960s when the Milk Marketing Board promoted the meal to boost cheese sales in Britain.

In essence, a ploughman's lunch resembles what a ploughman might have eaten during a midday break from working in the fields, for bread, cheese, and ale were the traditional lunchtime foodstuffs of rural workers for the foods were filling, easy to transport, and did not need to be cooked. Pubs, especially those in market towns, found that serving ploughman's lunches made excellent commercial sense as the meal required little preparation, was made from easily available, inexpensive ingredients, and the saltiness of the cheese made customers thirstier and thus likely to buy more beer.

In southern England, cheese was especially common as a lunchtime source of protein rather than expensive meat, and so the ploughman's lunch is particularly associated with southern England. Indeed, the 1787 book *Provincial Glossary with a Collection of Local Proverbs and Popular Superstitions* by Francis Grose, a guide to the local customs of England and Wales, notes that in the southeast English county of Kent, ploughmen ate bread and cheese washed down by beer. Meanwhile, in the 1870s, farm laborers in Devon, southwest England, were famous for eating bread and cheese washed down with local cider. The use of cheese as a source of protein meant the ploughman's lunch was often considered humble and associated with rural poverty. The ploughman's lunch was not exclusive to England, however, for in 1891, the Scottish *Dundee Courier* newspaper reported that a group of Scottish ploughmen were so outraged at being served something other than bread, cheese, and beer for lunch that they took their employer to court.

Even at the start of the twentieth century, bread, cheese, and beer were the only lunchtime refreshments offered by many country pubs in England, though the meal was referred to as "bread and cheese" rather than a ploughman's lunch as the term was yet to enter common usage. Wartime cheese rationing (1942–54) severed cheese's relationship with beer leaving cheese sales depressed. Therefore, in 1955, the Cheese Bureau was established to represent British and Commonwealth cheese producers and, in particular, to promote sales of Cheddar and Cheshire cheese. As part of this move to increase cheese sales, the Cheese Bureau aimed to reaffirm the traditional affinity of cheese served with bread, beer, and pickle as enjoyed at pubs throughout the centuries. While publicans were quick to start serving cheese with bread and beer, an advertising campaign consisting of special events to explain what was meant by the term "ploughman's lunch" was needed to convince the British public that cheese was a natural accompaniment to bread and beer and, moreover, to associate the name "ploughman's lunch" with the meal.

In the 1970s, the popularity of the ploughman's lunch grew rapidly. The growth in popularity was in part because the meal chimed with a wave of distrust of modernity felt by some Britons at the time, and also because the meal was quick and easy to prepare from cheap ingredients, meaning caterers could get less skilled staff to create the dish resulting in the meal yielding high-profit margins.

Sunday Roast

The Sunday roast is eaten as either lunch or dinner on Sundays across Britain. The meal consists of a roast meat (typically beef, lamb, pork, or chicken) accompanied by roast potatoes, and a selection of vegetables, usually some combination of cabbage, carrots, parsnips, Brussels sprouts, cauliflower, and peas, plus gravy and a sauce. The sauce served depends on the type of roast meat included in the meal. For instance, the traditional accompaniment to roast beef is horseradish sauce, while roast pork is served with apple sauce, lamb with mint sauce, and chicken with cranberry sauce. Roast beef is also accompanied by a Yorkshire pudding. Vegetarians tend to substitute the roast meat with a nut roast (a dish comprising nuts and seasoned grains formed into a loaf shape, then roasted). Britons eat Sunday roasts both at home as a family meal and at other eateries, especially pubs.

The Sunday roast is a cherished British culinary tradition. Indeed, such was Britons' love of the Sunday roast, particularly roast beef, that in the eighteenth century, the French referred to the English as the *rosbifs*. Additionally, the ceremonial guardians of the Tower of London called The Yeomen Warders of Her Majesty's Royal Palace and Fortress the Tower of London, and Members of the Sovereign's Body Guard of the Yeoman Guard Extraordinary, are commonly referred to as the "Beefeaters." There are several theories as to the origins of this name including the fact that during the seventeenth century, the term "beefeater" was used as a slang name for the English.

Originally, Britons roasted their meat on spits in front of open fires as this meant that the heat from the fire cooked the flesh but prevented the meat from tasting of smoke. A pan placed under the meat caught any dripping fat. Today, Britons roast their meat in the oven—though technically this method is baking, it is generally accepted as the way to "roast" meat. In earlier times, less affluent Britons did not have houses with large fireplaces on which to roast a joint of meat nor could they afford to eat meat several times per week. Therefore, many Britons bought meat once per week and dropped it off at a local baker on their way to church so that the meat could be cooked in the baker's ovens as they cooled (for bread was not baked on Sundays). In this way, the traditional Sunday lunch began.

In the 1790s, the invention of the coal-fired kitchen range allowed Britons to cook meat in the home oven rather than in front of a fire. In the nineteenth century, the advent of gas and electric ovens meant even more people could roast meat at home, and thus a British culinary institution was born.

Cornish Pasty

A pasty is a type of baked pastry found across Britain that is made by placing an uncooked filling, usually comprising meat and vegetables in the middle of a pastry circle, and then bringing the edges of the pastry together around the filling before crimping over the top of the pastry to form a seal. The most famous example of a pasty is the Cornish pasty, which in 2011 was granted Protected Geographical Indication status in Europe by the European Union authorities. In 2020, this designation was upheld by the UK government following Brexit. Under this designation, to be classified as a Cornish pasty, a pasty must have been made within the southwest English county of Cornwall to the west of the River Tamar. Although Cornish pasties must be made in Cornwall, thousands of

Cornish pasties are sent all over Britain where they are sold in shops, pubs, and other eateries. Sometimes, these pasties are baked and packaged in Cornwall before being sent outside the county, while others are prepared in Cornwall before being freshly baked at their end destination. Additionally, a true Cornish pasty must contain only the following uncooked ingredients: diced or minced beef, diced or sliced potato, diced swede (rutabaga) or turnip (in Cornwall the word 'swede' refers to a 'turnip' so the two vegetables are interchangeable), onion, and salt and pepper. Moreover, to be classed as a Cornish pasty, a pasty must contain a minimum of 12.5 percent meat and a minimum of 25 percent vegetable. The pastry may be shortcrust, puff, or rough puff but must be able to hold all the ingredients throughout the cooking time without cracking. Furthermore, the pasty's pastry must be crimped into a "D" shape, with the crimp toward one side. Cornish pasties that have their pastry crimped to the left are known as a cock pasty while those with a right-hand crimp are called a hen pasty. In Cornwall, a Cornish pasty is known as a tiddly oggie. The exact derivation of the name is unclear. Tiddly may stem from "tiddly" meaning proper in naval slang or "tiddy" being the local word for a potato in Devon and Cornwall, while "oggie" may derive from the expression "Hoggan," which was shouted down Cornish tin mine shafts when pasties were cooked and ready to eat. Today, British sports crowds, especially those at rugby union matches, are known to chant "Oggie, oggie, oggie" to which other fans in the sports stadium reply "Oi, oi, oi!"

Although in Britain, pasties are most strongly associated with Cornwall, the word "pasty" derives from the Old French word *paste* meaning "a pie." One of the earliest references to pasties in British documents occurred in a charter granted by King John of England in 1208 to the town of Great Yarmouth in the eastern county of Norfolk, for the town was bound to send to the sheriffs of the nearby city of Norwich one hundred herrings baked in twenty-four pasties annually. Meanwhile, the thirteenth-century monk and historian Matthew Paris documented that the monks of St. Albans Abbey in southeast England lived upon pasties. By this time, the pasty had become part of the British diet though they were eaten mostly by the upper classes and royalty. The fillings at this time were varied, and it was possible to find pasties containing venison, lamb, eels, or fruits.

The earliest written reference to pasties in southwest England can be found in the city records of the Devon town of Plymouth dated 1509 and 1510. This documentation has led some historians to believe that Cornish pasties may have originated in Devon before spreading westward to Devon's neighboring county of Cornwall. However, this belief is countered by others who suggest cave paintings dating from 8000 BCE found at Lizard in Cornwall that depict two people eating a pasty-like food wrapped in crimped leaves.

After about the mid-1600s, the word pasty fell out of use in Britain save for when used to refer to the Cornish pasty. Nonetheless, the Cornish pasty was by then firmly established as an important food of the poor for the pasty's vegetable ingredients were easily attainable and the meat component of the pasty could be made up of cheap meat scraps. It is for this reason that traditionally Cornish pasties contain much less meat than they do vegetables.

Since Cornish pasties were made from humble ingredients, they became both an affordable and a filling meal enjoyed by working families. In the nineteenth century, the importance of the Cornish pasty increased for the wives and mothers of Cornish tin miners prepared the pasties as easily transportable, takeaway meals to provide sustenance for their husbands and children who worked grueling days down the mines. The miners worked at such deep depths that it was not possible for them to surface for food at lunchtime, so some mineshaft were equipped with stoves that allowed miners to cook raw pasties. The heated pasties not only provided the miners with a hot lunch but also kept them warm for a pasty could keep warm for 8–10 hours if worn close to the body thereby warming the miner too. In order to give miners a culinary treat, it was common for Cornish pasties to have a savory filling at one end and a sweet filling at the other end. It has been theorized that the miners gave rise to the Cornish pasty's distinctive crimped edge for the pasties' crust functioned as a handle that was discarded after the rest of the pasty had been eaten so as not to ingest toxic substances on the miners' hands (many Cornish tin mines contained high levels of arsenic). However, other historians maintain that miners ate their pasties from muslin or paper bags.

There are many superstitions surrounding the Cornish pasty. One such superstition suggests that the Devil refused to cross the River Tamar into Cornwall for fear of becoming the filling of a Cornish pasty. Additionally, according to tradition, Cornish wives would imprint their husbands' initials on to pasties so that they could be distinguished from each other. Another reason for imprinting the initials was that a miner could leave part of his pasty and the crust to placate the mischievous underground, gnome-like creatures called tommyknockers or knockers that were thought to inhabit the tin mines of Cornwall and Devon, making a knocking sound either when miners had found a rich vein of ore or to warn that a mine's tunnel was about to collapse.

In order to maintain friendly relations with the knockers, the tin miners would leave a morsel of pasty inside a mine for the knockers to eat so the initials

> ### The Knockers
>
> In Cornwall, the knockers are described as being around 2 ft tall, with large heads, long arms, wrinkled skin, and white hair. They are said to wear a miniature version of a miner's clothing and commit random acts of mischief, such as stealing miners' equipment and food. As miners faced numerous hazards underground including mineshaft collapses, they were constantly alert to the sounds of the mines. Creaking timbers would strike fear into miners' hearts, and they would attribute the knocking sound of the timber to the knockers. Indeed, some miners felt the knocking sound came from knockers attacking the timber supports in order to cause shafts to collapse.

carved into the pasties meant that those miners who had left their crusts for the knockers could be determined from those who failed to feed the creatures. Cornish fishermen, however, believed it was bad luck to bring a Cornish pasty onboard a ship. This belief likely originated because Cornish tin miners did not want their traditional food to be adopted by others, transported by ship to places near and far. Nevertheless, when political unrest broke out in Europe in 1848, this resulted in a collapse in mineral prices, leading to mine closures and widespread unemployment in Cornwall. Consequently, Cornish tin miners began to migrate to other parts of Britain as well to across the globe, taking with them the concept of the Cornish pasty and led to regional variations on the food. For example, in the nineteenth century, a sweet-savory pasty called a Parys pasty was eaten by copper miners on Parys Mountain, on the Isle of Anglesey off the Welsh coast. This pasty took the form of a thick, shortcrust pastry shell filled with a meat and vegetable mix on one side and a fruit and jam filling on the other side so as to create a two-course meal in one pasty. The thick pasty also allowed the miners to keep their food uncontaminated by their dirty hands. Traditionally, the pasties had the miner's initials cut into the savory side in order to designate which side contained the meat and vegetables. Additionally, the Parys pasty was glazed on the sweet side so that the miner knew which side of the pasty to eat first (the meat side, followed by the sweet side for pudding). While early Parys pasties contained cheap cuts of meat, today they are made using prime cuts of Welsh lamb.

A similar pasty called a Bedfordshire or Hertfordshire clanger (also called a Trowley dumpling or simply a clanger) can be found in the southern English county of Bedfordshire and adjacent counties including Buckinghamshire and Hertfordshire. This pasty dates back to at least the nineteenth century when the pasty was a staple food of field laborers. The etymology of the name clanger is unknown though it may be related to the dialect word "clung" denoting a heavy food. This would be apt because a clanger is a substantial food—a suet crust pastry with a savory filling at one end and a sweet filling at the other end with a piece of pastry between the two ends to keep the sweet and savory fillings separate. Alternatively, the name could derive from the dialect word *clang* from nearby Northamptonshire meaning "to eat ravenously."

Originally, Bedfordshire clangers were made using the remains of the Sunday roast meat, which was then boiled. The farm workers kept the clangers in muslin cloths and heated the clangers on a hot stone before eating them as they worked in the fields. Today, local bakers still make Bedfordshire clangers using potatoes and gammon for the savory filling and stewed apples for the sweet end, though in the past jam was used instead of apples. It is possible to differentiate between the sweet and savory ends of the clanger for the end containing the meat has two holes baked into the pastry while three knife slits denote the sweet end. Bedfordshire clangers are sold by local shops, cafés, and restaurants.

Dinner

Dinners served in Britain vary greatly between individuals and households for the choice of meal depends on factors as varied as time, people's cultural heritage, income, and the time of year. For example, if people are in a hurry, then they may eat a microwavable ready-meal from a supermarket whereas someone with more time might cook a casserole. Similarly, in summer, people tend to eat more salads and cold dishes whereas in winter, hearty, warming stews and the like are eaten widely. Since Britain is hugely multicultural, dinners can range from pizza and pasta to curries and stir-fries. Sausages are another popular dinner food being eaten with mashed potato (a meal commonly referred to as bangers and mash) or cooked in a Yorkshire pudding as "toad in the hole." Mashed potato also features as the topping to dinner dishes such as shepherd's pie (minced lamb topped with mashed potato and baked in the oven) and cottage pie (the same as shepherd's pie but made with minced beef instead of lamb). There are also a number of regional dishes that are served traditionally as dinner around Britain.

Lancashire Hotpot

Lancashire hotpot (often called simply "hotpot") is a dish originating in the northwest English county of Lancashire. The dish comprises lamb (or mutton), onion, and possibly carrots and other root vegetables such as leeks and turnips, stock to keep the dish moist, and flour to thicken the liquid. The whole dish is then topped with thin slices of potatoes before being baked slowly in a deep pot at a low temperature. The dish is popular across Britain but most particularly in the northwest of England. Since Lancashire hotpot is such a hearty dish, it is enjoyed especially in winter. While Lancashire hotpot is a homely dish, it is also frequently served in pubs.

The origin of the name hotpot is unknown, but it may refer to the tall, earthenware pot in which the stew is made traditionally. Alternatively, the name may derive from the word *hodgepodge*, meaning a confused mixture, which may be a reference to the jumble of layered ingredients that make up the dish for traditionally Lancashire hotpot comprises alternating layers of the meat (usually mutton or maybe sheep kidneys but today more often diced lamb), the root vegetables, and then the sliced potatoes.

The exact history of Lancashire hotpot is unknown too, but in Lancashire, the dish certainly has a long history. That said, the first published recipe for Lancashire hotpot appeared only as recently as 1859 in *The English Cookery Book* by J. H. Walsh, which gave a recipe for Lancashire hotpot made with mutton chops. The recipe was well received and made hotpot popular across Britain. *Mrs Beeton's Cookery Book* (1861) popularized the dish further for the cookbook contained a recipe for a one-pot stew called Hotch Potch that was very similar to hotpot.

The development of Lancashire hotpot is tied to Lancashire's history of industrialization. Pre-industrialization, many Lancastrian families worked at home spinning thread and so ate meals such as hotpot that would slow-cook over a fire at home. During the Industrial Revolution, Lancashire became the center of the English textile industry along with Manchester and other towns in the historic county of Lancashire which came to be known as Cottonopolis. Manchester was the epicenter of England's cotton industry when Britain produced 80 percent of global cotton yarn and fabric, and industrialization meant many Lancastrians (people living in Lancashire) started to work away from home in the area's many cotton mills. The development of England's textile industry had a fundamental impact on every aspect of Lancashire life so that by the end of the nineteenth century, over 500,000 Lancastrians out of a population of around four million people were employed by the textile industry, principally in work connected to the production of cotton. While the cotton industry boomed, however, many of the cotton industry's workers lived in poverty. Cotton mill laborers regarded hotpot as a filling, warming dish that could be left to cook while households were at work in nearby mills. This made hotpot an extremely convenient meal for workers who were hungry after hours of physically challenging labor and who would race home at the end of their shift to find a hearty hotpot dinner waiting for them. That the hotpot's ingredients were easily accessible and affordable only helped the popularity of the dish. The ingredients needed for hotpot were easy to find for the root vegetables used to make hotpot could be cultivated in northwest England and required minimal tending by people out at work, while mutton, being the meat of older sheep, was a cheaper alternative to lamb. For this reason, in the nineteenth century, lamb-based hotpots were enjoyed by the wealthy, whereas the hotpots of the working class were made with mutton. The association of Lancashire hotpot with the cotton mills of northern England are evinced in Elizabeth Gaskell's novel *North and South* (1854–5), which details how the cotton mill owner John Thornton eats hotpot with his workers.

Today in Britain, mutton is not as easily obtainable as lamb, hence most Lancashire hotpots are made with lamb rather than mutton. Another change to occur to Lancashire hotpot is that in some early versions of Lancashire hotpot, oysters were added to the meat mix in order to bulk out the hotpot filling. However, oysters are not included in modern hotpots because oysters are now regarded as something of a luxury food unlike in the nineteenth century when they were a food of the poor. Traditionally, Lancashire hotpot is accompanied with a side dish of pickled red cabbage as the vinegary tang of the vegetable cuts through the fattiness of the hotpot.

Cawl and Scouse

Cawl (pronounced cow-al) is a traditional Welsh broth comprising Welsh lamb or beef (sometimes meat leftover from a roast dinner), slow-cooked for several hours together with such vegetables as leeks (one of the national emblems of Wales), swede, onions, cabbage, and carrots as well as herbs such as rosemary and thyme. A vegetarian cawl known as *Cawl cennin* (leek cawl) is eaten widely and is made in the same manner as meaty cawl but with the meat replaced by lima beans.

As cawl contains quite a lot of liquid when served, it tends to be eaten from a deep bowl rather than a plate. Traditionally, cawl should be eaten using a wooden spoon as the wood does not get hot and so prevents the diner from burning their lips when eating the broth. Traditionally, some Welsh families would remove the meat and vegetables from the cawl broth as this allowed the broth to be saved to be eaten the next day. As cawl is a warming, hearty dish, it is enjoyed particularly on winter and early spring evenings and is typically accompanied by bread and a Welsh cheese. In Wales, cawl is a traditional staple dish of school dinners, Friday night dinners, and weekend lunches. However, although the dish is popular in Wales, cawl is not so well known outside of the principality, unlike the similar Irish stew, which is also a broth-type meal consisting of root vegetables and lamb or beef.

The origin of the name cawl is uncertain. On the one hand, the name may derive from the Latin word *caulis*, meaning the stalk of a plant that is also sometimes translated as cabbage. On the other hand, cawl could also be related to another Latin word *calidus* meaning "fiery," from which the word *caldo*, meaning "hot" derives to give the name of a broth eaten in northern Spain and Portugal. The origin of cawl predates written records but archeologists believe that prehistoric cooks in Wales cooked using pots of water warmed by stones heated on flames for throughout Wales are scattered "burnt mounds" (burnt fragments of rock and charcoal) that date back to around 2500 BCE. In some parts of Wales, the cooking technique using pots of water and hot stones persisted well into the Roman era in some areas. While some early Welsh cooks would have cooked food in cauldrons suspended over fires, the Romans introduced to Wales the three-legged iron cooking pot. Cawl was cooked in such three-legged pots well into the twentieth century.

According to the *Cyfraith Hywel* (Laws of Hywel Dda, the system of law practiced in medieval Wales), cabbages and leeks were the vegetables most commonly grown at the time, and therefore, cawl featured these vegetables. Similarly, although today Wales is famous for producing lamb, sheep only became common in Wales as the country's highlands became deforested allowing space for the sheep to graze. Instead, pigs and cows were more common animals at the time, with beef being especially prized and exported to England. Indeed, in medieval times, the indigenous Welsh Celts measured their wealth in cattle. Therefore, early cawl featured not only leeks and cabbage, but also pork and beef. Potatoes were not commonly used in Welsh cuisine until the eighteenth century so although they are now considered intrinsic to cawl, they were not included in early versions of the dish, which was instead thickened using oats. Once potatoes became popular in Wales, they overtook other vegetables as the main ingredient of cawl. When cereal crops failed and land enclosures started to cause hunger among the Welsh poor due to the loss of common land, eighteenth-century Welsh farmers turned to potatoes as their main crop rather than growing a variety of vegetables as they once had. Consequently, potatoes became the main vegetable ingredient of cawl. Other late additions to cawl include turnip and swede, which were not grown in Britain before the eighteenth century. By the end of the 1900s, cawl had evolved into the dish that is enjoyed today.

According to some food historians, traditionally, in south Wales, cawl should be made using lamb, while in north Wales, it is should be made with beef. However, the beef version is known as lobscouse (or lobscows) and is therefore almost indistinguishable from scouse, a very similar stew from nearby Liverpool in northwest England. Scouse is the name given to both the accent of people native to Liverpool and a stew hailing from the city. Similarly, people from Liverpool are often referred to in Britain as Scousers. These terms derive from the traditional northern European sailor's stew called *lobscouse*, which was made from beef, potatoes, onions, and seasoning. Indeed, versions of scouse can be found across northern Europe and Scandinavia. In the eighteenth and nineteenth centuries, Liverpool was a major port where seaman from across the globe converged. Consequently, many of the sailors in Liverpool at this time came from Scandinavia, and it is probable that the Liverpudlian dish scouse originated from a Norwegian recipe for a beef stew called *lapskaus* that was brought to Liverpool by Norwegian sailors. Another theory suggests, however, that scouse has its origins in the lobscouse eaten at Baltic ports, especially those in Germany. In Germany, the dish *labskaus* typically comprises boiled salted meat, potatoes, and onion that may be served with beetroot and soused herring.

Scouse is similar to cawl, Irish stew, and Lancashire hotpot, for meat, usually beef but sometimes lamb, is simmered together for hours. Usually the meat is seared first, then removed from the pan while some of the potatoes are boiled. As the potatoes cook, they break apart and thicken the boiling liquid. The meat is then returned to the pan along with the rest of the potatoes and onions. The scouse is then left to finish cooking. Meat is not essential to scouse, however, for scouse made without meat (either through preference or because the cook cannot afford meat) is known as a "blind scouse." Scouse is still popular in Liverpool being a staple dish found in Liverpudlian pubs and cafés, though these eateries may embellish the dish and use more luxurious ingredients than the original thrifty ingredients traditionally associated with scouse.

Despite its northern European roots, today, scouse is synonymous with Liverpool. The nickname Scouser to describe Liverpudlians (people from Liverpool) began as a derogatory term that suggested an individual was so poor that they could afford to eat only leftovers cooked with potatoes. However, Liverpudlians have reclaimed the word as their own and started to use it with pride to describe themselves. In 2018, research by *The Liverpool Echo* newspaper found that most Liverpudlians add carrots to their scouse, while some also add ingredients including lentils and sweet potato, as well as such herbs as rosemary and basil. The most popular meat for scouse-making was beef, but the survey found many respondents used whichever meat was cheapest and some included marrowbone (the spongy tissue found in the center of bones) to thicken the broth. Like Lancashire hotpot, scouse is often served with red cabbage or, like cawl, with a chunk of bread. Sometimes, scouse may be served with pickled beetroot instead of pickled cabbage.

Chicken Tikka Masala

Chicken tikka masala comprises boneless chicken chunks that are marinated in spices and yogurt before being roasted in a traditional tandoor oven and then served in a creamy sauce. The ingredients of the sauce vary, but tomato, coriander, coconut cream, and cream are common. Additionally, the sauce is often colored orange by the presence of such spices as turmeric and paprika. Chicken tikka masala is a hugely popular takeaway dish in Britain as well as a staple dish of curry houses, especially those in Brick Lane, a street in London's East End that is famous for the presence of myriad restaurants serving curry. Additionally, in 2016, chicken tikka masala was the third best-selling ready-meal sold by UK supermarkets (after shepherd's pie and lasagne).

The origins of chicken tikka masala are disputed. The dish may have been invented by a Bangladeshi chef in the Scottish city of Glasgow during the 1970s who likely added a creamy sauce to his chicken tikka (pieces of boneless chicken marinated in spices and yogurt then served on a skewer). Some food historians have also claimed that the dish may have originated in 1970s London when an Indian chef cooked chicken in spiced, canned tomato soup. Celebrated British Pakistani restauranteur Ali Ahmed Aslam has also been credited with inventing the dish when he improvised a sauce made from a can of condensed tomato soup. However, a recipe for Shahi chicken masala occurs in Balbir Singh's 1961 cookbook *Indian Cookery* and thus predates the other potential dates of origin. Alternatively, chicken tikka masala may be derived from the popular north

Indian dish of *murgh makhana* or butter chicken, which is a chicken curry served in a spiced tomato and butter sauce.

Whatever the origins of chicken tikka masala, the dish is extremely popular in Britain and has a huge cultural significance as a symbol of Britain's multicultural society. Indeed, in 2001, the then British foreign secretary Robin Cook hailed chicken tikka masala as representative of the way in which Britain absorbs and adapts global influences, and the meal is sometimes cited as Britain's national dish. In 2009, Mohammed Sarwar, a member of the Scottish Parliament, sought unsuccessfully for chicken tikka masala to be granted an official Protected Designation of Origin status by the European Union.

Fish and Chips

Fish and chips is one of the most iconic of British dishes. Traditional fish and chips comprises a fillet of fish (often cod or haddock) deep-fried in a crisp batter served together with fried chips (French fries). Often the fish and chips are accompanied by mushy peas (dried marrowfat peas that are simmered in water until very soft) and a pickled onion (an onion pickled in vinegar with salt and spices added). Tartar sauce, tomato ketchup, malt vinegar, or curry sauce are sometimes added accompaniments, but this depends on the personal preference of the diner. Fish and chips can be eaten for lunch or dinner at home or in all types of British eateries—from the humblest takeaway fish-and-chip establishments (often referred to as "chippies") to the fanciest restaurant (though these tend to serve a much more refined version of the dish) to pubs and restaurants dedicated to serving only fish with chips. Indeed, according to the National Federation of Fish Friers, today there are 10,500 specialist fish-and-chip shops in the UK (compared to just 1,200 McDonald's branches), which sell 382 million meals annually, just over half of which are eaten at home as takeaways. Such is the UK's love of fish and chips that the industry is worth £1.2 billion annually. Although fish and chips is a fried dish, it is not necessarily unhealthy for it contains only 2.8 percent saturated fat. The dish also provides a third of an adult man's recommended daily allowance of vitamins (or nearly half of the allowance for an adult woman).

The exact history of fish and chips in Britain is debatable though may be related to several continental European culinary traditions. For example, in the sixteenth century, Western Sephardic Jewish refugees fleeing persecution in Portugal and Spain sought sanctuary in London and in so doing brought with them a tradition of frying fish. The refugees prepared their fried fish in the manner of *Pescado frito*, a traditional Shabbat fish dish eaten by Spanish and Portuguese Jews in which fish is coated in flour and then deep-fried in vegetable oil. On a visit to London in the eighteenth century, U.S. president Thomas Jefferson noted this Jewish tradition of eating fried fish, and the 1845 cookbook *A Shilling Cookery for the People* by Alexis Soyer contains a recipe for fish fried in the "Jewish manner." Meanwhile, Belgian housewives of the late seventeenth century are credited with inventing chips (French fries) for when the Meuse River that flows through France, Belgium, and the Netherlands froze during winter, meaning fishing could not take place, the women would fry potatoes in place of the unavailable fish.

In 1837, Charles Dickens's novel *Oliver Twist*, which is set in London, refers to a "fried fish warehouse," which was the forerunner of today's fish-and-chip shop, though at these warehouses, fish was served alongside baked potatoes and bread. Victorian London was home to a baked-potato trade, but this trade tended to stay separate from the emerging fried fish trade. Therefore, it is not known, when fried fish began to be sold with chips. Recipes for fried potatoes were available in cookbooks such as William Kitchiner's *The Cook's Oracle* (1817) that contains a recipe for "Potatoes fried in Slices or Shavings," while both Soyer's *Modern Housewife or Mènagére* (published from 1848 to 1849) and *A Shilling Cookery for the People* contain a recipe for thinly cut fried potatoes as well as for fried fish. Therefore, it may be that London fish friers took inspiration from these sources and combined their fried fish with the newly popular fried-potato slices. However, it should be noted that some historians point to Lancashire being the hub of the Victorian fried-potato trend, rather than London. It is generally accepted that Britain's first fish-and-chip shop opened at some point during the Victorian era, possibly in the late 1850s or early 1860s somewhere in London, possibly in Soho. Indeed, an Ashkenazi Jewish immigrant, Joseph Malin, is often cited as opening the world's first fish-and-chip shop, Malin's, located in London's East End. Malin's proved so popular that it remained open until the 1970s. However, a fish-and-chip shop opened by John Lees in Mossely, Lancashire, in the1860s is also reputed to be the world's first chippie. Lees's fish-and-chip business began operating from a wooden hut but was soon so popular that in 1863 he moved to a permanent shop.

From the 1870s onward, the fish-and-chip industry spread rapidly, particularly in London and in the manufacturing towns of northern England where fish and chips served as an easily accessible, hot, nourishing meal for industrial workers. The spread of the fish-and-chip trade was boosted by growing mechanization for the development of North Sea steam trawler fishing provided Britain with plentiful supplies of white fish, while the invention of new ice machines kept the fish cold. Meanwhile, the development of Britain's rail network meant fish that landed at such ports as Grimsby and Whitby could be transported easily to heavily populated areas. By the start of the Edwardian era, fish and chips were widely available throughout England and Wales, including in genteel resorts on England's south coast such as Bournemouth as well as in such southern naval port towns as Portsmouth and Southampton. Fish and chips continued to be popular in northern England too with numerous chippies in operation in seaside towns such as Blackpool and in such northern English fishing towns as Hull.

Soon, fish and chips were considered an integral part of the British diet. By 1910, there were around 25,000 British chippies, peaking at 35,000 British chippies by 1927. Consequently, every British industrial town had a chippie on virtually every street. Going into the First World War, the British government recognized the importance of fish and chips to the British working classes and ensured fish supplies remained off ration for not only did preserving Britons' access to fish and chips help national morale, but the meal fed munitions workers and their families. In the interwar years, the fish-and-chip industry used up around two-thirds of Britain's fish catch, while the demand for fish caught by the trawler fleets in various parts of northern England and in Scotland meant new rail links had to be developed to keep up with demand. The development of these new rail links fueled the development of many of Britain's great industrial fishing ports. As in the First World War, during the Second World War, the British government ensured fish and chips were not rationed as the meal both kept up morale and fed hungry workers. Thus, fish and chips became an invaluable supplement to Britons' wartime diet with lengthy lines forming when a chippie had fish in stock.

Traditionally, fish and chips was sold wrapped in newspaper from which the meal could be eaten directly, for eschewing fancy packaging kept the prices low for both the chippies and the consumer. However, this practice was banned in the late 1980s as it was judged unsafe for food to come into contact with newspaper ink unless greaseproof paper was placed in between. Therefore, today some fish-and-chip shops wrap their fish and chips in greaseproof paper that is printed specifically to resemble newspaper.

Cullen Skink

Cullen skink is an iconic Scottish dish that is served both as a main course and as a starter. While the dish is often made at home, it also appears on many restaurant menus throughout Scotland. Cullen skink takes the form of a hearty soup made using smoked haddock, potatoes, and onions. In order to be considered authentic, purists maintain that Cullen skink should feature finnan haddie, a cold-smoked haddock from northeast Scotland. However, the soup can be made with any smoked haddock.

Cullen skink takes its name from Cullen, a small town in northeast Scotland, and "skink" is a Scottish word for the knuckle or shin of beef from which most Scottish soups are made traditionally. When the inhabitants of northern Scotland were unable to afford beef, they decided to make soup from smoked fish; they had already applied the name skink to this soup even though it did not contain meat. Regional variations of Cullen skink see the soup made either with water or milk, or with single or double cream. Some variations suggest that potatoes should be mashed prior to being added to the soup in order to act as a thickener, while other recipes use waxy potatoes that hold their shape during cooking.

Further Reading

Arndt Anderson, Heather. *Breakfast: A History*. Lanham, MD: Rowman & Littlefield, 2013

BBC. "Why do the French call the British 'the roast beefs'?" *BBC News* (April 3, 2003). http://news.bbc.co.uk/1/hi/2913151.stm (accessed August 17, 2023).

Bule, Guise. "The traditional Full English Breakfast." *English Breakfast Society: Research* (2012–2023). https://englishbreakfastsociety.com/full-english-breakfast.html (accessed April 2, 2023).

Cocks, Simon. "Brits buy over 3 million ready meals each day." *Good Housekeeping* (February 24, 2016). https://www.goodhousekeeping.com/uk/food/food-reviews/a669695/brits-buying-over-3-million-ready-meals-each-day/ (accessed August 17, 2023).

Collingham, Elizabeth M. *Curry: A Tale of Cooks and Conquerors*. Oxford: Oxford University Press, 2007.

The Cornish Pasty Association. "About the pasty" (2023). https://cornishpastyassociation.co.uk/about-the-pasty/ (accessed April 17, 2023).

Cuff, Madeleine. "Kippers, the breakfast dish that fell out of favour, are back on British menus." *The Guardian: Business: Retail: Fish* (April 7, 2012). https://www.theguardian.com/lifeandstyle/2012/apr/07/food-kippers-smoked-fish-sales-revival (accessed April 24, 2023).

Davis, Laura. "Revealed: Liverpool's favourite Scouse ingredients." *The Liverpool Echo* (February 27, 2018). https://www.liverpoolecho.co.uk/whats-on/food-drink-news/revealed-liverpools-favourite-scouse-ingredients-10953251 (accessed April 19, 2023).

Fone, Martin. "Curious questions: Who invented the Ploughman's Lunch?" *Country Life: Food and Drink* (April 9, 2022). https://www.countrylife.co.uk/food-drink/who-invented-the-ploughmans-lunch-241426 (accessed April 12, 2023).

Mason, Laura. *Roasts*. London: National Trust Books, 2019.

Morris, Steve. "Hats off to the great British greasy spoon." *The Critic* (March 27, 2012). https://thecritic.co.uk/hats-off-to-the-great-british-greasy-spoon/ (accessed April 5, 2023).

National Federation of Fish Friers. "Everything you need to know about fish and chips." Fish and Chips. https://www.nfff.co.uk/pages/fish-and-chips (accessed April 24, 2023).

Naylor, Tony. "How to eat: A ploughman's lunch." *The Guardian: Lifestyle* (March 31, 2014). https://www.theguardian.com/lifeandstyle/wordofmouth/2014/mar/31/how-to-eat-a-ploughmans-lunch (accessed April 12, 2023).

Panayi, Panikos. *Fish and Chips: A History*. London: Reaktion Books, 2022.

Seal, Rebecca. "Deconstructing cawl, the hearty Welsh stew." *National Geographic: Travel* (October 14, 2021). https://www.nationalgeographic.co.uk/travel/2021/09/deconstructing-cawl-the-hearty-welsh-stew (accessed April 19, 2023).

Specification Council Regulation (EC) No. 510/2006 on Protected Geographical Indications and Protected Designations of Origin. "Cornish pasty." https://assets.publishing.service.gov.uk/media/5fd34f3dd3bf7f3059ef3cd2/pfn-cornish-pasty-pgi-pdf.pdf (accessed April 24, 2023).

Vogler, Pen. *Scoff: A History of Food and Class in Britain*. London: Atlantic Books, 2020.

Walton, John K. *Fish and Chips, and the British Working Class, 1870–1940*. London: Leicester University Press, 2000.

5

Desserts

Britons use the words "dessert" and "pudding" fairly interchangeably (pudding is also often shortened to "pud"). However, while the word "pudding" can denote a dessert, the term dessert does not always refer to a pudding. Instead, the word "pudding" usually indicates a sweet or savory steamed dish, the outside of which is made from suet and flour. When used to denote a dessert, traditionally, the word "pudding" refers to a homely, rustic dessert such as spotted dick or rice pudding, which in the past tended to be eaten by the lower classes. Contrastingly, in the past, the term "dessert" referred to refined sweet indulgences enjoyed by the upper classes at the end of a meal. Such desserts would often reflect international cuisine, for example, mousses, soufflés, and jellies. Today, in Britain, these class-based boundaries are blurred with sweet dishes that were originally enjoyed by the lower classes now being enjoyed by all, and homely puddings served by fine dining restaurants, albeit usually with more refined presentation than they would be served at home. Meanwhile, dessert recipes once favored by the upper classes are now attainable to all Britons through myriad television cookery shows, magazines, and websites. Thus, the delineation between "dessert" and "pudding" is blurred, and the two words are taken to mean the same thing.

Whereas in, for example, France, people may eat a cheese course before the dessert course, in Britain, it is traditional to have the cheese course after dessert. Thus, in Britain, desserts are more than a sweet treat, for they are the sweet finale to a meal. Additionally, both "dessert" and "pudding," when referring to the sweet course at the end of a meal may also be substituted by the word "afters." For instance, when enjoying an informal meal, a Briton might enquire "what's for pud?" in order to ask what is for dessert with "what's for afters?" an alternative way of asking the same question.

Britons enjoy both hot and cold desserts. Popular hot desserts eaten in Britain include crumbles, pies, and puddings that are usually served with ice cream, cream, or custard. When ice cream is served alongside a hot pudding, the ice cream melts to create a thick, sweetened, creamy sauce that is eaten together with the dessert dish. Popular cold desserts include trifle, ice cream, and banoffee pie. British cities and towns are crammed with places to enjoy something sweet, from bakeries, tea shops, and cafés offering an array of cakes and cookies to gelateries serving artisan ices. In 2019, the kitchen equipment company Breville analyzed Google search data to discover the UK's favorite desserts and sweet treats and found that the most frequently searched-for dessert was apple crumble. Other desserts (as opposed to cakes, which are rarely eaten as dessert) searched for included jelly, bread and butter pudding, cheesecake, and banoffee pie. The most searched-for cakes were Victoria sponge, carrot cake, and red velvet cake as well as scones and churros. While crumbles are popular throughout Britain, Breville's analysis showed that apple crumble was more popular in northern Britain than in southern Britain. While most desserts and sweet treats in Britain are enjoyed across England, Scotland, and Wales, certain sweet foods are associated with particular countries of Britain.

English Desserts

Many of the desserts eaten in modern England have historical roots. The Norman Conquest (the military conquest of England by William, duke of Normandy, during the period 1066–71) was significant for many reasons, not least that the Normans replaced England's ruling classes with French aristocrats and royalty. This change in the ruling class meant that England's upper classes came to enjoy foreign influences on their food including the Arab flavors that the Normans enjoyed in their colony of Sicily, off the southern coast of Italy. Soon the British elite had come to enjoy the spices popular in Arab cuisine including saffron, ginger, and nutmeg. Almonds, as used in Arab cuisine, also became a favored British dessert ingredient. Britons' fondness for such flavors increased after the Crusades for British fighters returned home from the Crusades with an even stronger penchant for cinnamon, saffron, mace, nutmeg, and ginger, as well as sugar. Britons' fondness for these ingredients transformed British food, including desserts.

The introduction of sugar to medieval England had a profound impact on the diets of the English elite for once sugar became available as a sweetening agent, those that could afford it started to consume large quantities of sweet treats. Indeed by 1287, the court of Henry III (king of England 1207–1272) consumed 677 lb of regular sugar, 300 lb of violet-flavored sugar, and 1,900 lb of rose-flavored sugar. While initially the upper classes used these sugars as medicines to treat conditions such as colds, by the late thirteenth century, sugar was very much used as a sweetener. However, sugar remained expensive so while the elite could afford to use sugar, most other Britons ate honey and dried fruits as sweet indulgences.

During the reign of Elizabeth I (1558–1603), England started to import considerable quantities of sugar from places including Madeira and the Canary Islands off of Africa's northwest coast in order to satisfy the English upper classes' love of such sweet treats as gingerbread, sugared almonds, and jelly. Sugar continued to be a luxury throughout the sixteenth century however, meaning most English people used honey and dried fruits in sweet recipes instead of sugar. Indeed, such was the upper classes' love of sugar that during the Elizabethan era, it became fashionable in England for people to blacken their teeth with coal because having black teeth indicated that the wearer could afford to eat sugar, since sugar was available only to the wealthy. It was also during this period that the English developed a taste for vanilla, which had arrived in Europe via Spanish explorers in the Americas. The introduction of vanilla resulted in Elizabethan recipes for custard made using eggs, milk, sugar, vanilla, and almonds. Elizabethan custards were often flavored with spices and decorated with nuts, candied citrus peel, and preserved fruits and were sometimes colored a bright yellow through the inclusion of marigold (*Calendula officinalis*) petals. Contrastingly, another sweetened milk-based dessert, junket, which was popular in medieval England, started to fall from favor during the Tudor era. Instead of junkets, fashionable Elizabethans opted for syllabubs for dessert.

Marzipan (known to Elizabethans as marchpane) was also popular at this time, being made from almonds, sugar, and rose water. Marchpane was often the centerpiece of lavish banquets, shaped into elaborate constructions including castles, ships, and chessboards.

Gingerbread was also popular in Elizabethan England where it was eaten after meals as a tasty indigestion remedy. Moreover, Elizabeth I is credited with the invention of gingerbread men for she would have gingerbread figures baked to resemble dignitaries visiting her court. Over time, gingerbread festivals called Gingerbread Fairs started to be held in England with the gingerbread biscuits served at the festivals known as "fairings." The shape of the fairings sold changed with the season, with gingerbread flowers sold in the spring and gingerbread birds sold in the autumn. Today, fairings are synonymous with the English county of Cornwall to the extent that the biscuits are known as Cornish fairings. A traditional Cornish fairing takes the form of a ginger biscuit decorated with comfits (sugar-coated almonds and caraway seeds) and crystallized angelica, though nowadays, Cornish fairings are usually sold undecorated. It was also in the early seventeenth century that blancmange morphed from being a dish of poultry and rice stewed in almond milk to a molded dessert made using gelatin from calves' feet or pigs' trotters, almonds, rice flour, rose water, ginger, and cinnamon.

Whitepot (or white-pot), a dessert popular from the 1600s, was especially associated with Devon in southwest England with recipes published in most cookery books from the seventeenth century onward. Whitepot was so called because the creamy ingredients that went into the oven were a glistening white color. Once cooked, however, whitepot emerged from the oven a golden color due to the inclusion of cinnamon, egg yolks, and sugar. Typically, whitepot was made with rice. Rice was first introduced to Europe via Spain's trade with India during the tenth century before being grown widely in Spain and northern Italy from the fifteenth century. Initially, Britain started to receive both long- and short-grain rice from these areas, but by the seventeenth century, short-grain Arborio rice had started to predominate in parts of Europe that were importing rice to Britain, and thus, whitepot came to be made using mostly short-grain rice. However, the first recipe for rice pudding, as opposed to whitepot made with rice, appeared in Britain and was published in fourteenth-century *The Forme of Cury*. This recipe was free of sugar but did contain spices that gave the mellow rice a sweetness. In the Middle Ages, rice pudding was served at breakfast, while in the Victorian era, rice pudding was given to convalescents because it was easy to digest. For many modern Britons, however, rice pudding is a comfort food redolent of school dinners and so is eaten at times of stress. This nostalgic attitude to rice pudding is evident during the cost-of-living crisis for recently sales of rice pudding through major food stores have increased including 45 percent year-on-year at Aldi and 49 percent month-on-month at Ocado. Meanwhile, Waitrose noted a 54 percent rise in searches for tinned rice pudding while recipe searches for rice pudding have risen by 233 percent. This trend for rice pudding comes despite the fact that the price of rice has increased at a much faster rate than general inflation. The price of milk and butter are also rising sharply. Despite the rise in the price of ingredients, rice pudding remains increasingly popular with vegan versions made using coconut and almond milks coming to the fore, along with such toppings as pistachios and edible flowers.

Whitepot was also sometimes made with bread. For instance, an alternative version of whitepot appears in 1723's *The Cooks and Confectioners Dictionary: or the Accomplished Housewives Companion* by John Nott, who had served as cook to several English aristocrats including the duke of Bolton. Although this recipe dates from the Georgian period, the bread-based dish would have been baked as early as the 1600s. As whitepot could be made with bread to make a dessert of bread, cream, and dried fruit, it is often cited as the forerunner of the bread and butter pudding, an ever-popular English dessert made from buttered bread, dried fruit, and a spiced custard mix layered in a dish and baked in the oven. Bread and butter pudding has a rich and comforting, indulgent quality for the crisp, sugar-coated crust contrasts with the luscious soft bread and dried fruit beneath. Bread and butter pudding can be served hot or cold and eaten at any time of the year but is especially popular as a winter pudding.

Toward the end of the seventeenth century, chocolate became the most popular sweet treat of the English. Whilst in Jamaica, Sir Hans Sloane (1660–1753), a notable Irish, London-based physician and collector, tasted a local cocoa drink but he only came to enjoy the taste once he had added milk to the drink. Sloane brought the cocoa drink back to England where it was mass produced and sold as a medicinal drink. Around the same time, the Cocoa Tree Chocolate House became a popular London destination, and sugar started to be added to the desserts served in coffeehouses. Biscuits also became increasingly popular in the seventeenth century as sugar became cheaper. Later, the advent of the Industrial Revolution allowed the mass manufacture of both chocolate and biscuits, as well as sweets.

The Victorian era (1837–1901) was a time of great innovation for desserts during which many classic English desserts originated. It was during this period that the mass manufacture of kitchenware allowed housewives lacking both cooks and culinary training to create their own desserts. For instance, the advent of pudding tins allowed housewives to invent new puddings, which were decidedly sweeter than the puddings of previous eras. English desserts that came into being during this period and are still enjoyed today include the spotted dick, a steamed pudding made using suet rather than butter and flavored with lemon. The name "dick" derives from the Old English name for a pudding—*puddick*—while the pudding has a "spotted" appearance due to the inclusion of currants that protrude from the sponge mixture. Spotted dick was first mentioned in print in *The Modern Housewife, or Ménagère* (1849) by the pioneering celebrity chef Alexis Soyer.

As well as puddings, in Victorian England, people also enjoyed cream ices, water ices, and sorbets. Cream ices were made from flavored frozen custard or sweetened cream while water ices consisted of sweetened, flavored water. Sorbets were made from frozen, flavored alcohol and tended to be served as a distinct course at special occasions, whereas cream ices and water ices were served after a pudding or fruit tart as part of the dessert course. Ices and sorbets were often molded into elegant shapes and served highly decorated with fruit, nuts, and wine biscuits (biscuits intended to be eaten with wine).

In Victorian England, ice creams were incredibly popular despite the fact that they were extremely labor-intensive to produce. Hand-cranked ice cream–making machines were invented during the Victorian era—prior to their invention, Britons made ices by putting ingredients into a lidded pewter jar called a sorbetier, which was placed inside a wooden bucket and spun by hand to churn the ice-cream ingredients together. While this method of ice cream–making was less labor-intensive than using a hand-cranked machine, the hand-cranked machine made ices much more quickly. The doyenne of Victorian ices was Anne Marshall, the author of *The Book of Ices* (1885), who also traveled around Britain teaching people to make ices and patented a zinc-lined ice cream–making machine that could make ices in 3 minutes. Marshall's machine used a combination of salt and ice placed around a pewter jar to churn ice cream at temperatures as low as −20°C depending on how much salt a user added. Since people in Victorian England did not have access to freezers, people used a contraption called an ice cave (a metal box set inside a wooden chest filled with salt and ice) to freeze their homemade ices into molded shapes. Once ices were frozen, they were stored in so-called ice houses, large wells packed with ice that were either taken from rivers in winter or imported from Newfoundland and Alaska. A drain at the base of the ice house let the melted water flow into the soil or waterways. On top of the well was a small building that was designed to allow people to enter but keep heat out.

Victorian ice creams came in what might be considered unusual flavors including brown bread and cucumber. Cooked cucumber was a popular Victorian side dish, and soon it became incorporated into a refreshing ice that was a popular way for Victorians to end summer dinner parties. Cucumber ice cream combined puréed cooked cucumber with sugar, ginger wine, lemon juice, either custard or sweetened cream, and green food coloring. Victorians enjoyed using chemical food dyes and artificial flavorings as the dyes chimed with the era's love of scientific discovery. Today, frozen desserts, including ice cream, sorbet, and frozen yogurt, continue to be popular in all areas of Britain, with some Britons claiming they eat ice cream from a tub on a daily basis. In the UK, the ice-cream industry revenue has grown steadily in recent years, despite the Covid-19 pandemic with revenue in the UK ice market reaching £610 million in 2022. It is expected that this revenue will fall to £520 million by 2025, however, for British consumers are starting to eat ice cream less frequently. From 2013 to 2014, ice-cream sales in the UK fell by over 100 million liters and have remained around this level ever since.

It is likely that one of the quintessential English summer desserts, Eton mess—a combination of whipped cream, fresh strawberries, and broken meringue—was invented toward the end of the Victorian era for it is generally agreed that the dessert was created accidentally in the late nineteenth century with a recipe for Eton mess first appearing in print in 1893. According to food lore, a dessert made from strawberries, cream, and meringue that was intended to be eaten after a cricket match between Eton and Harrow (exclusive schools located near London) was dropped on the floor and rather than throw the ruined dessert away, it was scooped up and served in individual portions. Ever since, Eton mess has been served at the annual cricket match between Eton and Harrow held at Lords' cricket ground in London. There are several possible reasons why Eton mess is so named. For example, while the name may refer to the dessert's untidy appearance, "mess" may also be derived from the Old French word *mes*, meaning "a portion of food." Another classic English dessert, the summer pudding also originated in the late nineteenth century. Summer pudding, which features sliced white bread, layered in a deep bowl with fresh summer berries that is left to soak overnight before being turned out onto a plate, was known at the end of the nineteenth century as hydropathic pudding because it was eaten at English health resorts where less healthy desserts were forbidden. By the start of the twentieth century, the dessert had been renamed as summer pudding, possibly because the name hydropathic pudding did not look good in print when printed recipes for the dessert started to circulate around 1904. Typically, the summer fruits used to make a summer pudding are raspberries, strawberries, blackcurrants, redcurrants, and blackberries though sometimes more unusual berries such as tayberries and loganberries are included too, alongside blueberries and cherries.

New desserts started to appear with the outbreak of the Second World War in 1939 for wartime food rationing across Britain resulted in a lack of butter and sugar needed to make pastry. Consequently, the food shortages led to the invention of crumbles, which used less sugar and butter to make than pastry. Soon crumbles were enjoyed as a popular dessert alternative to pies. Bread pudding also became popular around this time because the pudding is made with leftover stale bread soaked in water, very little sugar, and dried fruit. Fruit cobblers also became popular during the Second World War as they made use of whichever fruits were in season and were topped by pastry made with flour, margarine, a small amount of sugar, and some milk. Crumbles, bread pudding, and fruits cobblers are still enjoyed today with crumbles being a particularly popular dessert eaten at home, as well as served in all sorts of eateries ranging from pubs to high-end restaurants.

Not all British desserts have a lengthy history, however. For instance, sticky toffee pudding dates from much more recent times though its origins are disputed. It has been claimed variously that the pudding was invented by the owner of the Gait Inn in Millington, Yorkshire, in 1907, while the owner of the Udny Arms Hotel in Aberdeenshire, Scotland, claims to have invented the dessert in the 1960s. Whatever the truth of these claims, sticky toffee pudding was undoubtedly popularized in the 1970s by Francis Coulson and Robert Lee, who served the pudding at the Sharrow Bay Country House Hotel in Cumbria, northern England. Sticky toffee pudding has two key elements: a layer of moist, spiced sponge containing chopped dates and toffee sauce. Typically, the pudding is served with custard, single cream, or vanilla ice cream. Another British pudding invented recently is the banoffee pie, which is made from bananas, whipped cream, and caramel sauce layered over a buttery biscuit base ("banoffee" is a portmanteau name combining the words "banana" and "toffee"). The invention of banoffee pie is credited to Nigel Mackenzie and Ian Dowding, the owner and chef, respectively, at The Hungry Monk Restaurant in Jevington, East Sussex, southeast England, who are said to have invented the dessert in 1971 with the dessert based on a recipe from San Francisco. The San Francisco recipe used apple or mandarin orange, but Mackenzie and Dowding swapped these for banana. In 1974, the pair's banoffee pie recipe was published in *The Deeper Secrets of the Hungry Monk* cookery book.

Scottish Desserts and Sweet Treats

As in England, most traditional Scottish desserts have a long history. For example, cranachan, which is generally considered the most iconic Scottish dessert, may date from the Viking invasion of Scotland in the eighth century. Made by combining cream, raspberries, toasted oats, and whisky, cranachan takes its name from the Scottish Gaelic word for "to churn." In earlier times, cranachan was a celebratory harvest dish eaten when raspberries were plentiful, but today cranachan is enjoyed all year-round and is particularly associated with Burns Night held in January. Traditionally, the host that is offering cranachan as dessert will bring the cranachan ingredients to the dining table separately so that diners can create their own individual cranachan dish made to their own personal preference. Cranachan owes its invention to crowdie, which is both a Scottish cream cheese and a traditional Scottish breakfast dish of finely ground oatmeal mixed with water. When this breakfast dish was sweetened with honey and made with buttermilk rather than water, it was called "cream crowdie" and was served on special occasions. There is some disagreement among Scots as to whether this more luxurious form of crowdie should be considered crowdie or as a type of cranachan.

Another famous Scottish dessert, the clootie dumpling most likely dates back to the eighteenth century though one of the earliest printed recipes for the dessert appears in the 1929 edition of *The Scots Kitchen: Its Traditions and Lore with Old-Time Recipes* by the Scottish folklorist and writer Florence Marian McNeill. There is no definitive recipe for clootie dumpling as the recipe for clootie dumpling is passed down through generations of families meaning each family's recipe is different. That said, typically, a clootie dumpling consists of flour, breadcrumbs, dried fruits, eggs, treacle, spices, sugar, and milk with the combined ingredients boiled in a large ball-shape within a flour-dusted "cloot," the Scottish word for cloth. As the dumpling cooks, the presence of the flour on the outside of the fruit mixture creates a tasty outer crust around the dumpling. Traditionally, good luck charms or coins were hidden within a clootie dumpling with the dessert served with either cream or custard, as well as a dram of whisky. Clootie dumpling can be served either as a homely dish or the finale to a special occasion meal such as Christmas lunch, a Burns Night feast, or a Hogmanay celebration.

Florence Marian McNeill

Florence Marian McNeill (1885–1973) was born in Orkney but later moved to London where she organized a women's suffrage society and worked for an abolitionist organization. Post–First World War, McNeill wrote for various Scottish newspapers. In the 1920s, McNeill worked on the *Scottish National Dictionary* and published *The Scots Kitchen*. The book's success led McNeill to produce additional works celebrating Scottish cuisine. In 1934, McNeill became a founding member of the Scottish National Party (SNP). From 1957 to 1968, McNeill published her most famous work, *The Silver Bough*, a four-volume study of Scottish folklore.

Tipsy laird is a Sottish version of an English trifle that, like clootie dumpling, can be eaten either as a dessert or as a sweet treat enjoyed at Hogmanay or following a Burns Night supper. Tipsy laird differs from an English trifle as it is made with whisky or Drambuie (a Scottish liqueur made from whisky, heather honey, aromatic herbs, and spices) rather than sherry. Other ingredients in a tipsy laird usually include sponge fingers that have been soaked in whisky or Drambuie, custard, raspberries, raspberry jam, and heavy cream layered one on top of the other. The origin of tipsy laird is unknown, but recipes for trifle appeared in cookbooks from 1585, so it is likely the Scots made their own version of the dessert from around this time. The name tipsy laird denotes the alcoholic nature of the dessert for tipsy is a British slang to describe being slightly drunk while "laird" is the Scottish word for a wealthy landowner.

Tablet is a popular Scottish sweet treat that takes the form of a type of crumbly, grainy fudge. The origins of tablet are undetermined, but tablet is certainly a centuries-old candy that has stood the test of time. One of the reasons that tablet has been so popular for so long is that it is easy to make the treat using inexpensive ingredients (sugar, butter, and condensed milk) that are boiled together until the soft-ball stage is reached, then stirred briskly until the mixture starts to crystallize. Once the mixture crystallizes, it is poured into a pan to cool before being cut into small pieces. While tablet may look like fudge, it is a much firmer candy than fudge and has a coarse texture. Another crumbly Scottish candy is Berwick cockles, a white and red striped crumbly peppermint candy dating from 1801. Although Berwick cockles originate from Berwick-upon-Tweed, a town in the northernmost English county of Northumberland very near England's border with Scotland, Berwick cockles are considered a specialty food of southeast Scotland. The unique flavor of Berwick cockles is due to the inclusion of brown sugar in the candy mixture. Hawick Balls are another traditional Scottish peppermint candy. According to oral history, Hawick Balls were invented in the southeast Scottish town of Hawick in the 1850s by "sweetie wives" (street sweet-sellers) Jessie McVittie and Aggie Lamb who pulled boiled sugar by hanging the melted sugar over a nail so that gravity could stretch it downward to harden. Although the recipe for Hawick Balls is a secret, it is known that nowadays the candies are made in open copper pans that allow the caramelized sugar to combine with peppermint oil and harden into candies. The resulting candies are crunchy on the outside yet buttery and chewy on the inside. Another Scottish peppermint-flavored candy is Jethart snails. Jethart snails date back to the Napoleonic Wars (1803–15), when French prisoners of war were held in the jail of the southeast Scottish town of Jedburgh (called Jethart in Scottish

Gaelic). A local family called the Millers treated the prisoners with particular kindness, and in return, a French prisoner presented the family with a recipe for hard minty boiled candies in a twisted shape reminiscent of snail shells. The recipe was handed down through generations of the Miller family, and today, Jethart snails are still made in Jedburgh. Another hard Scottish candy is the *soor plooms* ("sour plums"), which originated in the southeast Scottish town of Galashiels. Soor plooms have a distinctive bright green color that matches their characteristic sour taste. According to Scottish lore, soor plooms got their name because in 1337, a group of men from Galashiels encountered a party of English soldiers eating the unripe plums that grew wild in the area. The Galashiels men decided to kill the soldiers and left their corpses strewn amid the sour plums. This event is integral to Galashiels' history and as such is commemorated not just by the candy but also in the Galashiels coat of arms, which depicts two foxes reaching up to eat plums from a tree, and above the motto is *Sour Plums,* as well as the town's weathervanes.

Perhaps the most famous Scottish sweet treat is, however, the traditional Scottish shortbread biscuit, sometimes called shortbread petticoats. Shortbread derives from a type of twelfth-century biscuit that was made from leftover dough containing yeast. The dough was cooked at a low temperature until it formed rusk-type cookies known as bread biscuit (the word biscuit deriving from the French *bis cuit* meaning twice cooked). Over time, butter came to replace the yeast in the dough recipe. The addition of the butter prevents long gluten strands from forming within the biscuit mixture to create a cookie with a crumbly, sandy texture. Indeed, since medieval times, in Britain, the word "short" has been used to describe something that crumbles easily while historically, the term "shortening" describes any form of cooking fat such as butter. Therefore, shortbread may take its name from either its crumbly texture or the inclusion of butter. It has also been suggested that the name shortbread petticoats is a corruption for the French *petites galettes* meaning little cakes. Scottish food was greatly influenced by France for Mary, Queen of Scots (1542–1587), spent her formative years at the French royal court and in 1588 married the heir to the French throne, the dauphin François (later King Francis II of France). Over time, Mary, Queen of Scots, has been credited with improving upon the early version of shortbread by favoring crisp, buttery biscuits flavored with caraway seeds. Another theory suggests that the triangular shape of shortbread petticoats echoes the shape of the cloth used to make a full-gored petticoat during Mary's reign. This would also explain the term petticoat tails, the name given to individual shortbread segments. Indeed, traditionally, shortbread is made in one of three shapes: a large circle divided into petticoat tails that have been scored into the biscuit (the large biscuit is left intact for the eater to break off the individual tails), individual round biscuits called shortbread rounds, and thick rectangular slabs of biscuit known as shortbread fingers. In earlier times, shortbread was a luxury food eaten only on special occasions such as Christmas and Hogmanay, while in Shetland, it was traditional for a decorated shortbread to be broken over the head of a bride as she crossed the threshold of her new home. The tradition of cooking shortbread at Hogmanay in a round shape can likely be traced back to ancient pagan round Yule cakes that symbolized the sun. Today, however, shortbread is eaten year-round and has become a ubiquitous souvenir of travel to Scotland with the biscuits often available in large tartan-patterned tins. The tins are also popular Christmas gifts in England that are available from most supermarkets.

Another iconic, or perhaps more accurately, notorious Scottish sweet treat is the deep-fried Mars bar. This dish sees a chilled Mars-brand chocolate bar enrobed in batter before being deep fried in boiling oil—chilling the chocolate first prevents the chocolate from melting during the cooking process. The origins of the dish are disputed, but the deep-fried Mars bar may have originated as a novelty item at a fast-food outlet in Stonehaven, northeast Scotland. Once the British media started to report on the dish in the early 1990s, its popularity spread. Indeed by 2000, Scottish chef Ross Kendall had started to include deep-fried Mars bar on the menu of Le Chipper restaurant in Paris to a mixed reception with some critics claiming that to serve the dish in France was to insult Gallic gastronomy. Other critics of the dish have even gone so far as to suggest that Scots' fondness for the deep-fried Mars bar may help account for the fact that Scotland has the lowest life expectancy at birth of any country in Western Europe for each deep-fried Mars bar contains around 1,000 calories, a quarter of an adult's daily fat allowance, and contains such ingredients as glucose syrup that can hamper the body's ability to absorb nutrients.

Welsh Desserts

In times past, the Welsh were predominantly farmers, fishers, and miners, so Welsh desserts and sweet treats tended to be substantial dishes filling enough to satisfy people working in physically demanding jobs. Moreover, traditional Welsh desserts and sweet treats tend to be uncomplicated, making the best use of humble, seasonal ingredients including locally grown fruit, bread, and milk.

For instance, *Pwdin Mynwy* (called Monmouth pudding in English), which is named after the southeast town of Monmouth that lies just inside Wales' border with England, is made using cooked seasonal fruit, particularly apples or plums. Monmouthshire, the county in which Monmouth is located, was once one of Wales' main fruit-producing areas so fruit was often plentiful in the area and was used to make the dessert *Pwdin Mynwy*, though jam can also be used to make the dish instead of fresh fruit. To make Pwdin Mynwy, the cooked fruit or jam is layered with breadcrumbs soaked in heated sweetened milk that has been flavored with lemon and enriched with butter. The milky breadcrumbs are then topped with another layer of cooked fruit or jam that is then itself topped with meringue before being baked until crisp. In Wales, Pwdin Mynwy is enjoyed on St. David's Day (the day dedicated to David, the patron saint of Wales) on March 1 and at other times of the year. Pwdin Rhaglan is a similar dessert to Pwdin Mynwy for it is named after the Monmouthshire town of Raglan and typically features apples, plums, pears, or blackberries topped with a smooth batter and then baked. In Wales, fruit pies tend to be made using apples, plums, damsons, rhubarb, gooseberries, and whinberries (a type of blueberry) for not only were these fruits grown in orchards, but most gardens in south Wales would grow these fruits too. Other desserts made using these fruits include *Ffwl Eirin Mair* (gooseberry fool) though fools (desserts comprising stewed fruit combined with cold custard or whipped cream) could also be made using other fruits. Local fruit is also poached for dessert or used to make jams. As in England and Scotland, Wales also has a traditional fruit pudding steamed in a cloth bag: *Pwdin Eryri* (Snowdon pudding) dating from the nineteenth century, which comprises suet, raisins, sugar, eggs, flour, and breadcrumbs, as well as lemon marmalade.

Dried fruits including raisins are a major ingredient of *Bara brith* (speckled bread). Originally, Bara brith was a yeasted bread, but today, it is made as a moist cake comprising dried fruit soaked overnight in tea flavored with such spices as cinnamon, nutmeg, and cardamom. Normally, Bara brith is stored for a couple of days before eating as this allows the bread's flavors to develop. Bara brith is usually served buttered, and in Wales, it can be a component of afternoon tea.

Some of the most traditional Welsh sweet treats are cooked on a griddle. For instance, griddle-baked *picau ar y maen* (Welsh cakes) are a traditional Welsh delicacy and are made from a simple base of flour, lard or butter, sugar, and eggs to which are added spices (usually cinnamon or nutmeg), lemon zest, and dried fruit. The cakes are also called bakestones because traditionally they can be cooked on a bakestone, a cast iron griddle that is placed in a fire or oven.

Griddle cakes are eaten as a dessert or as a sweet snack. Welsh cakes are usually eaten plain, but if served as part of afternoon tea, they may be accompanied by butter and jam that can be spread on top of the cakes. Similar griddle cakes are found elsewhere in Britain, for example, the singin' hinny made in northern and northeast England, particularly in Northumberland, and fatty cutties eaten in Scotland. Welsh pancakes, usually called *crempog*, are made from a batter made from some combination of buttermilk, butter, flour, sugar, salt, vinegar, bicarbonate of soda, and eggs (there is no one specific recipe). To make crempog, the batter is poured on to a hot griddle and cooked until the thick pancakes are golden brown on both sides. To serve, crempogs are usually stacked in a pile and smeared with butter before the pancake stack is sliced like a cake and eaten as dessert. While crempog is the most common name for these pancakes, they were known by different names across Wales. For example, *crempog* is the name used in north Wales, while in Carmarthenshire and Glamorgan, they are known as *cramwythen* (in some areas of Glamorgan, they are also called *ffroes*), while in Cardiganshire, they are called *poncagau* or *pancosen*. The *ffroes* eaten in Glamorganshire are almost undistinguishable from Scottish drop scones, which may have been brought to Glamorganshire by Scottish coalfield workers who settled in south Wales in the nineteenth century. However, slicing into the stacked, buttered crempog is a particularly Welsh way of serving pancakes.

While the exact history of griddle cooking in Wales is unknown, a *gradell* (griddle) appeared among the objects recorded as being made by blacksmiths in thirteenth-century *Cyfraith Hywel* (Laws of Hywel Dda, the system of law practised in medieval Wales).

Another Welsh sweet treat that dates back to the thirteenth century is the Aberffraw biscuit, which is sometimes cited as Britain's oldest biscuit. Aberffraw biscuits are shortbread-type cookies made from butter, flour, and sugar and shaped like a scallop shell. According to legend, a Welsh king was holding court in the village of Aberffraw, located on the southwest coast of the Isle of Anglesey, when his wife found a beautiful scallop shell on the beach and requested a cake to be baked in the same shape of the shell. A less fanciful explanation for the biscuits' shape is that thirteenth-century Welsh pilgrims influenced the shape for when they went on pilgrimage to Santiago de Compostela in Galicia, northwest Spain, the pilgrims wore badges on their hats in the shape of a scallop shell. The scallop shell is the symbol of both the Camino de Santiago (the ancient pilgrim routes across Europe that culminate at the tomb of St. James in Santiago de Compostela) and the routes' pilgrims (*los peregrinos*).

Camino de Santiago

The Camino de Santiago pilgrimage sees pilgrims walk to the Cathedral of Santiago de Compostela in Galicia in northwest Spain. The pilgrimage is of medieval origin. The Camino de Santiago encompasses many different routes but the most popular is the Camino Frances (the French Way). This route is 497 miles long if started from the traditional departure point of St. Jean Pied de Port Camino Frances in the Pyrénées-Atlantiques department of southwest France. The Camino de Santiago trails are marked by scallop shells painted on trees and walls. Since 1993, the Camino de Santiago has been listed as a UNESCO World Heritage Site.

After completing their pilgrimage, the Welsh peregrinos returned to Wales and started to impress scallop shells into the biscuits they made in remembrance of their travels. It is for this reason that Aberffraw biscuits are occasionally called James cakes.

Further Reading

Breville. "The UK's favourite desserts revealed." *Breville: Blog* (2019). https://www.breville.co.uk/blog/UK-favourite-desserts-revealed.html (accessed August 17, 2023).

Chrystal, Paul. *The History of Sweets*. Yorkshire: Pen and Sword History, 2021.

Conway, Jan. "Ice cream and frozen desserts in the UK—statistics & facts." *Statista: Food & Nutrition* (January 19, 2023). https://www.statista.com/topics/7237/ice-cream-in-the-uk/#dossier-chapter1 (accessed February 23, 2023).

Freeman, Bobby. *First Catch Your Peacock: The Classic Guide to Welsh Food*. Ceredigion: Y Lolfa Cyf, 1996.

Goldstein, Darra, ed. *The Oxford Companion to Sugar and Sweets*. Oxford: Oxford University Press, 2015.

MacEacheran, Mike. "The contentious origins of England's famous pudding." *BBC: Hidden Britain: Food & Drink: Lake District* (July 16, 2021). https://www.bbc.com/travel/article/20210715-the-contentious-origins-of-englands-famous-pudding (accessed March 8, 2023).

MacEacheran, Mike. "The strange story of Britain's oldest sweet." *BBC: Food & Hospitality: Food & Drink: England* (July 11, 2019). https://www.bbc.com/travel/article/20190710-the-strange-story-of-britains-oldest-sweet (accessed March 8, 2023).

Roufs, Timothy G., and Kathleen Smyth Roufs. *Sweet Treats around the World: An Encyclopedia of Food and Culture*. Santa Barbara, CA: ABC-CLIO, 2014.

Ysewijn, Regula. *Pride and Pudding: The History of British Puddings, Savoury and Sweet*. London: Murdoch, 2016.

6

Beverages

Most Britons start the day with a hot drink of either tea or coffee at breakfast then enjoy a soft drink with their lunch. Tea or coffee is usually drunk again during mid-afternoon. Soft drinks, in the form of juices, smoothies, cordials, and carbonated products, are widely consumed throughout the day. Some Britons enjoy alcoholic beverages, and there is a long history of alcoholic drinks being widely available across Britain. This is a very generalized pattern of behavior however—for instance, some Britons do not drink alcohol for religious or health reasons.

Water

Britons have long associated water with the sacred as evinced by pagan well-dressing ceremonies (a custom of rural England, especially the Peak District, in which wells, springs, and other water sources are decorated with designs created from flower petals) and Christian baptisms. Yet, there is also a long history of water in Britain being unclean, even deadly, to drink. The Romans recognized the need for clean drinking water when they invaded Britain, for they built aqueducts to transport water from springs to Roman settlements. After the Romans left Britain, Roman water-bearing infrastructure became dilapidated. However, British monasteries and castles employed similar methods of fetching water from rivers, wells, and springs. It had long been recognized that water was hazardous to drink, so at this time, water was consumed in hot foods such as soup, as well as in distilled and brewed drinks, all of which were relatively safe to consume as they involved heating water.

Through the fifteenth to the seventeenth centuries, such English towns as Southampton, Oxford, and Rye established their own waterworks to ensure clean water for public use, and by the sixteenth century, Londoners had started to pay laborers to bring better quality water to them from outside the city. From 1711 to 1830, numerous new waterworks opened across Britain to pipe supplies to houses in wealthy areas. Additionally, many Georgian doctors advised wealthier patients to partake of spa water in towns such as Harrogate, Bath, and Tunbridge Wells. Since spa water contained health-giving properties such as iron and sulfur, they were felt to combat the ill-effects of over-indulgent diets. By the 1750s, tea and beer were Britons' main drinks and to drink plain water was considered a sign of poverty.

By the mid-nineteenth century, much of Britain's water supply had ceased to function as rapidly increasing urban populations strained existing infrastructure's ability to deliver water. The situation was exacerbated by the need to provide water to industry too. In many cities, both human and industrial waste entered waterways making the water unsafe to drink. For instance, in 1848, the establishment of the Metropolitan Commission of Sewers in London declared that properties should be cleaned and connected to sewers. However, when homes were cleaned, typically, waste was dumped into the River Thames, thereby worsening the problem of water contamination. At the same time, the increasing popularity of the flushing water closet (lavatory) in wealthier homes added to the amount of sewage entering the river. The unsanitary state of the city's water resulted in the cholera epidemic of 1848 and 1849 that killed over 14,000 Londoners.

By the start of the twentieth century, Britain's water supply and quality issues had been largely fixed. However, even as late as 1910, some people in rural areas

Dr. John Snow

In 1849, Dr. John Snow suggested that cholera was spread through ingesting contaminated water after noting that a particular water pump in London was the source of a deadly cholera outbreak. Despite the evidence Snow presented to them, public health officials were reluctant to believe him. Then, however, the "Great Stink" occurred during the hot summer of 1858—with politicians unable to stand the smell of the River Thames flowing past their offices in the Houses of Parliament, they became determined to clean up the river. Consequently, Prime Minister Benjamin Disraeli tabled a Bill that within a record 18 days brought into law improvements to London's water quality.

preferred to take their water straight from streams. This was because parts of England were well served for clean water—in counties such as Yorkshire, water came from numerous springs and streams while villages in southern England could draw water from deep wells that were free from contamination.

At the start of the nineteenth century, most British waterworks were owned and maintained by private companies. However, by the start of the twentieth century, various parliamentary regulations meant the government assumed control of the water industry, with the responsibility for the majority of water and sewerage systems being assumed by local councils. Hot, dry summers such as those in 1933 and 1935 sometimes interrupted supplies leading to calls for the unification of water supplies for by this time the water in England and Wales was provided by nearly 1,000 different suppliers. The Water Act of 1945 united some water suppliers into Joint Water Boards. Then in 1973, the government virtually nationalized the water industry by creating ten large Regional Water Authorities (known colloquially as water boards) responsible for the supply and safety of their water. The Water Authorities had to cover their own costs, so subsequently, Britons' water bills rose rapidly. In the late 1980s, the increase in the cost of water led to heated debate about the ethics of how to manage a natural asset essential to public health. The Regional Water Authorities lasted until 1989, when the government privatized the water industry.

Virtually all Britons receive their water from a company that abstracts supplies from surface water (rivers and reservoirs) or groundwater aquifers. Before water reaches the consumer, public water supplies are treated to remove impurities, and distributed through a network of pipes, before local water mains transport water to people's homes. Around 1 percent of Britons living on farms or in very remote areas get their water from a well, spring, or borehole. Today, British tap water is among the safest in the world with millions of tests conducted annually to guarantee its quality. In Britain, drinking water contains some lead that enters the supply via plumbing present in some older buildings while nickel can sometimes be found in water having traveled through new chrome household taps. Iron and manganese are found in tap water as these metal deposits occur naturally in source waters and accumulate in the pipe network. Iron is also used in the water treatment process. The mineral fluoride occurs naturally in British water, but the amount varies across Britain due to geological variations. Since fluoride can help fight tooth decay, in some parts of Britain, fluoride is added to drinking water through the process of fluoridation. Today, roughly 5.8 million people in England receive fluoridated tap water whereby 1 mg of fluoride is present in each liter of water. This is a level that can reduce tooth decay.

Despite the high-quality drinking water available in Britain, some Britons opt to drink bottled water. Foreign water brands including Evian and Perrier are popular in Britain, but homegrown water brands are also available including Highland Spring, which was established in Scotland in the 1970s, and Buxton, from England's Peak District region where water has been bottled since the 1850s. The original Buxton water was derived from St. Ann's Well, an ancient spring that since Roman times has been reputed to hold medicinal properties. Some Britons shun bottled water, however, arguing that it is an unnecessary expense and that the bottles contribute to plastic pollution and other environmental issues. Recently, however, some bottled water companies have switched to using 100 percent recycled plastic bottles or have started to sell their product in cans and cartons. Many Britons also carry with them reusable metal water bottles that they can refill from taps or drinking fountains when on the move.

Beer

Beer has a long history in Britain. Neolithic farmers on the Orkney Isles brewed beer using poisonous ingredients such as hemlock, while in the third and fourth centuries, strong ale was enjoyed by wealthy Britons. In the sixth century, Welsh princes drank *bragawd* (or braggot), a spiced, honeyed ale.

During Norman times, most ale was created by women known as ale-wives who brewed beer in their homes using readily available ingredients. Up until the fifteenth century, the words beer and ale were used interchangeably—ale came from Danish, while Anglo-Saxons used the word beer to describe a sweet, unhopped drink. Around 1362, the first beer to include hops as a flavoring was imported from the Netherlands to Great Yarmouth in eastern England, while the first British beer brewed using hops was made in 1410 by Dutch and Belgian immigrants who used hops imported from their home nations. In 1441, beer was so central to British life that it became subject to an official maximum price per gallon. After this time, the word ale came to mean an unhopped drink, while beer was the term used in southern England to denote the same drink.

The cultivation of hops in Britain began in Kent, far southeast England circa 1520. The Dissolution of the Monasteries in the 1530s (the destruction of the English monasteries under King Henry VIII) ended most monastic brewing in Britain, however, including the production of bragawd at Tintern Abbey located on the border between Wales and England. Nonetheless, some British monks continued to develop the brewing industry by finding employment in breweries attached to inns and by keeping records of beer recipes.

Beer made from malted barley, water, and spices was the preferred drink of the Elizabethan era for drinking water then tended to harbor such diseases as typhoid, cholera, and dysentery. At this time, most British households brewed their own beer, which was drunk with every meal by both adults and children. In the sixteenth and seventeenth centuries, numerous wholesale breweries developed, based in London, Edinburgh, York, Nottingham, and elsewhere, which supplied beer to inns and ships. The mass production of beer was possible partly because the use of hops allowed a more standardized product to be made. By this time, hops were grown in the Midlands, especially in the county of Herefordshire. Another reason for the increase in beer production was that growing urban populations meant there was a ready market for beer. Also, from this time, Britain's influence over trading networks created a global demand for beer as British ships carried beer to be used by sailors in place of drinking water, as ballast for ships, and as a trading commodity. In 1790, a London-based brewer began to supply East Indian Company ships with lighter ale for long journeys as this ale lasted longer than dark ale. Consequently, the brewer won a monopoly on supplying India with beer. Eventually, rival brewers from the Midlands entered the Indian market and came to dominate the market with what became known as India Pale Ale, which is still popular in Britain. Over time, possibly around the eighteenth century, ale fell out of favor with the public, and beer came to dominate the brewing industry. At the same time, beer started to be referred to as ale.

The eighteenth century saw major changes in British beer consumption and production. The proportion of beer brewed by businesses increased while the amount of home-brewed beer fell except in the Midlands and north of England where abundant forests and coal-pits meant people could access the fuel needed for the home-brewing process. Beer consumption also faced competition from Britons' growing enjoyment of tea. Home-brewing was especially popular in the northern English county of Yorkshire where locals used foraged herbs instead of hops to create strong ales served at celebrations. London's commercial brewers were especially dominant at this time as they brought out a new product, a hearty beer called porter, which was so-called because it was nourishing and thus good for people with jobs that kept them on the move such as porters. By the end of the century, beer was no longer a drink drunk by everyone. Rather it was enjoyed by the wealthy for pleasure when not at home.

In the nineteenth century, home-brewing all but died out in Britain, replaced by industrialized production. By 1815, a dozen London brewers produced around two million barrels of beer per year, which equated to a fifth of all British beer production. From then on, London beer production was concentrated on a handful of large breweries with whom many London pubs were tied into deals thereby providing the breweries with a guaranteed market. Soon the dominance of the major London brewers attracted the ire of authorities who sought to increase competition in the beer industry by introducing measures such as the 1830 Beerhouse Act that allowed more inns to open. The move resulted in cheaper beer prices and a short-lived rise in beer consumption. By 1834, there were 134 commercial brewers in Britain producing over 10,000 barrels per year, but by the 1870s, this number had almost trebled as higher wages meant Britons enjoyed more beer. As part of the expanding brewing industry, more large breweries were built, especially in the Midlands where ample building land was available as well as transport links via the developing canal network. In 1881, the Austro-Bavarian Brewery of Tottenham, Britain's first purpose-built lager brewery, opened in London. However, the brewery failed, and for the next 80 years, lager comprised only a small percentage of British beer sales. Though Victorian beer was weaker than the beer drunk today, there was disquiet in some sections of British society about alcohol's influence on Britons. Consequently, from 1855, a number of laws were introduced to restrict pub opening hours initially on Sundays and later on weekdays too.

Beer consumption fell from 1880 to 1914 mainly because the working class opted to drink tea when at home (beer became a drink for men when they were out of the house). The working class also started to spend their disposable income on newly available manufactured goods, such as clothes and toys, and on entertainment. Also, since many members of the working class aspired to be seen as middle class, they adopted the middle-class disdain for drunkenness and began to shun beer. By 1914, the influence of the temperance movement on the ruling Liberal Party meant authorities brought about ever-tightening controls on alcohol sales. In 1914, the government introduced the Defence of the Realm Act that gave the government wide-ranging powers to ensure victory in the First World War. Under the law, pub opening hours were reduced, as was the strength of alcoholic drinks. It also became illegal to buy drinks for other people, and the duty on beer rose steeply, thus making beer more expensive to purchase. These measures were intended to prevent munitions workers from suffering hangovers that might impede their work and prevent drunken disorder that could impinge the war effort.

From 1919 to 1939, beer consumption reached a historic low partly because the early 1930s was a time of mass unemployment among working-class men and partly because the working class chose to spend their money on other things including sport, cafés, gardening, and holidays. High beer taxes and continuing strict licensing laws also curtailed beer sales. To combat falling consumption, brewers began an advertising campaign that associated beer with good health while pubs became cleaner, brighter, and more comfortable in order to appeal to women and the middle classes.

During the Second World War, pubs became essential to maintaining public morale, and unlike in the First World War, beer consumption rose during the conflict despite higher beer prices. At the same time, with so many pub workers fighting overseas, numerous pubs became short-staffed meaning many British women became publicans. After the war, beer consumption fluctuated. In the 1950s, British leisure activities tended to be family-orientated and homely so did not usually involve alcohol. Then in the 1960s, mild ale began to decline in popularity, while bitter, especially "keg" bitter, became popular, as did lager. Since keg bitter was pasteurized and easier to keep than cask beers, it became ubiquitous. Thus, by 1970, almost all British pubs served only keg draught beers, which not only kept well but needed less training on the part of bar staff to serve. Both keg beer and lager were also suitable for canning and so became popular supermarket buys. In the 1980s, Britons began to get a taste for foreign and British-brewed lagers, so that by 1989 lager was Britain's best-selling beer type.

In 2002, the Progressive Beer Duty was introduced to Britain. This taxed smaller breweries at a lower rate than bigger, market-dominant breweries and stimulated an increase in the number of British breweries and microbreweries (small-scale, often independent breweries). Today, there are around 3,018 British breweries. In 2020, pubs were closed for 161 days under lockdowns aimed at combatting the Covid-19 pandemic. Nonetheless, the number of new breweries in Britain has continued to grow. Indeed, some economists suggest lockdowns may have acted as a catalyst for entrepreneurs to start new brewing businesses. Despite the number of breweries in Britain, in 2022, the most popular beers in Britain were European—San Miguel, Guinness, Heineken, Peroni, Stella Artois, and Kronenbourg 1664. The Campaign for Real Ale (founded in 1971), which represents British beer drinkers and pub-goers, has around 180,000 members. Among other concerns, the organization considers pubs a tangible part of British heritage and aims to ensure they are supported by the government. Nonetheless, in July 2022, it was reported there are fewer pubs in England and Wales than ever before, for the total number of pubs fell below 40,000 during the first half of the year, a fall of more than 7,000 compared with 10 years ago. The biggest reduction came in the West Midlands, followed by London and eastern England. The fall is partly because many pubs have been demolished or converted into homes and offices. Also, while pubs managed to battle through the pandemic by selling take-away beer or through online sales, they now face record-high inflation and exorbitant energy bills. According to the British Beer and Pub Association, the British Institute of Innkeeping, and UK Hospitality, only 37 percent of hospitality businesses currently turn a profit, meaning the British pub, and thus breweries and beer sales, faces an uncertain future.

Gin

Gin was developed by the Dutch in the sixteenth century and became popular in England after English soldiers enjoyed the drink while in the Netherlands around 1570. By 1575, small amounts of gin were being exported from the Netherlands to England. Gin became widespread in England after the 1688 Glorious Revolution, when Queen Mary II and her husband William III of Orange (the leader of the Dutch Republic) came to rule England, Scotland, and Ireland. Under William and Mary, prohibitive import restrictions on French brandy and wine were imposed as well as heavier duties on strong beer, moves that steered Britons toward drinking gin rather than brandy, wine, or beer. Under William, the Act for the Encouraging the Distilling of Brandy and Spirits from Corn (1690) was introduced that gave tax breaks for grain farming and, by default, the distillation of grain-based spirits like gin. The act resulted in a huge increase in the number of distilleries in England and so fueled the availability of gin in England. Subsequently, gin emerged as England's national alcoholic drink, and soon after, England entered into a period known as the "Gin Craze." The gin mania was most prevalent in London, which in 1725 was home to at least 6,187 gin sellers. Gin was especially popular with women for not only was it a favorite tipple of Queen Anne (successor to William III), but, at this time, gin was heavily sweetened to make it palatable and thus tasted similar to the herbal cordials many women drank for medicinal reasons. The association of women with gin led to the drink being nicknamed "mother gin" or "mother's ruin."

Gin's low cost and easy availability was problematic, however, for without any form of regulation, some distillers added harmful substances such as turpentine and sulfuric acid to their gin in an effort to produce an intensely intoxicating effect. The gin craze also led to a surge in public drunkenness, especially among the poor. Therefore, in 1736, the government introduced the Gin Act, which brought in a retail tax on gin, heavy duty on gin production, and annual licenses for gin sellers that were prohibitively expensive to acquire. The measures aroused much anger among the English and were widely ignored. Faced with more expensive gin, the English started to drink illegal gin that was even more dangerous to drink than previous adulterated gins. This fact, coupled with riotous public outrage, meant that in 1739, the act was dropped. By 1743, official figures put England's gin consumption at 8.2 million gallons, but the figure was likely nearer 19 million gallons. Such was the dissipation in London caused by the gin craze that the artist William Hogarth depicted gin-soaked Londoners in various works. Hogarth's print *Gin Lane* (1751) is particularly notorious as it depicts London as a hellspace inhabited by those made syphilitic, debt-ridden, and ravenous by their gin addiction. Soon after the print appeared, the Gin Act of 1751 was enacted, which reduced the number of gin shops and increased the tax on importing gin substantially as part of a range of measures to curtail gin consumption. The public accepted this act and external factors also helped curb the availability of cheap gin, including a succession of poor corn harvests in the late 1750s that meant available corn was prioritized for bread making rather than distilling. After 1760, gin production fell to a low of around 2 million gallons per year before rising to 4 million gallons per year at the end of the century. By this time, gin producers had started to make better quality gin that found favor among the English upper classes. The British living in India during the colonial era boosted gin's popularity further. In the early nineteenth century, malaria was rife in India so British officials and soldiers stationed there took medicinal quinine as an antimalarial. However, since quinine tasted awful, the British mixed it with recently invented carbonated water and sugar to mask the taste, thus creating tonic water. In 1825, British Army officers started to mix tonic water with gin and thus created the gin and tonic, the quintessential British cocktail. When British colonials returned home, they brought with them a love of gin and tonic. Also, around this time, it was discovered that Angostura bitters helped combat seasickness, and so the British Navy began to use the bitters. As with tonic water, it was found that the bitters tasted good mixed with gin and the combination became known as "pink gin." Pink gin soon became popular among the British public. Pink gin was usually made with Plymouth gin, which originates in Devon, southwest England, and is sweeter tasting than the more common London gin.

By the late nineteenth century, gin had fallen out of fashion and was once again considered a drink for the poor. By the 1950s, British gin consumption had fallen further as the drink had become thoroughly unfashionable. The lack of demand together with rising property values meant distilleries in London began to close, until only the famous Beefeater distillery remained. Recently, however, London's transformation into a global gastronomic capital has resulted in Londoners becoming interested in gin again, partly because gin has a retro appeal and also because as a local product, it chimed with the move toward eating local foods. Today, gin has been re-embraced by all sections of English society and is currently fashionable again.

In 2009, London's first copper pot distillery in 189 years, Sipsmith, based in Chiswick, opened and paved the way for countless artisan gin-makers. Today, small gin producers compete with big name brands such as Booth's Gin, G&J Greenall, Gordon's, and Plymouth Gin (all dating from the eighteenth century), Beefeater (opened in 1820), Tanqueray (whose recipe has remained unchanged since 1830), and Gilbey's, which started as a merchant business in 1857. Today, Beefeater is the only premium-brand distillery to own a London premises.

Tea

Tea is ingrained in the British psyche for it is drunk by most Britons at all times of the day, with or without food, and holds a unique place in people's affections. Tea was first introduced to Britain around the start of the seventeenth century when it was imported from the Netherlands via a Dutch company that enjoyed trade relations with China. Initially, tea's popularity in Britain lagged behind that of coffee and hot chocolate but this changed when Catherine of Braganza (1638–1705), the Portuguese wife of King Charles II (king of England, Scotland, and Ireland), introduced tea to the English aristocracy. Previously, tea had been drunk in England only for its health benefits whereas the Portuguese aristocracy had a penchant for recreational tea-drinking because of Portugal's colony of Macau in southeast China. Soon, tea was adopted by the English upper classes as an accoutrement of gentility while the burgeoning middle classes regarded tea as a symbol of sober respectability. Tea helped transform British breakfasts into a light meal featuring tea, cakes, and jam as opposed to meat and ale. Tea was also served after dinner (at the time taken around 2 p.m.) by the lady of the house who presided over the serving of tea using paraphernalia including fine china tea sets. In this way, tea became the drink of polite society. In time, loose-leaf tea came to be sold by various traders including chinaware vendors, silk sellers, and hat-makers, all of whom attracted predominantly female shoppers.

As a luxury good, from 1689, tea was subject to customs duty. By this time, tea imports from China were brought to Britain by the East India Company that enjoyed a monopoly on Chinese tea. The customs duty made little difference to Britons' fondness for tea however, and by 1700, Britain imported 90,000 lb of tea per year. Gradually, tea became Britain's national drink, drunk by all sections of society. Initially, British tea consumption was centered around London, but throughout the eighteenth century, tea-drinking spread first to fashionable resorts such as Bath in southwest England, then to rural areas. Later, tea became popular in the north of England, and by 1744, in Scotland too. Growing demand for tea meant the East India Company had to import ever-increasing amounts of tea—from 142,000 lb in 1711 to 15,000,000 lb in 1791. However, since tea was highly taxed and thus expensive to buy, a huge tea smuggling industry operated simultaneously. In 1783, Prime Minister William Pitt the Younger slashed tax on tea in order to ruin the smuggling trade. The move was successful for the reduced tax meant legal tea imports tripled in volume and tea consumption in Britain skyrocketed.

Part of the reason eighteenth-century Britons loved tea was that at this time tea was much more cost-effective than coffee—tea leaves could be reused, and, unlike coffee, was palatable without milk or sugar. Tea was also readily available for by 1760, a quarter of all British shops sold tea. The teas sold at this time included various types of black and green tea including Bohea, Souchong, Congou, and Gunpowder. Shops would also combine teas to create bespoke blends.

By the start of the nineteenth century, tea was drunk at all times of the day. Consequently, from 1800 to 1900, tea consumption in Britain increased from 23,720,000 lb per year to 224,180,000 lb. In 1853, tax on tea was reduced further thereby stimulating a further sustained fall in the price of tea to the consumer. Now, tea was not only cheaper, but grocers started to sell tea in packets. This innovation allowed even more Britons to enjoy tea not just at home, but also at work as packets made tea easier for workers to transport.

The East India Company started to import tea from India in 1839. Soon after, in around 1840, the concept of afternoon tea was originated by Anna Maria Russell, the seventh duchess of Bedford, who was a lady-in-waiting to Queen Victoria. The duchess would become peckish around 4 p.m., which was unfortunate because the Victorian custom was for evening meals to be served at around 8 p.m. Therefore, feeling frustrated at having to suffer a lengthy wait between her lunch and dinner, the duchess asked that a tray carrying tea, buttered bread, and cake be brought to her room in late afternoon. The late afternoon snack became the duchess' habit and soon she started to invite friends to join her for the afternoon meal. Soon, the late afternoon tea became a fashionable social event, and by the 1880s, the women of high society would change into their best indoor clothes to enjoy afternoon tea, which typically was served in a household's drawing room between 4 p.m. and 5 p.m. Afternoon tea was a particularly feminine affair for the occasion allowed women to entertain company at home with their husbands absent. In this way, afternoon tea became a liberating experience that enabled women to share ideas and gossip.

Traditionally, afternoon teas consist of a plentiful selection of delicate sandwiches (including those famously filled with thinly sliced cucumber), scones served with clotted cream and jam, cakes, and pastries. Typically, tea is served from silver tea pots and drunk from elegant china cups, while the cakes and sandwiches are served on a tiered stand. Although the components of an afternoon tea are inherently light, when eaten together, they form a fairly substantial meal. Today, traditional afternoon teas can be enjoyed in a variety of locations including fine hotels such as London's the Ritz and such upmarket London shops as Fortnum and Mason, as well as quirkier venues such as cricket stadiums, art galleries, and even London buses. Afternoon teas are also a staple of rural tearooms with England's West Country (the counties of Devon, Dorset, Cornwall, and Somerset) synonymous with so-called cream teas, which consist of tea, scones, strawberry jam, and clotted cream. Although tea is the staple drink to accompany afternoon tea, today it is also possible to accompany the cakes and sandwiches with coffee or a herbal infusion instead. Some afternoon tea establishments also offer champagne alongside the sandwiches and cakes as a so-called champagne afternoon tea.

The tea industry in India expanded later in the nineteenth century. By 1900, India was producing 100 million lb of tea per year, which accounted for half of the tea consumed in Britain. Britain's love of tea continued up to the First World War. During the war, the government recognized tea was important to the British national psyche. To this end, the British government protected the supply of tea and allocated Britons 2 oz of tea per person per week. In the interwar years, tea was cheap as stiff competition between tea-exporting countries kept the price low, and a peak of tea consumption was reached in 1929. This was during a time of economic depression and highlights that in Britain tea is often considered a comforting drink. It is for this reason that when misfortune occurs, it is quite usual for a Briton to ask: "how about a nice cup of tea?" while proffering a cup of hot drink (a "cuppa"). In the run-up to the Second World War, the British government planned ahead to maintain tea supplies despite the fact that tea had to be imported via docks that were vulnerable to aerial bombardment. Once war was declared, all tea was requisitioned, and maximum tea prices were imposed by the government. Britain's tea supplies remained constant during the war, however, as India, Ceylon (now Sri Lanka), Uganda, and Kenya stepped up production. Tea came off ration in 1952, and its consumption revived to prewar levels. Since 1960, British tea consumption has started to fall as changing tastes, influenced by Continental Europe and the United States, meant Britons switched to drinking coffee, and other drinks. That said, Britons still drink around 100 million cups of tea each day, which equates to almost 36 billion cups per year. Britain remains a nation of tea lovers, with 75 percent of Britons drinking at least one cup per day and 13 percent drinking at least six cups daily. Black tea is the favorite amongst Britons, but interest in fruit teas, herbal infusions, and decaffeinated tea are driving growth in the British tea market, especially among younger tea drinkers who tend to be particularly adventurous in their tea choices. Similarly, British women are also more likely to drink fruit teas, herbal infusions, decaffeinated, or iced tea than men. English Breakfast (a blend of single-origin black teas, usually Assam, Kenya, and Ceylon) is by far the most popular tea blend, followed by Earl Grey and Darjeeling. British shoppers care about the ethical sourcing of tea, and the sustainability of tea production is particularly important to British shoppers aged 18 to 34 years.

Coffee

Coffee arrived in England in the seventeenth century, possibly as early as 1637 when a Greek student drank it at Oxford University. Subsequently, the first coffeehouse in England, The Angel, opened in Oxford in 1650. The first coffeehouse in London was opened in 1652 by a Greek servant named Pasqua Roseé who worked for a British merchant, Daniel Edwards, who imported Turkish coffee. Soon, such was Londoners' love of coffee that by 1663, the City of London alone contained eighty-two coffeehouses. It was at the coffeehouses that London's traders, bankers, and insurance underwriters met to conduct business. Southern England's love of coffee soon spread across Britain, reaching Edinburgh by 1707. The coffeehouses offered a space for men to socialize and network. This is reflected today, for in Britain, coffee is seen as more of a social drink than tea, hence Britons will often "go for a coffee," that is, meet up with friends in a café.

Toward the end of the seventeenth century, coffee was being enjoyed at home by the aristocracy who drank the drink at breakfast and after dinner. By 1685, powdered coffee for home consumption was available and despite increases in customs duty, was still cheaper to buy than tea. Over subsequent decades, the home consumption of coffee trickled down to the middle classes. The popularity of coffee at this time meant that soon many inns and taverns started to sell coffee alongside alcohol. Today, many pubs still sell coffee.

In order to meet demand, the East India Company started to import increasing amounts of coffee—5,000 cwt in 1711 but 28,852 cwt by 1724. In the first decades of the eighteenth century, coffee remained cheaper than tea, but tea was more economical to buy as 1 lb of tea produced up to four times the quantity of drink than 1 lb of coffee. Also, the tea leaves could be reused unlike with coffee. Tea's cost-effectiveness meant tea was far more popular with poorer Britons than coffee. Thus, coffee became the preserve of wealthy Britons who had traveled to the Continent and followed the European fashion for drinking coffee with breakfast and after dinner.

Between 1700 and 1950, coffee consumption in Britain fluctuated greatly. In the early eighteenth century, the coffee drunk in Britain came from Yemen via the port of Mocha, which was used by the East India Company. The price of this coffee was dictated by monopolistic local merchants so Britain, like several other European countries, decided to develop coffee production in its colonial territories. Thus, in 1730, Britain established a coffee plantation in Jamaica. As a result of colonial coffee production, by the late 1700s, the wholesale coffee price was around half that of tea. Despite Britons' ability to make coffee at home, coffeehouses continued to open across England throughout the eighteenth and nineteenth centuries. In London especially, coffeehouses were an important part of the city as they acted as hubs where writers, thinkers, and merchants could meet. Some Britons preferred to drink coffee in coffeehouses because the powdered coffee available to use at home was often stale and bulked out by such substances as cocoa shell, dandelion roots, and acorns.

In the first half of the nineteenth century, coffee consumption was a quarter of that for tea. However, in 1825, duty on coffee was lowered resulting in the strong growth of the British coffee market as well as a proliferation of coffeehouses selling cheap coffee aimed at lower-class male workers. These coffeehouses were seen as a straightlaced alternative to pubs and were backed by supporters of the temperance movement. Another reduction in duty in 1842 resulted in hundreds of late-night coffee stalls appearing in London that attracted a clientele comprising prostitutes and criminals. Coffee consumption peaked in 1847 before beginning a steady decline. The main reason for the decline was that cheap coffee was often adulterated with questionable ingredients. Indeed, in 1855, there was public outcry when the medical journal *The Lancet* claimed coffee often contained sawdust and red iron oxide. The loss of public confidence in coffee's safety at a time when tea was becoming cheaper was the chief reason for the fall in British coffee consumption. From 1900 to the start of the First World War, coffee consumption continued to fall. During the war, however, coffee consumption rose as it became a substitute for tea, which was in short supply. Postwar, coffee's popularity fell again, with coffee only drunk by the richest Britons as an after-dinner drink. Coffee was rationed during the Second World War but nonetheless, coffee's popularity increased as Britons had money to spend on little luxuries at a time when food was in short supply and greater African coffee output meant the supply of coffee was constant. From the 1950s, coffee's popularity rose quickly with the opening of espresso bars marketed as trendy establishments aimed at young workers with a disposable income. The first espresso bar in Britain to install the revolutionary Gaggia espresso machine, the Moka Bar, opened in London in 1953. By 1960, Britain was home to 2,000 espresso bars of which 500 were located in Greater London.

From 1950 to the present, coffee consumption enjoyed its fastest growth. This increase in coffee's popularity coincided with a general rise in living standards, an increase in the number of all-adult households, advertising and television series that presented coffee as a desirable drink, and the fact that people ate out more often and so tended to finish a meal with coffee. Moreover, Britons' liking for European travel meant they continued to enjoy European coffee-drinking habits when they returned home. More recently, it has become increasingly easy to make good-quality coffee at home through the availability of instant coffee, coffee pods, and coffee bags, as well as domestic coffee-making machines.

Today, Britons drink around 98 million cups of coffee per day with coffee typically drunk between meals rather than as an accompaniment to food, except for at breakfast. Instant coffee is bought by 80 percent of households and is especially popular with drinkers aged 65 years and older. Contrastingly, ground coffee and coffee pods are growing in popularity amongst Britons aged 16 to 34 years. Café culture is well established in Britain and continues to boom, for 80 percent of Britons visit a café at least once a week, whilst 16 percent visit a café daily. The popularity of coffee shops means that the coffee industry employs over 210,000 Britons.

Cider

It is thought that cider came to Britain from Normandy, France, in the twelfth century with large-scale production taking off in the thirteenth century following the introduction of new apple varieties. In many parts of England, especially southwest and western England, cider was the main alternative to beer. Initially, two types of cider were made—strongly alcoholic cyder, which was made only from apple juice, and cider, which was far less alcoholic as it was diluted with water or produced from apples that had been pressed several times. Cyder was enjoyed by the elite, while cider was drunk by the poor. The importance of cider in rural England is demonstrated by the number of religious rites that developed in association with apples. For example, wassailing, which dates from Anglo-Saxon times, is an annual tradition that sees people gather to perform various rituals they believe will encourage an orchard to produce a bountiful harvest. Wassailing still occurs in some rural parts of England from New Year to February.

In the seventeenth century, landowners in the West Country (an area comprising the English counties of Cornwall, Devon, Dorset, Somerset, Bristol, Wiltshire, and Gloucestershire) planted orchards of Redstreak apples as a cash crop. When pressed, the harvested apples greatly improved the taste and quantity of the resulting cider. For a time, cider made from Redstreak apples was as expensive as the best imported wine. However, by the late eighteenth century, Redstreak apples were already in decline and by the nineteenth century were virtually extinct because the trees could no longer be propagated. By this time, cider was important because it was used to part pay laborers. It was from the West Country that scrumpy, a type of rustic, unfiltered cider, originated. Unlike regular cider, traditionally, scrumpy is made using windfall apples and is neither sweetened nor pasteurized. Today, the word "scrumpy" is used to distinguish small-batch ciders made using traditional methods from branded ciders.

The modern cider industry developed when in 1887 Henry Perceval Bulmer of Herefordshire (an English county now synonymous with cider production) established his eponymous cider business and embarked on a tour of England to publicize cider with the intention of creating a domestic cider market. Later, Bulmer mechanized cider production by installing steam-powered apple presses and traveled to France to learn about fermentation from champagne producers. These innovations marked the start of the modern British cider industry. Consequently, cider production rose from around 20 million gallons in 1870 to

33 million gallons in the mid-1880s. After this time, the demand for cider fell somewhat in line with the demand for other alcoholic drinks but still hovered around the 20 million gallons mark. In the inter-war period, cider production fell as low as 16 million gallons partly because in the public imagination, cider was considered unsophisticated. That said, the proportion of cider made in factories rose during the time, which suggests an upswing in demand among city-dwellers. It was only in the 1960s that mass cider consumption evolved due to successful advertising aimed at popularizing cider among young adults. By 1993, consumption had risen to 123 million gallons from 18 million gallons in 1963. Today, almost half of all households in Britain and Northern Ireland buy cider regularly. The majority of cider drunk in Britain is made from apples but recently ciders made from other fruits have become very popular. Cider remains most popular among British drinkers aged 18 to 34 years and is slightly more popular with women than men.

Whisky

Whisky—also known as Scotch—is an important part of Scottish identity. As such, it is the national drink of Scotland. To be classed as Scottish whisky, a whisky must be produced in Scotland and matured in oak casks for at least 3 years. Though the whisky-making process is always the same, Scotland's five regions each produce a different tasting whisky. Malts from Islay have a peaty character while those from Campbeltown have a pungent saltiness. Highland is the largest whisky region in terms of area, and its whiskies are known for a heavy character containing hints of nut, honey, and heather. Speyside whiskies have fruity, spicy notes, while Lowland malts are triple distilled resulting in a lighter taste.

It is thought that whisky was first made by medieval Scottish monks who, without access to wine-making grapes, used malted barley to produce alcohol. The monks called the drink *uisgebeatha*, which translates from Gaelic as water of life (*uisge* means "water"; *beatha* means "life"). The first record of whisky dates from 1494 when a monk at Lindores Abbey in Fife was granted a king's commission to make the spirit. Over time, whisky's popularity increased, which, in 1664, led to the Scottish authorities introducing a whisky tax. The tax led to the growth of an illicit whisky industry, and whisky smuggling became pervasive. Excisemen (known as gaugers) tried to combat the illicit distillers, but Scots found increasingly ingenious ways to hide illicit whisky from the authorities, including members of the clergy transporting whisky in coffins. By the 1820s, over half the whisky drunk in Scotland was illegal. While the Act of Union (1707, when the Scottish and English Parliaments united to form the Parliament of Great Britain) meant Scotland became subject to English excise laws, in Scotland, these laws were not enforced strictly.

In 1730, commercial whisky production began in earnest in the Scottish Lowlands region and by the end of the century, Lowlands distilling was dominated by two families that began exporting whisky to England. Even after private distilling required a license in 1781, the licenses were not enforced. This was partly because the remoteness of the Highlands meant logistically it was impossible for the authorities to keep tabs on which households were producing their own whisky. Therefore, it is likely that at the start of the nineteenth century, there were many thousands of distilleries in Scotland, both legal and illegal. That in 1822 there were 6,000 prosecutions related to illegal whisky distilling in Scotland goes some way to highlight the irregularity of the industry around this time.

In 1820, the strength of the illicit whisky trade prompted the duke of Gordon, whose lands included the Glenlivet distilling region, suggested that the government should make it profitable to make whisky legally. Thus, the duke offered to suppress the illegal whisky trade in return for reductions in whisky duty. In 1823, the duke's offer was accepted by the authorities, and so, in 1823, the Excise Act was passed. The act allowed Scots to pay £10 for a whisky-distilling license and lowered excise duty on whisky. In 1825, the distiller George Smith from Glenlivet took out the first whisky-distilling license and soon became Scotland's biggest commercial whisky business. Following the introduction of the Excise Act, whisky smuggling died out. In 1830, Aeneas Coffey invented the Patent Still that allowed continuous distillation to occur thereby industrializing whisky production. Coffey's still produced a greater yield at lower cost to create a stronger spirit. The stills were expensive to install, however, so did not catch on immediately. In the meantime, the amount of whisky drunk in Scotland continued to grow from roughly 2 million gallons in 1822 to almost 7 million gallons in 1829. An accompanying rise in drunkenness led to the development of an anti-spirits movement in Scotland.

In the nineteenth century, famous names of the whisky industry including Johnnie Walker and James Chivas exported whisky across the British Empire to Hong Kong, Sydney, Mumbai, Cape Town, and elsewhere. Additionally, when an 1880s outbreak of phylloxera beetle devastated French vineyards resulting in far less French brandy on the international drinks market, whisky producers ensured whisky became the spirit of choice globally in place of brandy. Meanwhile, in England, Queen Victoria's love of Scotland, together with the popularity of the novels of Sir Walter Scott, began a Victorian craze for all things Scottish, including whisky.

In 1853, the first blended whiskies were produced that mixed a high-quality single malt whisky with less expensive whisky to produce a lighter, cheaper drink. Blended whisky proved especially popular among city-dwellers in the Scottish Lowlands and in England. Thanks to effective advertising campaigns, blended whisky was soon the most popular spirit in England with brands such as Johnnie Walker and William Teacher becoming household names. Indeed, whisky did not follow the decline in spirit consumption after the 1870s, but rather, its consumption in England increased from 2.1 million gallons in 1876 to 7.2 million gallons by 1900. However, a 1909 rise in duty saw this figure fall to 2.1 million in 1913. When the First World War broke out, the prime minister, Lloyd George, thought of banning alcohol but reconsidered as to do so would be unfair to the Scottish. Instead, the government doubled the duty on spirits and ordered the dilution of spirits, including whisky. The actions proved hugely unpopular and were modified quickly, with pub-opening hours amended so that people had less chance to buy spirits. The modified opening hours included pubs in parts of Scotland being closed on Sundays and banned from selling spirits on Saturdays. It also became illegal to sell spirit chasers with beer. Whisky producers suffered greatly under these rules and suffered further in 1917 when whisky production using pot-stills was banned. The measures succeeded at reducing Britons' alcohol consumption until after the war when there was a brief upsurge in spirit consumption as people celebrated the end of the war. The 1930s saw the consumption of spirits fall further still, partly because of unemployment and the global economic downturn. The Scottish whisky industry also suffered because exports to the United States dried up during Prohibition. At the end of the 1930s, the fashionableness of cocktail parties boosted whisky sales so that whisky, along with gin, was the most popular spirit of the era. Cocktail parties were the preserve of the middle and upper classes, however, and whisky's trendiness did not extend to the working class who only drank expensive spirits on special occasions. When the Second World War erupted, the British government convened the Committee on Brewing and Distilling that prioritized grain supplies for whisky production as the whisky could be exported to the United States in exchange for food and weapons. Nonetheless, war disrupted grain supplies, and in 1942, Scottish distilleries were forced to close temporarily. By 1945, the distilleries had reopened, but their output was far less than prewar.

Scarcity together with postwar increases in duty made spirits more expensive for Britons to buy and led to a fall in consumption that extended into the 1950s. However, from 1953 to 1990, spirit consumption in Britain tripled mainly because Britons had more disposable income to spend on alcohol. Another important factor was the availability of spirits in supermarkets. Whereas off-licenses were traditionally seen in Britain as frequented by men, women were now able to buy bottles of spirit while supermarket shopping.

During the Covid-19 pandemic, whisky-makers produced significant quantities of ethanol for hand sanitizer that was supplied to frontline workers across Britain. At the peak of demand, the Scottish whisky industry was producing more than 1.4 million liters of ethanol a week, which was sufficient to produce over 12 million 500 ml bottles of sanitizer per month. In 2021, whisky accounted for 75 percent of all Scottish food and drink exports. The whisky industry remains an important employer, for over 11,000 people are employed directly in the industry in Scotland with 7,000 of these jobs being in rural areas of the Highlands and Islands (an area of Scotland broadly covering the remote Scottish Highlands, Orkney, Shetland, and Outer Hebrides islands). The whisky industry also provides indirect employment for it attracts many tourists—in 2019, 2.2 million people visited Scotland's 138 whisky distilleries, making the distilleries Scotland's third biggest tourist attraction.

Wine

It is not known when wine was first enjoyed in Britain, but it has been consumed in Britain since at least Roman times, when Britons drank around a liter of wine (roughly two pints) per day. While there is some evidence that wine was imported to Britain from Italy during the second century, it was under the Romans that viticulture took off in Britain, with vineyards established in southern England. The *Domesday Book* (Britain's earliest public record, a survey of land and landholding compiled in 1085–6) lists 130 vineyards in England, 52 of which were owned by the Church. This indicates that in early Britain, wine was not just part of people's diets but a medicine, an anesthetic, a disinfectant, and also used in religious rites. Later, wine became central to the celebration of the Eucharist as part of Christian church services.

Wine was popular in medieval times, but its popularity never rivaled that of beer for while beer was enjoyed by the masses, wine was the preserve of the elite. After 1152, when King Henry II married the French queen Eleanor of Aquitaine, wine-producing areas of France came under English rule and caused claret to become popular in England. Similarly, when England agreed a trade deal with parts of modern-day Portugal, Iberian wines became popular in England. Later, wealthier Elizabethans enjoyed wine imported from France, Italy, Germany, Spain, and Greece, as well as English wine. Fortified sweet wines including sack from Jerez (later known as sherry) and madeira from the Madeira Islands were popular, as were mead, metheglin, aqua vitae, and wines made from seasonal fruits such as elderberries.

In the seventeenth century, wine consumption in England fell under the austere rule of Oliver Cromwell. However, around the same time, a trade deal struck between England and Portugal meant port (fortified Portuguese wine) became popular in England. Under Cromwell, however, the 1651 Navigation Act banned some foreign ships from entering English ports. This move was aimed at hurting Dutch trade, but in reality, prevented French and German wine from reaching England. Under the rule of Cromwell's son Richard, the Wine Act (1688) imposed heavy duty on French wine with lower duty imposed on wine from Spain and Portugal. Consequently, in England, French wine became the preserve solely of the rich. In the eighteenth century, all wine was taxed heavily, and so an extensive network of wine smuggling developed along England's south coast. Partly in response to the smuggling, in 1786, the government halved the duty on French wine. However, despite the reduction in duty, wine consumption in Britain did not increase significantly. This was because a range of other drinks had become available in Britain including tea, beer, gin, and brandy. The adulteration of wine to make poor-quality produce more palatable through the addition of substances ranging from berries to litharge (a mineral form of lead oxide) increased toward the end of the century when duty on wine rose due to the French Revolutionary Wars (1792–1802). The war made imported, good-quality wine both scarce and expensive.

The growth of the British middle classes during the nineteenth century did not increase wine consumption substantially. This was likely because wine was still regarded as a drink of the wealthy and also due to a move toward temperance, which deemed excessive consumption uncouth. As a result of strong alcohol consumption becoming unfashionable, port and sherry fell out of favor among the rich. Instead, the wealthy opted for lighter German wines that reflected the royal ties between Britain and Germany (Queen Victoria's husband, Prince Albert, was German).

In 1860, the British government restructured the duty on wine and allowed restaurants to apply for a license that enabled them to sell wine from their premises. As a result of these changes, wine became cheaper and more popular with the British lower middle class of affluent workers. The availability of good-quality, cheaper wine all but ended the selling of adulterated wine though despite the greater availability of affordable good-quality wine, wine did not become popular with the British working class who in the main continued to prefer beer. That said, some working-class British women did start to drink "port and lemon" (port diluted by lemonade). Also, during the nineteenth century, Britons started to match their food to their wine, for example, drinking dry white wine with fish, claret with roast meats, and brandy at the end of a meal. By the Edwardian era, it was usual at dinner parties for gentlemen to enjoy a post-dinner brandy before they joined female diners for coffee. Wine continued to fall out of fashion during the First World War, partly because supplies of French wine were severely disrupted by fighting. A postwar boom saw wines sales rise before sales of table wine fell to a historic low during the years leading up to the Second World War. At the same time, sales of port and sherry held steady. By 1938, Australian and South African wine had become available in Britain for the first time following a change in import taxes intended to encourage trade across the British Empire. There was also an increase in British wines made from fruits and herbs. By this time, medicated wines sold as health tonics, such as Wincarnis (a fortified wine made from grape juice, malt extract, herbs, and spices dating from 1881), had become popular, especially with women. Nonetheless, only a minority of wealthy Britons drank table wine at home ordinarily for pleasure. For the majority of Britons, wine meant port or sherry and was enjoyed typically by women on special occasions or while at the pub. During the Second World War, wine availability was hugely disrupted by the fighting in Continental Europe, and the wine that was available was taxed heavily. Postwar, wine remained little drunk. In the 1960s, however, British wine consumption rose dramatically and continued to increase throughout the 1970s for a number of reasons: rising living standards allowed more people time and money to enjoy alcohol recreationally, foreign travel whetted Britons' enthusiasm for European drinks, and more Britons identified as middle class and thought it the done thing to have wine with their meals. Wine also became increasingly available with the advent of the wine bar (a bar where wine is the main drink available) and the growth of supermarkets. Both factors boosted wine sales, especially with British women. Wine consumption continued to grow throughout the 1980s and 1990s despite these being decades of high unemployment. By the late 1990s, 61 percent of wine was sold by supermarkets. This reflects that wine has become an everyday product bought with the weekly shopping to be enjoyed at home. At the same time, wines such as champagne continue to be associated with celebrations.

In 2020, Britain was the world's second largest importer of wine, importing just under 1.5 billion liters, valued at over $US 4 billion. Although Britain imports most of its wine from the European Union countries (especially France and Italy), Australian and New Zealand wines are also popular as are wines from Latin America. In 2022, a poll found that the Californian rosé Blossom Hill was the most popular wine brand in Britain. Other wines in the Top 10 include white Jacob's Creek from Australia and red Casillero del Diablo from Chile. The champagne brands Moët & Chandon, Dom Pérignon, and Bollinger were also in the Top 10, perhaps reflecting that many Britons chose to celebrate the Queen's Platinum Jubilee.

There is a small but rapidly growing British wine industry. In 2018, Britain produced a record 15.6 million bottles of wine, beating the previous record of 6.3 million bottles in 2014. Exports of British wine have risen greatly in recent years, and English and Welsh wines are now exported to forty different countries, with the top importers being Scandinavia, the United States, and Japan. The area of land used as vineyards in Britain has also increased by 160 percent over the last 10 years to reach 7,000 acres. In recent years, English sparkling wines have won prestigious international awards including the Decanter World Wine Awards. Moreover, it is thought that by 2024, the British wine industry will produce forty million bottles a year with a retail value of £1 billion. Exports of English wine alone are expected to reach £350 million.

Further Reading

Bossart, Celine. "The complete and slightly insane history of gin in England." VinePair (May 21, 2018). https://vinepair.com/articles/england-gin-history/Brewers Journal (accessed August 23, 2022).

British Beer and Pub Association. "Beer through the ages." Beer History. https://beerandpub.com/passions/beer-through-the-ages/ (accessed September 11, 2022).

British Coffee Association. "Coffee consumption" (2022). https://britishcoffeeassociation.org/coffee-consumption/ (accessed August 17, 2023).

Burnett, John. *Liquid Pleasures: A Social History of Drinks in Modern Britain.* London: Routledge, 1999.

Campaign for Real Ale. "What we stand for." CAMRA.org.uk (2022). https://camra.org.uk/about/about-us/what-we-stand-for/ (accessed September 12, 2022).

Carling. "The current market and future trends of cider: Part 2—the current market and future trends." Carling: Insights. https://www.carlingpartnership.com/insights/where-is-cider-going-2/ (accessed September 8, 2022).

Clark, Peter. "The 'mother gin' controversy in the early eighteenth century." *Transactions of the Royal Historical Society* 38 (1988): 63–84. JSTOR, https://doi.org/10.2307/3678967 (accessed August 23, 2022).

Cohen, Billie. "The true story behind England's tea obsession." *BBC Travel: Food & Hospitality* (August 28, 2017). https://www.bbc.com/travel/article/20170823-the-true-story-behind-englands-tea-obsession (accessed September 13, 2022).

Crown. "Fluoride." *NHS: Health A to Z* (August 21, 2021). https://www.nhs.uk/conditions/fluoride/ (accessed September 11, 2022).

Department for Environment, Food and Rural Affairs. "Drinking water quality in England: A triennial report 2017–2019" (December 2021). https://assets.publishing.service.gov.uk/government/uploads/system/uploads/attachment_data/file/1042163/drinking-water-quality-england17-19.pdf (accessed September 11, 2022).

Department for International Trade and The Rt Hon Liam Fox MP. "UK wine exports pouring into overseas markets." Gov.uk (May 30, 2019). https://www.gov.uk/government/news/uk-wine-exports-pouring-into-overseas-markets (accessed August 23, 2022).

El-Beih, Yasmin. "How coffee forever changed Britain." *BBC Travel: Food & Hospitality: History: London* (November 19, 2020). https://www.bbc.com/travel/article/20201119-how-coffee-forever-changed-britain (accessed August 31, 2022).

French, Phoebe. "Record 15.6m bottles of wine produced in England and Wales last year." The Drinks Business (February 1, 2019). https://www.thedrinksbusiness.com/2019/02/record-15-6m-bottles-of-wine-produced-in-england-and-wales-last-year/ (accessed August 23, 2022).

Jennings, Paul. *A History of Drink and the English, 1500–2000*. Abingdon: Routledge, 2016.

Johnson, Ben. "The great British pub." Historic-UK (June 1, 2015). https://www.historic-uk.com/CultureUK/The-Great-British-Pub/ (accessed August 17, 2023).

Mitchell, Ian. "Taking the pledge." *Whisky Magazine: History* https://whiskymag.com/story/taking-the-pledge (accessed September 13, 2022).

PA Media. "Number of pubs in England and Wales falls to record low." *The Guardian: Hospitality Industry* (July 4, 2022). https://www.theguardian.com/business/2022/jul/04/number-of-pubs-in-england-and-wales-falls-to-record-low-covid-19-soaring-costs (accessed September 14, 2022).

The Scotch Whisky Association. "Story of scotch." Scotch Whisky Association: Discover. https://www.scotch-whisky.org.uk/discover/story-of-scotch/ (accessed September 6, 2022).

The Scotch Whisky Association. "Facts & figures." Scotch Whisky Association. https://www.scotch-whisky.org.uk/insights/facts-figures/ (accessed September 6, 2022).

Taylor, Elise. "How gin bounced back from decades of decline to become London's latest It drink." *Vogue: Food* (June 11, 2018). https://www.vogue.com/article/how-gin-became-londons-it-drink-again (accessed September 4, 2022).

Thomas, Louis. "The 10 most popular beer brands in the UK." The Drinks Business (July 5, 2022). https://www.thedrinksbusiness.com/2022/07/the-10-most-popular-beer-brands-in-the-uk/ (accessed August 29, 2022).

Thomas, Louis. "The 10 most popular wine brands in the UK." The Drinks Business (July 12, 2022). https://www.thedrinksbusiness.com/2022/07/most-popular-uk-wine-brands/ (accessed August 29, 2022).

"UK brewery numbers increase 7.5%, surpassing 3,000." *Brewers Journal* (March 15, 2021). https://www.brewersjournal.info/uk-brewery-numbers-increase-7-5-surpassing-3000/ (accessed August 17, 2022).

UK Tea and Infusions Association. "FAQs about tea." Tea.co.uk (2022). https://www.tea.co.uk/tea-faqs (accessed August 30, 2022).

The Whiskey Exchange. "Glenlivet: Single malt scotch whisky." The Whiskey Exchange: Scotch Whisky: Single Malt Scotch Whisky (1999–2022). https://www.thewhiskyexchange.com/b/40/glenlivet-single-malt-scotch-whisky (accessed September 7, 2022).

William Reed Ltd. "Tea addicts, gender splits and the love of a traditional cuppa: 10 charts explaining UK attitudes to hot beverages." *The Grocer: Trend Reports* (September 16, 2019). https://www.thegrocer.co.uk/trend-reports/10-charts-explaining-uk-attitudes-to-hot-beverages/597574.article (accessed August 17, 2023).

Williams, Victoria. *London: Geography, History and Culture*. Santa Barbara, CA: ABC-CLIO, 2022.

7

Holidays and Special Occasions

In Great Britain, particular times of the year are associated with certain foods as are special occasions. For instance, Twelfth Night, Burns Night, Easter, Allhallowtide, Bonfire Night, and Christmas are all associated with particular dishes. When calendar customs have religious connotations, the foods associated with the custom will be enjoyed by most Britons whether or not they are religious. Meanwhile, certain months see people choose not to partake of certain food and drink. For example, each January, some Britons take part in Dry January and Veganuary.

British Calendar Customs and Food

Britain is home to myriad calendar customs, some of which are marked by all of the home nations while others are celebrated more in one country than another. For example, while Christmas and Easter are celebrated in England, Scotland, and Wales, Burns Night is a particularly Scottish tradition (though Scottish people living in England and Wales also mark the occasion). From boozy Twelfth Night wassailing to the Easter custom of Pancake Day, harvest festivals, and Christmas feasting, food and drink are essential components of these annual events.

Twelfth Night Cake and Wassailing

For many British people, Twelfth Night on January 5 marks the culmination of the Twelve Days of Christmas (the 12 days following Christmas Day that are called Twelvetide by some Christians) and is marked by certain customs that mark the day as special.

The custom of wassailing is particularly associated with Twelfth Night and dates back to before Christianity arrived in Northern Europe. The word "wassail" is Old Norse in origin and derives from the Old English *waes Pul háel*, a drinking toast meaning "be thou healthy" to which the response is "*Drinc hael*," which translates along the lines of "drink and be healthy." Wassailing takes many forms depending on local customs but typically sees revelers known as wassailers visit an orchard in order to sing songs such as the English folk carol *Here we come a-wassailing* to the orchard's fruit trees thereby ensuring that orchard spirits bestow a bountiful harvest. In return for ensuring a plentiful harvest, the wassailers are rewarded by the orchard's owner with wassail—a warm, spiced alcoholic drink (usually cider, but sometimes perry or ale) served in a communal bowl known as the wassail bowl.

Sometimes, the alcoholic drink is called the lamb's wool. The origins of this name are unknown, but may derive from the white, wool-like froth that forms on the drink, or it may be a corruption of *La Mas Ubhal* (pronounced lamasool), which was the ancient Celtic day for gathering apples and which occurred on November 1. Traditionally, a drink called lamb's wool that took the form of hot mead made using roasted crab apples was also enjoyed during the late summer Christian holiday of Lammas.

Wassailing is practiced throughout Britain in areas where orchards, particularly apple and pear orchards, are located. For instance, in the southwest English county of Gloucestershire, wassailing sees torchlit processions of singing villagers led by the Wassail King and Queen enter orchards before the Wassail Queen is hoisted onto the branches of a fruit tree where she places toasted bread that has been soaked in wassail punch. After this, the Wassail Queen is brought back to earth before a gun is fired at the tree's branches, and the villagers leave the orchard making much noise so as to drive away evil spirits. Some villages also choose to pour the wassail drink over the tree's roots. A similar form of wassailing occurs in the neighboring county of Somerset where in the village of Carhampton, wassailing takes place on January 17. This date is the "old" Twelfth Night dating from when the British calendar was altered in the eighteenth century. Here, villagers form a circle around the local orchard's largest tree and place alcohol-soaked toast in the tree's branches as a gift for a robin—the bird being symbolic of the orchard's benevolent spirits.

Calennig, another old January calendar custom involving apples, endures in Wales, especially in rural areas and the south of the country. The name *calennig*, which derives from the Latin *kalends* (from which the word calendar comes), translates as "the first day of the month" and sees children rise early on New Year's Day (*Dydd Calan* in Welsh) and carry an apple resting on a tripod of three sticks from house to house. The apple is decorated with flour, and has nuts, oats, and wheat stuck to it as well as a topping of a fragrant herb such as thyme, or a twig of box, or hazelnuts. As they carry the apple, the children sing a song conferring good wishes for the year ahead on the houses they visit. In return for wishing households good fortune, the children are rewarded with gifts of food (nowadays bread and cheese) and money.

Some Twelfth Night traditions, such as the eating of Twelfth Night cake, fell out of fashion in the sixteenth century following the Reformation when the Church of England broke away from the Catholic Church, and consequently, Epiphany was observed less keenly as a religious feast day. Nonetheless, during the Tudor period, Twelfth Night Cake was still eaten and took the form of a fruity brioche cake leavened with yeast and containing good luck charms such as a bean and a pea—those who found a charm in their piece of cake would be proclaimed king or queen for the day. At the start of the eighteenth century, Britons began to add beaten eggs to the cake as a raising agent instead of yeast, and, gradually, the fruity brioche was usurped by baked fruitcakes. By the nineteenth century, Twelfth Night had morphed into a secular festival, and the good luck tokens had evolved into silver charms such as thimbles. Although the Twelfth Night cakes of the eighteenth and nineteenth centuries were decorated elaborately with intricate sugar figures, nuts, and marzipan, the cakes began to be usurped by Christmas traditions popularized during the reign of Queen Victoria, such as the Christmas tree and Christmas cards. Over time, the Twelfth Night cake gave way to the Christmas cake, and the idea of hiding charms in Christmas foods transferred to the Christmas pudding. At the moment, there is a resurgence of interest in Twelfth Night cake, possibly as a result of European immigrants bringing with them the European idea of the king cake (an Epiphany cake containing a figurine that symbolizes Christ Child—whichever diner finds the figurine is declared king for the day), or simply because baking a Twelfth Night cake allows British home-bakers an opportunity to make a cake to mark the end of the festive season.

Burns Night Supper

Burns Night is held every January 25 to celebrate the birth of the Scottish poet Robert Burns in 1759. To mark the occasion, many people in Scotland and elsewhere in Britain attend a Burns Night supper. The first Burns Night supper was held in 1801 when some of Burns's friends gathered together to mark the fifth anniversary of his death. The night was so successful that the friends decided to congregate again, only this time in honor of their friend's birthday. The food served at a Burns Night supper celebrates some of Scotland's most famous dishes. For example, to start, diners may be served the traditional Scottish soup cock-a-leekie. This soup dates back to at least the sixteenth century and has its roots in the culinary tradition of meat and fruit pottages. Alternatively, Scotch broth may be served as a starter.

Haggis is Scotland's national dish and the traditional centerpiece of a Burns Night supper. Although haggis is strongly associated with Scotland, it has been eaten in England since at least the seventeenth century and is readily available in English shops. Nevertheless, in Scotland, haggis is so celebrated that in 1786, Burns wrote his poem "To a Haggis" (1786), and the dish has become an intrinsic part not just of Burns Night suppers but also of the Scottish New Year celebrations known as Hogmanay.

It is also possible to buy vegetarian haggis. For Burns Night celebrations, pescatarians swap the haggis for the thick smoked haddock soup known as Cullen skink.

Typically, the haggis is accompanied by mashed neeps (swedes) and tatties (potato). Whisky is the traditional drink to accompany the Burns Night haggis though ale, fruit wine, or Scotland's popular non-alcoholic carbonated drink Irn Bru, may be drunk instead of the whisky. It is also traditional for a dram of whisky to be poured over the haggis before it is eaten. Customarily, the haggis is piped into the supper, that is, its entrance into the dining area is accompanied by the playing of bagpipes. Before the haggis is eaten, it is also usual for Burns's poem "Address to a Haggis" (1787) to be recited. Typically, a traditional Scottish dessert such as clootie dumpling, tipsy laird, or cranachan is served to end the Burns Night supper.

Easter

Shrove Tuesday (or Pancake Day) is the feast day before Lent begins on Ash Wednesday, according to Christian tradition, and is the day on which Christians confess their trespasses to become "shriven" (absolved from their sins). The date of Shrove Tuesday varies annually, but it always falls 47 days before Easter Sunday (so any day between February 3 and March 9). Shrove Tuesday marks the last opportunity for Christians to use up eggs and fats before starting their fast for Lent in recognition of the days that according to Christian teaching, Jesus spent fasting in the desert prior to his Crucifixion. Traditionally, Britons mark Lent by abstaining from a range of foods, including meat, eggs, fish, fats, and milk, so before Lent could begin, all edible temptations needed to be removed from the home. Historically in Britain, meat and dairy products were banned during Lent with dairy products replaced with almond milk and butter. Christians were permitted to eat fish, bread, and vegetables, however (fish was thought a virtuous food because two of Jesus's disciples were fishermen). The removal of banned foods from the home takes place over several days known as Shrovetide. Traditionally, meat is eaten up on Collop Monday, while on Shrove Tuesday, eggs, butter, and fats are used up by making pancakes. Since pancakes are made from eggs and fat, they use up all the ingredients proscribed by Lent and thus became associated with this particular time of year. A traditional British pancake consists of batter cooked in a frying pan and served thin and flat, usually topped with lemon juice and caster sugar. Pancakes have a very long history in British culture and feature in cookbooks dating back to 1439.

In Britain, pancake races take place on Shrove Tuesday. The races see competitors, often in fancy dress, race around a course (usually local streets) flipping cooked pancakes in a frying pan as they run. The winner is the person who reaches the finishing line first with their pancake in their pan. The most famous British pancake race takes place in Olney, in the southeast English county of Buckinghamshire. According to legend, the race originated when, in 1445, an Olney woman heard the shriving bell while she was cooking pancakes and ran to church in her apron, still clutching the frying pan in which she was making her pancakes.

Other foods associated with Easter in Britain are the Simnel cake, hot cross buns, and Easter eggs. Simnel cake is eaten throughout Britain during Lent and Easter as well as on Mothering Sunday. Indeed, sometimes, Simnel cake is topped with sugared violets in reference to the traditional act of giving of violets to mothers as a Mothering Sunday gift. Mothering Sunday was known originally as Laetare Sunday, which was the day on which the 40-day fast of Lent would end and thus cake could be enjoyed. The name "Simnel" is thought to derive from the Latin word *simila*, the fine wheat flour that was used by Romans to make cakes and which was traditionally used in the cakes eaten on Mothering Sunday.

Traditionally, hot cross buns are eaten throughout the Easter period as they symbolize the crucifixion of Jesus on Good Friday. The Ancient Greeks, Romans, and Saxons all made buns to mark the changing seasons. For instance, buns decorated with crosses were eaten in April by the Saxons to honor Eostre, the goddess of dawn and fertility whose name may be the origin of the word Easter. The cross associated with Eostre represented the four quarters of the moon as well as the intersection of the Earth and the human (the horizontal line) with the divine (the vertical line). Therefore, it may be that the Christian symbol of the crucifix was added to these buns to transform the pagan festival celebrating Eostre into a celebration of Christ. However, the invention of hot cross buns is generally accredited to Thomas Rocliffe, a monk at St. Albans Abbey in southeast England. In 1361, Rocliffe baked Alban buns made from flour, eggs, fresh yeast, currants, and grains of paradise or cardamom, which he then distributed to the poor on Good Friday. Alban buns differ from hot cross buns, however, for they do not feature a cross piped across their top. Instead, the lines of a cross are cut into the top of the bun before they are baked.

In 1592, Protestant queen Elizabeth I banned the eating of hot cross buns except on specific days as she considered them too Catholic. In time, the ban was lifted, and by the 1700s, sweet, fruity buns were sold across Britain. By the nineteenth century, Alban buns were eaten by Britons on Good Friday to mark the end of Lent. Nowadays, Alban buns are baked as a limited-edition Easter product by a local bakery once owned by St. Albans Cathedral and which uses Rocliffe's original recipe. Meanwhile, hot cross buns continue to evolve with shops vying to produce innovative new flavors including chocolate, mocha, and cheese with Marmite (a yeast extract spread).

Throughout history, many people have considered eggs to be a symbol of fertility and rebirth and so have given eggs to each other to mark the coming of spring. In the historical region of western Asia known as Mesopotamia, early Christians dyed eggs red in order to mimic the blood shed by Christ during his crucifixion, a practice adopted by the Orthodox Churches. The custom then spread to Western Europe and was absorbed into Easter celebrations as can be seen in various parts of England where the tradition of creating pace eggs endures. Deriving its name from the Latin name for Easter (*paschal*), pace eggs are hard-boiled hen, duck, or goose eggs whose shells are dyed. Pace eggs grew in popularity throughout the eighteenth century and are still given as presents. Sometimes, pace eggs are rolled along the ground in a kind of race perhaps echoing the rolling away of the stone from Jesus's tomb as recounted in Christian lore. Additionally, annual pace egg–rolling events occur across northern England, especially in the counties of Lancashire and Yorkshire. Egg-rolling events see competitors hard boil and paint an egg, then roll it down a hill with the person whose egg is the first to reach the bottom of the hill intact declared the winner. In Lancashire, local superstition tells that if a competitor's egg breaks while rolling down the hill, then the shell debris must be crushed lest witches use it to make boats.

Since traditionally Christians do not eat eggs during Lent, eating an egg on Easter Sunday became an edible treat. In 1873, the first English chocolate Easter eggs were made by Fry's, the Bristol-based chocolate company that in 1853 had also produced the first filled chocolate bar, Fry's Cream Sticks. Fry's, which was founded in 1759, patented a method of using a steam engine to grind cocoa beans that enabled the company to mass produce chocolate and quickly become Britain's largest commercial producer of chocolate. In 1919, Fry's merged with its increasingly popular rival, Cadbury. Cadbury had produced its first Easter egg in 1875, and over the next century, Cadbury's went on to produce a wide range of chocolate eggs including Cadbury Dairy Milk, launched in 1905, which greatly increased sales of Easter eggs and helped Cadbury corner the British Easter egg market.

In the 1920s, Easter eggs became more decorative with colors and relief patterns added to their appearance. Then, in the 1930s, Cadbury launched Easter eggs filled with assortments of chocolates that appealed to adult shoppers, unlike earlier mass-produced Easter eggs that had appealed more to children. Since the 1960s, the Easter egg market has grown considerably. It was in the 1960s that Britons' perception of Easter changed to be seen less as a religious occasion and more as a bank holiday to be enjoyed by all. Easter eggs became the main gift to give at Easter, and thus all major chocolate manufacturers strove to provide a variety of eggs including eggs aimed specifically at children that were packaged in illustrated cartons. In 1975, the Cadbury Creme Egg became a huge Easter success thanks in part to television advertising and now dominates the British Easter egg market. Around 500 million Cadbury Creme Eggs are made annually with two-thirds of the eggs enjoyed by Britons rather than exported.

In the 1980s and 1990s, innovations in Easter egg production and presentation meant chocolatiers could extend their ranges. Consequently, Easter is now the biggest chocolate-gifting occasion in Britain with new egg ranges attracting increasing numbers of consumers each year. In a typical year, Britons spend in excess of £220 million on Easter eggs with sales increasing annually as the range of chocolate eggs available grows. Cadbury dominates the British Easter egg market, selling over half of all British Easter eggs. Indeed, one in every three chocolate eggs sold in Britain is made in the Cadbury's factory in Bournville, central England.

Lammas and Harvest Festival

Lammas, which derives its name from the Anglo-Saxon *loaf-mass*, is a Christian celebration that sees loaves of bread made from newly collected, consecrated grain. Lammas falls on August 1 and as such celebrates both the start of autumn and the first rewards of the wheat harvest. Lammas' association with wheat involves special foods, chiefly bread baked in the shape of a wheatsheaf. The bread eaten at Lammas is made using freshly picked corn that has been blessed at a local church. Lammas coincides with the Celtic festival of Lugnasad that celebrates the grain harvest.

The autumn harvest is an important time in British farming for crops are collected as both humans and animal feed. Typically, a festival to celebrate the harvest occurs at the end of September or in early October. In the past, entire communities including children would help collect the crops as people's existence depended on the harvest's success—a bountiful harvest guaranteed that a community would not go hungry during the winter. Once the harvest ended, harvesters would gather at their farm to take part in the Harvest Supper (or Harvest Home), a feast accompanied by singing, drinking, and games.

Over time, agricultural technological advances lessened Britons' reliance on the harvest so that nowadays, harvest festivals are largely symbolic in nature. Harvest festivities differ across Britain, but the most common harvest celebration is a church festival that originated in Morwenstow, Cornwall, in 1843, when Reverend Robert Hawker held a service of thanksgiving for the harvest with bread made from the first cut of harvest corn used in the communion. Modern harvest festivals see parishioners bring fruit, vegetables, tinned goods, and other foods to church where they are placed on the altar before being blessed by a member of the clergy. Typically, the foods are then distributed to charities and the needy. Oftentimes, a loaf in the shape of a wheatsheaf is also present as a reminder of Lammas.

While harvests are usually associated with farming, some British festivals give thanks to the sea and rivers for providing fish. For instance, on a Sunday in October, the Harvest of the Sea Thanksgiving service occurs at St. Mary-at-Hill Church in Billingsgate, London. For the service, the fish sellers of Billingsgate Fish Market decorate the church with fishing nets, a fishing boat, and a display of seafood supplied by the local traders. Meanwhile, in North Shields in England's far northeast, the Blessing of the Salmon Fishery service takes place in February and sees the first salmon caught given to the local vicar. The people living in

North Shields have long depended on the salmon that live in the River Tweed with records showing that fisheries have existed there since the eleventh century. The tradition of blessing the river's salmon dates to Victorian times, and while the tradition died out in the mid-1980s, it was revived in the 2010s. Originally, the blessing was held at midnight on Valentine's Day as this date marked the start of the net fishing season.

All Hallows' Eve, All Saints' Day, and All Souls' Day (Allhallowtide)

Soul cakes are small, round, spiced fruity cakes traditionally baked by British Christians to mark All Hallows' Eve (October 31, commonly called Hallowe'en), All Saints' Day (November 1), and All Souls' Day (November 2) as a way to commemorate the dead, most particularly souls lingering in Purgatory. Some folklorists theorize that the cakes were originally baked in bonfires in pre-Christian times as a type of lottery with the person who picked a burnt cake becoming a human sacrifice to ensure a bountiful harvest the following year. Another theory suggests the cakes were scattered across fields in order to appease malevolent spirits. Whatever the cakes' origins, by the eighth century, the cakes had been adopted by Christians as a means to aid the souls of the departed. In recent years, there has been a resurgence of interest in soul cakes via baking blogs and the availability of old cookbooks online.

In England, especially the county of Cheshire, an enduring All Souls' Day custom known as souling sees children sing and pray while visiting houses to collect soul cakes. The songs sung during souling vary but nearly always mention the desire for soul cakes. According to tradition, each cake eaten by the so-called soulers, that is, the children, represents a soul freed from Purgatory. The practice of doling out soul cakes to children who knock at the door is often viewed as the origin of today's Hallowe'en custom of trick or treating. A custom similar to souling, Caking Night (or Cakin' Neet) occurs in central and northern England either on October 30/31 or November 1 and sees children visit homes while chanting for cake. The children then produce a tin into which homeowners place soul cakes. The children's visit is supposed to protect homes from evil.

Souling has a long history in England but reached a peak of popularity during the nineteenth century. The tradition, nonetheless does still takes place, and in Cheshire and most especially Wales, also sees troupes of actors known as mummers perform souling plays on November 1. Mummers travel from pub to pub to perform plays that feature a ghastly character known as a souling horse. This is a horse's skull attached to a stick that is then covered in a blanket. The most famous souling horse is Mari Lwyd (or Grey Mare), which is included in Welsh mummers' plays and visits pubs in the hope of receiving cakes and beer. Mari Lwyd is also a feature of Welsh wassailing customs, as well as Christmas and New Year celebrations. While the Mari Lwyd character is most famously seen in the Welsh counties of Glamorgan and Gwent, it has similarities with other British customs that see hooded representations of animals accompany people as they entreat others for food in the depths of winter. These folk customs include the Hoodening held in the southeast English county of Kent and the Broad folk custom found in the Cotswolds area of southcentral England.

Another food-related custom that occurs on October 31 is Hop-tu-Naa that takes place on the Isle of Man (a self-governing British Crown dependency located in the Irish Sea between England and Ireland). Over time, Hop-tu-Naa has come to be seen as a version of Hallowe'en as it involves carving turnips (or swedes) in the manner of jack-o'-lanterns, and processions of children dressed as ghosts and witches visit houses in the hope of being rewarded with apples, sweets, and coins. As the children walk in procession along the streets holding their carved turnips, they sing Hop-tu-Naa songs such as *Jinny the Witch*. A similar tradition, Punkie Night, occurs annually on the last Thursday of October in Hinton St. George, in the southwest English county of Somerset. The word "punkie" is the local name for a hollowed-out mangel-wurzel (large turnip) that is lit from within by a candle in the manner of a jack-o'-lantern. On Punkie Night, all the local children parade through the village streets singing and carrying their punkies in order to be given candy by onlookers. According to legend, the event began when local men went to a nearby village and became so drunk that they could not find their way home. In order to guide their menfolk home, the women of Hinton St. George placed lit candles inside hollowed-out mangel-wurzels to prevent the flames from being blown out by strong winds. Today, the event is very popular with locals and visitors alike, a popularity that has led nearby villages to hold their own Punkie Nights.

Guy Fawkes Night

Guy Fawkes Night, commonly called Bonfire Night, is a British custom celebrated annually on November 5 in order to commemorate the failure of the Gunpowder

Plot (1605) that saw plotters aim to blow up the Palace of Westminster (i.e., the British Houses of Parliament), thereby killing the king and politicians in order to clear the way to reinstate Catholic rule in England. One of the conspirators, Guy Fawkes, was apprehended the evening before the attack, and the plot failed. In the plot's aftermath, Parliament declared November 5 a national day of thanksgiving, and the first annual celebration occurred in 1606. Today, Guy Fawkes Night is celebrated across Britain with parades, fireworks, bonfires, and special foods including parkin, bonfire toffee, and toffee apples.

Parkin is a dark, spicy gingerbread strongly associated with northern England. Indeed in nineteenth-century Leeds in the county of Yorkshire, Guy Fawkes Night was known as Parkin Day. Parkin has a dense texture as it is made using oatmeal as oats were the main cereal grown in northern England. Similarly, parkin is rich in ground ginger, as in the past, ginger was the cheapest spice people could buy while the ginger's spiciness provided edible warmth on cold November nights. Originally, parkin was made with dripping rather than butter and did not include eggs resulting in parkin with a very dense texture. Now that such ingredients as flour, eggs, and sugar are cheaper, they are incorporated into most parkin recipes resulting in parkin with a lighter texture. That said, parkin recipes from Yorkshire use more oatmeal than flour, while recipes from Lancashire usually include more flour than oatmeal. It is traditional for parkin to be slightly underbaked, so that the center remains sticky. Once baked, parkin should be kept in an airtight tin for at least 3 days before it is cut so that it can soften and the flavors mellow. Parkin can be stored in an airtight tin for up to 2 weeks.

Treacle toffee (also known as Bonfire toffee or as *claggum* in Scotland and as *losin du* or *taffi triog* in Wales) tastes very strongly of black treacle for this is the toffees' dominant ingredient and gives the toffee a slightly bitter flavor. Treacle has been used in Great Britain since the 1660s. Treacle toffee emerged soon after, although treacle was very expensive because it was considered as medicinal originally. Toffee developed in northern England around the mid-eighteenth century and in so doing replaced such popular sweets as candied fruit. By 1800, toffee was popular throughout Britain though it is not known why it became associated with Guy Fawkes Night. The mass production of treacle toffee began in the 1840s but from the 1890s to the early 1900s, the price of black treacle often rose above the price of sugar meaning shop-bought toffee was too expensive for many Britons to purchase. For this reason, treacle toffee remained a primarily homemade confectionary, often made in large sheets with individual pieces broken off using a special hammer. The use of a hammer to break the toffee has all but died out however on the grounds of health and safety.

Although in England treacle toffee is closely associated with Guy Fawkes Night, in Wales, it is also associated with Christmas. In parts of northern Wales, *Noson Gyflaith* (Toffee Evening) was a Christmas and New Year tradition that would see families invite friends to their homes for a dinner that was followed by making toffee, playing games, and storytelling. When the toffee mixture had melted to the correct consistency, it was poured on to the house's hearthstone, and partygoers would cover their hands with butter before pulling the still-warm toffee with their hands until it became a golden color. Toffee-making was also popular in parts of south Wales, particularly in coal-mining areas, but here it was not associated with a particular festive occasion. Today in Wales, the traditional Christian worship service *plygain* still occurs. The service is followed by celebrations during which Christmas treacle toffee (*cyflaith*) and other treats are eaten while decorating houses with mistletoe and holly. Recently, some Welsh parishes have started to incorporate Plygain into celebrations to mark the pre-Julian calendar custom of Welsh New Year held on January 12.

Christmas

In Europe, winter has long been a time of feasting as food was plentiful following the harvest, hunting season was at its peak, and alcohol made in autumn had enjoyed time to ferment. In particular, the Roman festival of Saturnalia running from December 17 to 23 that honored Saturn, the god of agriculture, and Dies Natalis Solis Invicti, held on December 25 to celebrate the birth of the sun god Sol Invictus, evolved into the festive time of Christmas enjoyed in modern Britain. A remnant of pre-Christian celebrations is still evident at Christmas in the form of the Yule log. Yule was the time of the Germanic New Year that extended from mid-November to January. In Britain, the Yule log (a specially selected log burnt on the hearth during winter) is now represented in chocolate as a popular Christmas specialty also called a Yule log. Today, the Yule festival is largely synonymous with Christmas with the two festivities forming an extended festive season.

While it is popularly thought that the Victorians invented the modern British Christmas, almost all British Christmas food traditions originate from before the nineteenth century. However, the Victorians did take the Christmas traditions of earlier times and transform them into domestic celebrations focused on the family and, in particular, children. This accounts for the importance of Christmas during the two World Wars—as Christmas celebrations fulfilled the yearning for home experienced by the military serving far from Britain, the government gave out extra rations so that Britons could enjoy better food at Christmas. Postwar, Britons had more disposable income to spend on Christmas. This meant that while Christmas became more egalitarian as more people could afford to enjoy festive treats, Christmas also became more commercial with shop shelves heaving with everything from turkeys to mince pies. Today in Britain, as elsewhere, Christmas is a time of communal feasting, enjoying food with family and friends, and preparing and eating foods reserved for a special time of year.

While many British Christmas food traditions can be applied to the whole of Britain, one particularly localized tradition occurs every December 23, when the inhabitants of the Cornish town of Mousehole (pronounced mowsel) eat stargazy pie (sometimes called starry gazey pie). This is a very unusual pie for it features whole pilchards (sardines) cooked so that their heads (and sometimes tails) poke through a pastry crust that also contains hard-boiled eggs, potatoes, bacon, and a mustard-flavored sauce. It is imperative that the pilchards retain their heads and look skyward as this give the fish the appearance of gazing at the stars, hence the name of the dish. According to Cornish tradition, stargazy pie is eaten during the festival of Tom Bawcock's Eve, which is held in Mousehole on December 23 annually to commemorate the efforts of local resident Tom Bawcock. Legend tells that one winter, Tom Bawcock went out to fish during a period of severe stormy weather in order to feed the village and thus prevented the other villagers from starving at Christmas. The fish were then baked with their heads and tails sticking out of the pastry to prove there was indeed fish inside the pie.

The unusual nature of stargazy pie has given rise to the Cornish legend that the Devil refuses to enter Cornwall for, on learning of the stargazy pie's filling, the Devil is said to have decided the Cornish would make anything into a pie including the Devil. Consequently, the Devil decided to stay in the neighboring county of Devon.

On Christmas Eve, many Britons attend a Christingle church service (Christingle church services usually take place at Christmas though they can occur at any time between mid-November and February). The name Christingle is also the name given to the candy-covered orange given to children, and sometimes adults, during a Christingle service. During a Christingle service, children in the congregation approach the church altar and are given an orange around which is wrapped a band of red tape and into which are stuck toothpicks adorned with various candies and dried fruits. A lit candle, or sometimes a glow stick, wrapped in aluminum foil is wedged into the hollowed-out center of the orange. The history of the Christingle dates back to 1747 when German pastor John de Watteville started the tradition at his Moravian Church as a way to get children to think about Jesus. The earliest days of the tradition saw children given just a candle decorated with a red ribbon. It was not until 1968 that British churchman John Pensom took up the Christingle service as a way to raise funds for the Children's Society charity. To raise money for the charity, children attended Pensom's Anglican church service, bringing their purses full of pocket money and receiving a decorated orange in return for a charity donation. It is not known exactly why Pensom decided upon an orange studded with candies on toothpicks to decorate the Christingle, but it may have been a reminder of pomanders—oranges studded with cloves—that were traditionally used to scent British homes at Christmas. The Christingle orange is rich in Christian symbolism. The orange represents the world while the lit candle represents the Christian view that Jesus is the light of the world bringing hope to the lives of those in dark despair (the foil wrapped around the candle is there purely to stop hot wax dripping on the children's hands). The red tape encircling the orange is symbolic of Jesus's blood, and the candies and dried fruit stuck into the orange represent both God's creations and the four seasons.

In Britain, the main Christmas meal is eaten on Christmas Day and tends to comprise a roast turkey served with various vegetables—most notoriously Brussels sprouts (a love-or-hate food subject to much discussion)—as well as bread sauce, cranberry sauce, pigs-in-blankets, and some form of stuffing. The custom of eating a roasted bird at Christmas most likely originates from earlier Christian autumn and winter festivals such as Michaelmas (September 29) and Martinmas (November 11) when roast goose was eaten. These festivals are largely unmarked today with their customs subsumed by Christmas. Turkey was brought to Europe by the Spanish conquistadors who had encountered the bird in the Americas. Unlike many American foods, turkey was adopted quickly in Europe (as early as 1518) and introduced to England sometime in the sixteenth century. Indeed, by 1577, turkeys were seen as upper-class food, and turkey farms had sprung up across England with hundreds of thousands of turkeys transported to market during turkey season. By 1573, turkey was the mainstay of the Christmas feast.

It is traditional to finish Christmas dinner by eating Christmas pudding (sometimes called plum pudding or, occasionally referred to as figgy pudding). The essence of Christmas pudding dates back to medieval England. At this time, fat, spices, and fruits were mixed with meat, cereal, and vegetables before being packed into animal stomachs and intestines that allowed the mixture to keep well. The flavors of today's Christmas puddings were also found in medieval pottages for these broths included dried fruit, spices, alcohol, breadcrumbs, and ground almonds as is evident in a recipe for fig pottage noted in the fourteenth-century English recipe collection *The Forme of Cury* that lists figs, raisins, ground almonds, ground ginger, and wine among its ingredients. However, at this time, fruity pottages were served at the start of a meal rather than as dessert. By the end of the sixteenth century, dried fruit was more readily available in Britain meaning people started to include more dried fruit in their pottages. Thus, pottages became more sweet than savory. In the 1600s, pottage also took on a more solid appearance for it was either served like porridge or sliced and cooked under a roasting joint of meat. It tended to be served as an entree or as an accompaniment to a main meal. Around this time, the invention of a floured piece of muslin or cheesecloth material that could mold and preserve a pudding (a pudding cloth) meant that puddings no longer had to be preserved inside animal body parts, though suet remains a key ingredient of Christmas puddings (today vegetarian suet is readily available).

During the 1700s, the so-called plum pudding became associated with Christmas (with "plum" denoting a boiled pudding containing dried fruit rather than a pudding made with plums). Nevertheless, it was the Victorians who made the eating of plum pudding such an intrinsic part of Christmas dinner that it became known as Christmas pudding. The Victorians established the tradition of making the Christmas pudding on the fifth Sunday before Christmas, which in turn became known as Stir Up Sunday. This remains the day on which, traditionally, Britons make their Christmas puddings. On Stir Up Sunday, each member of a household should stir the pudding mixture from east to west in celebration of the journey of the Magi (also called the Three Wise Men or Three Kings) in order to bring those who stir the pudding good luck for the coming year. It was during Victorian times that boiling puddings in a pudding cloth gave way to steaming the pudding in a ceramic basin, and so wealthy households would steam their Christmas puddings in elaborate ceramic molds. Before the pudding was cooked, small charms would be placed in the pudding mixture. The charms would be left inside the pudding as it cooked and so would be found by the pudding's eaters. The charms were thought to foretell the future and often included a silver coin to symbolize coming wealth, a ring to signify future marriage, and a thimble that foretold that the finder was destined never to wed. The Victorians accompanied their Christmas puddings with custard or a hard sauce called brandy butter, both of which are still enjoyed today as the usual accompaniment to Christmas pudding.

Other popular sweet foods enjoyed throughout the Christmas period include Christmas cake and mince pies. The Christmas cake originated in the sixteenth century. At this time, households would find they had mixture left over after preparing their Christmas pudding and so would add to the mixture flour and eggs. The mixture was then baked as a fruitcake and eaten at Easter. The Easter fruitcakes proved so popular that soon people started to make them for Christmas too. Later, Britons started to top their Christmas cakes with marzipan and royal icing (hard, thick frosting), though in the county of Yorkshire, it is traditional to eat Christmas cake alongside cheeses such as Wensleydale and Cheddar. The Dundee cake is a traditional Scottish cake that is a lighter, crumblier alternative to the richly fruited Christmas cake. This cake was invented in the 1790s by shop-owner Janet Keiller who had also invented a new type of Seville orange marmalade. The marmalade proved popular and soon entered mass production as Britain's (possibly the world's) first commercially produced marmalade. In the mid-1800s, the Keiller factory started to produce cakes as a non-seasonal food, and the recipe became established as Keiller's Dundee Cake. Although intended as a non-seasonal treat, over time, the cakes became especially associated with Christmas.

The history of mince pies reaches back to the medieval period though items found as part of excavations at Durrington Walls (the settlement inhabited by the builders of Stonehenge circa 2500 BCE) reveal that such ingredients as pork, hazelnuts, and fruit were likely used to make a precursor of the mince pies that were eaten to mark midwinter. It was in medieval times, however, that large self-standing pastry boxes called coffyns were filled with sweet-savory meat fillings (smaller pies known as chewets were also made). The filling's sweetness was provided by honey or dried fruits such as figs and dates while the filling was spiced with saffron and ginger. *The Forme of Cury* includes a recipe for Tart of Flesh that combined minced pork with dried figs, raisins, wine, pine kernels, lard, cheese, honey, and spices, while the English cookbook *The English Huswife* (1615) contains a similar recipe made with minced mutton. The expensive ingredients needed to make these pies meant they were reserved for important feasts such as Christmas and functioned as a status symbol for only the well-off could afford to eat them. As the coffyns were rectangular in shape, medieval Britons felt they represented the manger in which the baby Jesus was said to have lain. In time, dough effigies of the infant Jesus were placed on top of the coffyns in order to reinforce the religious symbolism. In the seventeenth century, however, Puritans considered the religious symbolism of the coffyns idolatrous, and so by the end of the century, mince pies had become round while people also abandoned the dough effigies of Jesus. It is unknown when meat stopped being included in mince pies. The mincemeat (mince pie filling) recipe included in Eliza Acton's *Modern Cookery for Private Families* (1845) includes ox tongue while *Mrs Beeton's Book of Household Management* (1861) gives two recipes for mincemeat, one with meat and one without. Later editions of the book only include the meat-free version. Today, the only remnant of the medieval recipes in modern mince pies is the inclusion of suet though this is usually vegetarian.

Life Customs Foods

In Britain, certain food traditions are associated with particular life customs including birth and marriage. As in most countries, Britons celebrate birthdays with cake—these can take many forms from sponge cakes to chocolate cakes and fruitcakes. Cakes also in feature British wedding receptions and Christening parties and are usually sponge cakes or fruitcakes. There are no particular foods associated with death or funerals.

Birth and Christening

Groaning cheese and groaning cake (sometimes called kimbly) are edible treats traditionally given to women either experiencing labor or recovering from childbirth. Groaning cheese and cakes originated during the sixteenth century when the word "groaning" was used to refer to the time extending from when a mother-to-be took to her bed to give birth to the moment she became strong enough to walk. During the expectant woman's confinement, she was waited on by attendants who provided her with food on a platter known as a groaning board. Both the pregnant woman and her visitors would eat from this platter, and all the foods placed upon it were prefaced with the word groaning to indicate that they were especially laid on for this time in the woman's life. Several different ways of serving the groaning cake evolved across England. In the central county of Oxfordshire, it is traditional to cut the cheese or cake from the middle outward once the child had been born so that gradually a large hole appears in the center of the food that is large enough to pass the newborn baby through on the day of its christening. Meanwhile, in the north of England, women are given gingerbread, rich fruitcake, or local cheeses, such as Cheshire cheese, to eat while female neighbors are invited to partake of the foods as a way of celebrating the new birth. Elsewhere in England, it is considered good luck to preserve a piece of uneaten groaning cake.

Today, groaning cake has become popular with British women seeking holistic approaches to the birthing experience. As a result of this growing popularity, recipes for groaning cakes appear in pregnancy and childcare books, blogs, and websites. As there is no set recipe for groaning cake, ingredients differ between recipes. There are, however, similarities between recipes, which tend to produce spicy fruitcakes made from the sort of nutritious ingredients that are important for postpartum well-being. Therefore, recipes for groaning cakes often include unrefined flours or spelt flour, warming spices, fresh fruits such as grated apples, dried fruits, nuts, honey or molasses, milk, and eggs. In these less superstitious times, groaning cake often takes the form of individual muffin-like cakes or mini loaf cakes that are intended to strengthen and energize the new mother rather than as part of old traditions.

Wetting the baby's head is for all intents and purposes akin to a British father's version of a baby shower for it is a way of celebrating the fact that his partner has given birth. To wet the head of the baby, the infant's father gathers together with his male friends and relatives to mark the birth by drinking one or more—usually several—alcoholic drinks. This occurs soon after the baby is born and is normally a very impromptu, informal affair. Wetting the baby's head usually takes place in the father's favorite pub. The tradition is seen as an homage to the pouring of water over a baby head that occurs during some forms of baptism.

In Scotland, wetting the baby's head is an inescapable cultural custom that is enacted to ensure that a newborn baby receives good luck. In the Orkney Islands off Scotland's northeast coast, a bottle of whisky is brought out for the occasion and drunk quickly by the new father and his male friends and family. It is also not uncommon for a baby to receive his or her first alcoholic drink from this same bottle of whisky for a drop of whisky fed to a baby on a teaspoon is regarded as a cure for infant ailments. In order to increase the healing power of the whisky and to confer good luck on the baby, it is thought to be preferable to feed the whisky to the baby using a spoon made from silver. However, as most Scottish households do not use luxurious silver cutlery in everyday life, a borrowed silver coin is often used in placed of a silver spoon.

The popularity of wetting the baby's head is such that even British royals enact the custom. When the Princess of Wales gave birth to Princess Charlotte in May 2015, it was widely reported that the baby's uncle, Prince Harry, arranged for a wetting of the baby's head to be held at a local pub.

> ## Coronation Foods
>
> Royal events such as coronations have given rise to various dishes. Coronation chicken, formally called Poulet Reine Elizabeth, was invented by London's Cordon Bleu Cookery School for the official lunch held to mark the coronation of Queen Elizabeth II in 1953. Typically, coronation chicken comprises cold cooked chicken in a creamy curried sauce. At the time of the coronation, the ingredients were luxurious for wartime rationing was still in place. In 2023, the coronation quiche was chosen by King Charles III and Queen Camilla as the dish of their coronation celebrations. The quiche featured a filling of spinach, broad beans, and tarragon.

Marriage

British wedding cakes tend to take the form of three tiers of fruitcake covered in marzipan and frosting (sponge cakes are popular too). The tiers of cake are of decreasing size with the largest tier at the base and the smallest at the top. This multi-tiered style of wedding cake was invented by the nineteenth-century English baking industry with the cake's shape likely deriving from that of the steeple of St. Bride's Church in the City of London that features tiers of decreasing upward size. The cutting of a newly married couple's wedding cake is the highlight of many British wedding receptions. Newlyweds normally cut into their wedding cake in a ceremonial fashion and are often photographed doing so. Traditionally at a British wedding reception, the newlyweds both grip the handle of the knife with which the cake is cut as they make the first incision into the cake. British wedding cakes tend to be fruitcakes as fruitcakes have a very long shelf life. Indeed, it is customary for newlyweds to keep the top tier of their wedding cake to eat at the party following the christening of their first child.

In the early history of the English wedding cake, there existed several different types of cake, each intended for different classes of wedding. For instance, so-called two-guinea bride-cakes were made for the poorer classes while expensive, lavishly decorated cakes were baked for those that could afford them. It was only during the latter part of the nineteenth century that the term wedding cake was used to describe such cakes, replacing the earlier term bride-cake. Cakes and breads baked specially to celebrate a marriage have, however, existed for a long time. In Elizabethan times, it was customary for many small spiced buns to be made to celebrate nuptials, and in a poem by Thomas Campion

(1575–1620), there is a reference to a bridal cake, which at that time may well have referred to a type of matrimonial spiced bun. The concept of the frosted wedding cake began to develop around 1660 when French chefs were brought to England by British king Charles II. The French chefs took the existing English tradition of making individual small buns to serve at a wedding and decided to envelop each bun in a hard sugar crust. Each sugarcoated bun was then decorated with toys and figurines before being broken into pieces and scattered over the bride's head.

Normally couples arrange for their wedding cake to be baked by a professional baker, but again, anecdotal evidence suggests it is now increasingly common for a friend of the couple that is a keen amateur baker to bake the couple a wedding cake in lieu of buying them a gift. This new tradition is partly informed by reality television as the smash hit BBC television amateur baking competition *The Great British Bake Off* has led to an increasing number of confident amateur bakers. Some British couples also bake their own wedding cake, partly to save money but also because doing so gives them a chance to show off their baking prowess. Meanwhile, a recent innovation in British wedding cakes is the popularity of cheese wedding cakes that see a selection of cheeses stacked one on top of the other to create the effect of a traditional multi-tiered fruit wedding cake.

An old British wedding cake tradition tells that unmarried guests, particularly female guests, should place a morsel of wedding cake under their pillow before going to sleep as this will increase their chance of finding a spouse. Moreover, bridesmaids that do likewise are said to dream of their future husbands.

Further Reading

Bilton, Sam. "A history of the Christmas pudding: The origins of a Christmas favourite." *English Heritage*. https://www.english-heritage.org.uk/visit/inspire-me/history-of-the-christmas-pudding/ (accessed August 17, 2023).

Coulson, Jim. "Nutty northern Easter traditions." *Northern Life* (March 23, 2021). https://northernlifemagazine.co.uk/nutty-northern-easter-traditions/ (accessed January 2, 2023).

CountryFile. "British harvest: How long does the season last, when is harvest day, plus history and traditions." *CountryFile: Food and Recipes* (October 5, 2020). https://www.countryfile.com/how-to/food-recipes/british-harvest-how-long-does-the-season-last-when-is-harvest-day-plus-history-and-traditions/ (accessed August 17, 2023).

Davidson, Alan. *The Oxford Companion to Food*, 2nd edition. Tom Jaine (ed.). Oxford: Oxford University Press, 2006.

Easter Brand Fact Sheet. CadburyWorld.co.uk. https://www.cadburyworld.co.uk/scholandgroups/~/media/CadburyWorld/en/Files/Pdf/factsheet-easterbrands (accessed November 14, 2022).

English Heritage. "Why do we have Easter eggs?" *English Heritage: History at Home: Blog* (April 6, 2020). https://www.english-heritage.org.uk/visit/inspire-me/blog/articles/why-do-we-have-easter-eggs/ (accessed November 14, 2022).

Gant, Andrew. *Christmas Carols: From Village Green to Church Choir*. London: Profile Books, 2014.

Goldstein, Darra, ed. *The Oxford Companion to Sugar and Sweets*. Oxford: Oxford University Press, 2015.

Hall, Daniel. "The curious tradition of blessing the River Tweed's salmon and the story behind it." *Chronicle Live* (February 6, 2022). https://www.chroniclelive.co.uk/news/north-east-news/river-tweed-norham-berwick-salmon-22973681 (accessed August 17, 2023).

Shanahan, Madeline. *Christmas Food and Feasting: A History*. Lanham, MD: Rowman & Littlefield, 2019.

Williams, Victoria. *Celebrating Life Customs around the World: From Baby Showers to Funerals*, volumes 1–3. Santa Barbara, CA: ABC-CLIO, 2017.

8

Street Food and Snacks

Street food as understood in other countries is a fairly new concept to Britain, where the term is generally taken to mean artisan foods sold on the street from kiosks or stalls. While Britain has a long history of enjoying takeaways ranging from pizzas to kebabs and burgers, curries to Chinese cuisine, these tend to be eaten at home rather than on the street.

Al fresco eating such as pavement restaurant dining and picnics are popular in Britain, however. Al fresco dining enjoyed newfound popularity in Britain during the Covid-19 pandemic when restaurants, cafés, and pubs were allowed to place extra tables temporarily on streets to enable social distancing among customers and staff. Under the government's Levelling Up and Regeneration Bill (due to be passed in 2023), these temporary protocols will be enshrined in law to become permanent. In Britain, picnics are informal affairs that tend to include either homemade foods or foods bought especially for the occasion rather than foods purchased from street vendors to eat outdoors. Snacks are an important part of picnicking, and most Britons snack regularly on both sweet and savory foods.

Street Food

The history of food being sold on British streets dates back to the eleventh century, however, for vendors selling pies, flans, and pasties filled with such meats as veal, goose, and goat were popular in cities including London, Norwich, Leicester, and York. By the nineteenth century, oysters, which were plentiful and cheap, were sold on almost every London street. Oysters were particularly popular with the poor who used them as a substitute for beef in stews and soups, for unlike oysters, beef was expensive. That oysters were a favorite food of the working class was noted by Charles Dickens in his novel *The Pickwick Papers*

(1837) for in it, Dickens says "poverty and oysters always seem to go together." In eighteenth- and nineteenth-century Britain, oysters were usually sold by women who worked on the streets, and thus, the term oyster-girl came to refer to both oyster sellers and prostitutes. Indeed, in the eighteenth century, numerous bawdy songs referencing oyster-girls entered British popular culture, as exemplified by *The Eating of Oysters* (1794), which includes the lines

> As I was walking down a London Street,
> A pretty oyster girl, I chanced to meet.
> I lifted up her basket and boldly I did peek,
> Just to see if she's got any oysters.
> "Oysters, Oysters, Oysters," said she
> "These are the finest oysters that you will ever see.
> I'll sell them three-a-penny but I give 'em to you free."

The association between oysters and sex continued in Victorian London where one of the city's most notorious erotic magazines was called *The Oyster*.

By the mid-nineteenth century, oysters were sold on a huge scale—in 1864, over 700 million oysters were consumed in London, and British oyster fisheries employed around 120,000 Britons. Other street foods popular in Victorian Britain included whelks, sheep's trotters, and pea soup. By the turn of the twentieth century, however, the British middle classes had come to view eating in public as something suitable only for the poor. The exception to this rule was picnicking, a form of *al fresco* dining which in Britain originated when medieval huntsmen would stop for lunch. Picnics really took off in popularity among Britons, however, when French aristocrats fled to Britain during the eighteenth century to escape the French Revolution and in so doing imported the French fondness for *le pique-nique*.

The advent of the farmers' market movement helped make street food popular again in Britain. Britain's first farmers' market was founded in Bath, southwest England in 1997. Within a year, farmers' markets were established in towns throughout England. Farmers' markets helped make the move toward eating local food for all the food at farmers' markets must come from within 30 miles of a market; thus, the markets are also seen as an environmentally friendly alternative to supermarket shopping. By offering seasonal, local produce, farmers' markets also provide shoppers with a link to the land.

Moreover, farmers' markets made it socially acceptable for the middle classes to eat in the street as the artisan foods sold at farmers' markets had a veneer of acceptability. Farmers' markets are intrinsic to Britain's recent street food development for at the start of the twenty-first century, stalls selling artisan foods began to sell foods such as soups and sandwiches made with artisan ingredients. Although the artisan nature of the ingredients meant dishes were more expensive to buy than the soups and sandwiches available from shops and cafés, they were made from better quality, traceable ingredients, were bought straight from the producer, and made the buyers feel good about purchasing from small businesses. Many of Britain's first street food traders in the modern sense of the term were inspired by American food trucks serving American street food. The British street food pioneers reinvented classic American street food dishes by stripping dishes down to their core ingredients and then reimagining them using improved cooking methods and ingredients, for example, luxury, artisan hot dogs and burgers.

Once street food became popular via farmers markets, music festivals also started to serve street food, and a new, younger generation of Britons latched on to the street food trend. Now, there are even British Street Food Awards (inaugurated in 2010) to recognize outstanding street food vendors, who tend to specialize in just one type of specialty dish. Street food in Britain is growing in popularity quickly, partly through word-of-mouth publicity and social media. Increasingly, Britons appreciate street food's refreshing sense of spontaneity for street food dishes tend to be made to order with few barriers between vendors and customers, who can provide sellers with instant feedback about the food they are served.

The British street food scene is changing rapidly as multicultural Britons establish street food businesses selling foods from their or their parents' homelands. At the same time, new street food markets continue to spring up, pop-up street food events occur in locations such as disused warehouses, as well as at food festivals and on local high streets.

Snacks

Both savory and sweet snacks are popular in Britain. Crisps (chips) are Britain's most popular snack, with 66 percent of Britons saying they eat crisps regularly. Biscuits are a close second to crisps with 63 percent of Britons enjoying them regularly. Chocolate bars are the third most popular snack in Britain. Healthier snacks such as dried fruits (eaten regularly by 23 percent of people polled) and vegetable crisps (21 percent) are also popular. Ice cream, milk products, nuts, and sweets also make the Top 10 British snacks. Moreover, 57 percent of

Britain's snackers eat snacks several times per week, while 17 percent eat snacks daily. Most British snacking occurs after 8 p.m. Below are some quintessentially British snacks, both savory and sweet.

Savory Snacks

Scotch Egg

A Scotch egg is a traditional British snack comprising a shelled hard-boiled egg wrapped in sausage meat that is covered in breadcrumbs before being deep-fried or baked until crispy. Scotch eggs are typically eaten cold and are a popular pub and picnic snack.

The origins of the Scotch egg are uncertain. The London department store Fortnum & Mason, which is known for selling luxury foods, claims to have invented the Scotch egg in 1738 as an easily portable snack for wealthy travelers to take with them on carriage journeys. However, an alternative theory suggests that the Scotch egg evolved from the Indian snack *nargisi kofta*, which consists of an egg covered in minced meat and was brought back to Britain by soldiers and employees of the East India Company returning from India to England. A conflicting belief states that Scotch eggs originated in nineteenth-century Whitby, in the northern English county of Yorkshire, where they were invented by William J. Scott & Sons. Since Whitby is on the coast, the Scott & Sons' eggs used fish paste instead of sausage meat. Another theory as to the origin of Scotch eggs is that they were invented by Scottish farmers, and hence the snack's name. According to Fortnum & Mason, however, the eggs became known as Scotch eggs because they contained anchovies added to the sausage meat to create a stronger flavor (similarly the British snack Scotch woodcock comprises hot toast spread with anchovy paste and topped with scrambled eggs).

During the Second World War, a meat shortage meant that the quality and taste of Scotch eggs deteriorated leading to them falling out of fashion among the British public. By the 1960s, Scotch eggs had become primarily a mass-produced snack made using poor-quality meat. Consequently, Scotch eggs became a very unfashionable food that was shunned by many Britons. Nevertheless, Scotch eggs remained popular with die-hard fans and home cooks who liked that the snack was easy and economical to make. The recipe for Scotch eggs is also highly adaptable, meaning today, the snack is popular again, reinvented by British gastropubs (pubs specializing in serving high-quality food), which make Scotch eggs from more luxurious ingredients such as venison meat and duck, goose, and quails' eggs. Vegetarian Scotch eggs are also available, while confectionery Scotch eggs can be bought at Easter.

Scotch eggs hit the headlines in Britain during the Covid-19 pandemic as there was much discussion as to whether they constituted a snack or a substantial meal. The debate came about because under legislation published in October 2020, British pubs in Tier 2 areas (locations with higher rates of Covid transmission that operated under stricter Covid restrictions) were told that they could only serve alcohol with a "table meal" that "might be expected to be served as the main midday or main evening meal, or as a main course at either such meal." In short, pubs in Tier 2 areas could only open if they functioned as a restaurant, and moreover the pubs could only serve alcohol as part of a "substantial meal." During a radio interview, Environment Secretary George Eustice said Scotch eggs constituted a substantial meal if they were served via table service. However, a spokesperson for the British prime minister Boris Johnson stated that bar snacks did not constitute a substantial meal. Meanwhile, the MP Michael Gove asserted originally that a Scotch egg constituted only an entrée before later asserting that a Scotch egg did indeed count as a meal.

Pork Pie

A pork pie is a traditional English meat pie comprising a filling of roughly chopped pork and pork fat, surrounded by jellied pork stock packed into a hot water pastry. Typically, pork pies are served at room temperature and tend to be eaten as a snack, picnic dish, pub lunch, or with salad. Britons spend £165 million per year on pork pies.

Variations on the pork pie include the gala pie, which is loaf-shaped and includes hard-boiled eggs along its length as well as the usual pork filling. Smaller, pork pies sometimes called picnic pies can include additional ingredients such as apples, pickles, and bacon combined with the pork. While pork pies usually have a solid pastry lid, it is possible to buy find pork pies that either have a lattice work pastry topping or a layer of cranberries instead of pastry. A northern English version of the pork pie called a growler is so-called because that is said to be the noise made by the stomach after consuming one of the pies. Growlers are smaller than most pork pies and have a distinctive crimped lid. They are also made from cured pork that is pink in color, and thus, the filling tastes more like ham than pork.

The first English dictionary entry for the word "pie" appeared in the fourteenth century. The pies of this era were descended from the twelfth-century English rectangular pastries called coffyns. These pie-like pastries were self-standing dough boxes that were created primarily to preserve the filling within the pastry—often the pastry case itself was not eaten. Typically, coffyns were filled with eel-like lampreys seasoned with mint and parsley, cinnamon, ginger, saffron, and ground almonds. Additionally, the medieval English recipe collection *The Forme of Cury* (1390) contains a recipe for mylates of pork, which was a pork pie–like dish of minced pork mixed with cheese, eggs, spices, and saffron, cooked in a pastry shell. The pork pie of today not only has its origins in the early coffyns, but also contains elements of mylates of pork. The earliest recorded pork pie from Melton Mowbray (a town in the English county of Leicestershire that is synonymous with pork pies) dates from the fourteenth century. Traditionally, English pork pies were made in September for pigs were slaughtered in autumn so that their meat could be stored over winter. Originally, Melton Mowbray pork pies were a favorite of huntsmen engaged in foxhunts who ate the pies for breakfast. However, soon news of the pies reached London where they became a hit in gentlemen's clubs (private social clubs frequented by upper class men). In 1831, the baker Edward Adcock became the first to produce Melton Mowbray pork pies commercially and was soon supplying London with the pies, which were transported by stagecoach.

Today, pork fat is still an intrinsic ingredient of quality pork pies for they are made with hot water pastry that is made with lard (white fat made from rendered pig fat). Often the pastry is raised by hand over a wooden implement called a dolly that creates the perfect pork pie shape. In 2008, the European Union awarded Melton Mowbray Protected Designation of Origin status in recognition of its pork pies. Under this status, Melton Mowbray pork pies must display a characteristic bow-shaped, golden pastry case while the filling must be the color of roast pork. Additionally, the pies must be free from artificial colors, flavorings, and preservatives. Only pork pies made within a designated area around Melton Mowbray, approximately 10 miles in radius, are permitted to be called Melton Mowbray pork pies and as such are allowed to display the words "Melton Mowbray" on their packaging.

Crisps

Typically, crisps (chips) are thin, round slices of fried potato sold in packets, though in Britain, crisps made from other root vegetables such as carrot, parsnip, and beetroot are also available. Ostensibly, healthier options such as baked crisps or those made from lentils, peas, and chickpeas can also be found.

The history of crisps is unknown though some food historians believe the first crisp recipe dates from 1817 when the English doctor William Kitchiner published his pioneering cookbook, *The Cook's Oracle*. The book included a recipe for "potatoes fried in slices or shavings." The first mass-produced crisps appeared in Britain at the start of the twentieth century while the first flavored crisp was marketed in the late 1950s by Joe "Spud" Murphy, who was the owner of the Irish company Tayto. The company developed a technique to add cheese and onion flavoring to their crisps during production. Then, in 1967, salt and vinegar–flavored crisps were launched throughout Britain. According to a 2019 report by the supermarket chain Waitrose & Partners, cheese and onion is the UK's favorite crisp flavor, though the Welsh and people living in southeast England buck the national trend by preferring salt and vinegar. Sour cream and onion crisps are more popular in East Anglia than anywhere in the UK. Across the UK, salt and vinegar and ready salted crisps are the second and third preferred flavors, respectively. On average, Britons consume 178 packets of crisps each per year, though the Welsh eat the most averaging almost four packets of crisps per week.

Despite cheese and onion being Britain's favorite flavor, crisps in Britain come in an ever-expanding range of flavors including masala chicken, katsu curry, and sriracha (a spicy Thai sauce), as well as seasonal novelty flavors that appear at Christmas such as Brussels sprouts flavor. Such sweet-flavored crisps as Christmas pudding, strawberry, sugar cookie, and pecan pie have also appeared on the market as have flavors that taste of alcohol such as pink peppercorn gin, and truffled cheese and sparkling wine. According to the Sainsbury's supermarket chain, British crisp flavors are particularly varied as this reflects Britain's multicultural population with Middle Eastern and Indian influences becoming especially prevalent. Street food dishes are also starting to influence crisp flavors, with flavors such as falafel and hummus and onion bhaji also available.

Sweet Snacks

Biscuits

The earliest British biscuits (cookies) were baked on stones during the Neolithic era. Roman Britain was home to rusk-type savory biscuits that consisted of thin slices of twice-baked bread. These biscuits kept for longer than bread and were included in the rations of Roman soldiers. By the fourteenth century, the word "biscuit" had appeared in English from the French *bis cuit* (twice cooked), which itself derived from the Latin words *panis biscotus* (bread twice-cooked).

Wafer-type biscuits were particularly popular in medieval times being made from sweetened batter cooked over a fire. Typically, these wafers were eaten after a meal as a digestive.

Despite the newfound popularity of wafers, Britons continued to eat other types of biscuits. Indeed, as British shipping expanded and Britons started to sail around the world, biscuits became an essential element of naval provisions for the biscuits kept well onboard ship. Although ships carried some fresh food, biscuits (known as ship's biscuits or hard tack) were one of sailors' staple rations. Ship's biscuits were made from stoneground flour, water, and salt, which were combined to form a stiff dough, then baked in a hot oven for 30 minutes. The biscuits were then left to harden and become dry. Sometimes, powdered bone was added to the biscuit mixture. As ship's biscuits were extremely hard to the teeth, sailors would sometimes leave the biscuits to become soft. However, by leaving the biscuits to go soft, they not only would taste musty, but they also became home to maggots and weevils. When King Richard I sailed from England in 1190, his ships carried onboard "biskit of muslin" (made of barley, rye, and bean flour), while British sailors facing the Spanish Armada of 1588 had a daily allowance of 1 lb of biscuits. After the Anglo-Dutch War (1672–4), the famous British diarist Samuel Pepys standardized Navy food provisions to improve the diets of British sailors. Consequently, every British sailor was given a daily ration of 1 gallon of beer, fish or salt beef, cheese, butter, and 1 lb of sweet, wheaten biscuits. Biscuits were central to sailors' diets in the eighteenth century and remained so until canned foods such as preserved beef in tins were issued from 1847. From the mid-1850s, bread became a standard Navy provision. The bread was referred to by sailors as "soft bread" so as to distinguish it from biscuits, which were also called "bread" occasionally. The earliest surviving example of a ship's biscuit dates from 1784. The biscuits were renowned for being unpleasant to eat and were near indestructible hence sailors were known to write on them like postcards.

As sugar became more affordable in Britain, the types of biscuits enjoyed by Britons began to change. In the seventeenth century, Britain experienced a biscuit boom as people had easier access to ingredients such as sugar while at the same time cooking technology changed, and Italian and French cuisine started to influence British food. The traditional guild system (associations of craftspeople) was breaking down, and, despite their best efforts, bakers' guilds could not prevent Britons from baking their own biscuits at home. As home-baking became popular, so new types of biscuits emerged in Britain including thin crunchy, knot-shaped cracknels, nutty macaroons, and gingerbreads.

> ## The Grasmere Rushbearing and Gingerbread
>
> Rushbearing is an English ecclesiastical tradition that sees parishioners collect rushes that they then scatter on the floor of their parish church. Every summer since 1680, Grasmere in the far northwest of England holds England's most famous rushbearing festival. During the festival, parishioners carry rushes entwined into symbolic shapes through the village to the church where they strew the rushes across the church floor. Afterward, a church service is held, and local children are given spicy-sweet Grasmere gingerbread to eat. The gingerbread was invented in 1854 by cook Sarah Nelson and is stamped with the name of St. Oswald, the patron of the Grasmere parish church.

Until the eighteenth century, biscuits in Britain were eaten more often as part of the dessert course than as a snack. However, as tea drinking became intrinsic to British culture, so biscuits became an integral part of the enjoyment of tea. The eighteenth century also saw two new types of biscuits emerge that would become staples of the British biscuit tin: savoys and ratafias. Savoys are long, thin, crisp biscuits sometimes called ladyfingers, while ratifias are almond-flavored and crunchy. Both biscuits are also often used as the bottom layer in the classic British dessert, trifle. By the Victorian era, biscuits were ubiquitous in Britain.

> ## London's "Biscuit Town"
>
> The Bermondsey area of southeast London is nicknamed Biscuit Town due to the historic location of the Peek Freans biscuit factory, which was founded on Mill Street in 1857 by James Peek. George Hender Frean and John Carr joined the company subsequently. In 1865, Peek Freans revolutionized British biscuits by introducing the Pearl biscuit, which was followed by the Marie, and the Pat-A-Cake (by the twentieth century, 400 million Pat-A-Cake biscuits were baked annually). When the Mill Street factory burned down, Peek Freans relocated to nearby Drummond Road where the factory remained until 1989. In 1929, the Peek Freans factory created the first Twiglets. The site of the Drummond Road factory is home to the Peek Freans Museum.

The middle and upper classes, who often ate meals featuring many courses, had biscuits for dessert alongside ice cream, fruit, and nuts. Popular nineteenth-century dessert biscuits included macaroons and mini-meringues, wine biscuits (eaten to accompany wine), and petit fours. Early petit fours were small, delicate, intricately shapes biscuits cooked in a low oven once foods cooked at a higher temperature had been removed from the oven. The petit fours were often colorful and highly decorated. Popular biscuits for snacking in Victorian Britain included plain sponge-type biscuits such as langues de chat that went well with a cup of tea.

Toward the end of the nineteenth century, industrial innovations and the advent of electricity meant biscuits could be mass-produced. Among Britain's new favorite biscuits were gems, which were launched in the 1850s (later these would acquire a layer of icing and be known as iced gems), and in 1860, round crackers called Osborne biscuits (named after Queen Victoria's favorite house Osborne House) were introduced. In 1861, garibaldis were introduced to Britain. These took the form of a layer of currants baked between two thin oblongs of biscuit. The first chocolate digestive biscuit was introduced in 1899. Digestive biscuits are extremely popular biscuits in Britain. These semi-sweet biscuits originated in 1839 when two Scottish doctors invented them to aid digestion. First manufactured by the food brand McVitie's in 1892, digestive biscuits are one of Britons' favorite biscuits for "dunking" (the British term for dipping a biscuit in a cup of tea). Digestive biscuits are also a popular accompaniment to cheese while crushed digestives are often used as the basis for cheesecakes or added to tiffin. Savory biscuits have long been important in Britain too, with the Jacobs's cream cracker launched in 1885.

In 1874, the government removed import duty on sugar meaning sugar became affordable to most Britons. This in turn meant even more people started to make biscuits at home, and sugar became a major part of the British diet. Similarly, after the First World War, as sugar from beet became prevalent, so increasing amounts of biscuits were baked in British homes. During the Second World War, biscuits' place as a comfort food was cemented in British culture as they offered quite literally crumbs of comfort in dark times. Today, Britons continue to love not just eating, but also baking, biscuits thanks to television programs such as the hugely popular *Great British Bake Off*. This is despite the efforts of health organizations to highlight the danger to health from eating too much sugar, fat, and carbohydrate. Although Britain is home to numerous biscuit types, the favorite biscuit of the UK is Lotus Biscoff, a caramelized rectangular biscuit from Belgium. The UK's second favorite biscuit is shortbread, the traditional buttery

Scottish biscuit. The third most popular is the bourbon biscuit, which consists of two thin rectangular pieces of dark chocolate–flavored biscuit sandwiched around a chocolate buttercream filling.

Chocolate Bars

In 1847, the British confectionary dynasty Fry & Sons (commonly called Fry's) invented a way to mix cocoa powder with sugar and cocoa butter to produce a smooth, moldable paste. This is considered to be the first solid chocolate bar intended for eating rather than as the basis of a drink. Then, in 1866, Fry's launched Fry's Chocolate Cream, the first mass-produced chocolate bar. By the end of the nineteenth-century, Fry's had become the world's biggest chocolate manufacturing company. In 1853, another British chocolate manufacturing company, Cadbury's, received a royal warrant to provide chocolate bars to Queen Victoria. However, Cadbury's were soon forced to admit that they adulterated their chocolate with starch, and in a bid to restore their reputation, the company started to market their chocolate as "Absolutely Pure, Therefore Best." Cadbury's also proposed that all chocolate manufacturers have to state the precise percentages of the ingredients in their chocolate bar on the bars' wrappers in order to show the purity of their ingredients. Cadbury's campaign to redeem their reputation worked, and by the end of the nineteenth century, Cadbury's had surpassed Fry's in terms of sales. Today, Cadbury Dairy Milk is the UK's top selling chocolate bar. Cadbury Twirl is the UK's sixth most popular chocolate bar while Cadbury Wispa is the eighth most popular.

Despite the enduring popularity of chocolate bars, since Britain has come out of Covid-19 lockdown, chocolate bars have suffered from falling demand. During the 12 weeks up to June 12, 2022, the British chocolate market was valued at £476 million. This figure has been falling steadily, from £508 million for the 12 weeks to June 13, 2021, and from £527 million in the 12 weeks to June 14, 2020. In particular, while sales of large chocolate blocks and sharing bags were boosted when people were confined together in lockdown, sales of these forms of chocolate are now falling.

Sales of smaller, individual chocolate bars have seen an increase in growth post-lockdown though their sales have not recovered to pre-pandemic levels (sales of single chocolate bars fell during lockdown as they are often bought to eat on the go). Conversely, sales of multipacks and sharing bars grew so much during lockdown that Britons' overall spending on chocolate during lockdown rose by £50 million year-on-year. While that £50 million increase represents only a 3 percent increase on the total value of British chocolate sales, the amount of chocolate eaten by locked-down Britons is probably two or three times higher than usual as the chocolate sold by supermarkets is so much cheaper than artisan chocolates that might have been available from so-called non-essential shops, which were shut periodically during lockdown. According to the supermarket chain Waitrose, during lockdown, sales of sharing bars such as Cadbury Dairy Milk increased by 37 percent as shoppers comfort-ate cheaper chocolate. That said, demand for Waitrose's premium own-label bars also rose by a fifth as Britons sought solace in small indulgences. As chocolate sales rose during lockdown, so half of Britons reported they found it more difficult to manage their weight since lockdown as the Covid-19 pandemic changed people's priorities, meaning Britons were more focused on enjoying treats during a stressful time than they were on weight-watching. At the time of writing, the cost-of-living crisis is causing some Britons to cut back on their spending on treat foods. Meanwhile, the rising costs of ingredients due to factors such as adverse weather and diseases that are impacting cocoa bean production in West Africa mean chocolate producers are reducing the size of their bars. By reducing the size of chocolate bars, chocolate-makers are able to make supplies last.

Britons' demand for chocolate is recovering, however, partly because people are now able to meet-up and are again buying single "grab-and-go" chocolate bars. Moreover, despite the cost-of-living crisis, some British consumers have, conversely, started to buy more expensive chocolate bars as they seek special, one-off treats.

Further Reading

Armstrong, Martin. "The UK's favourite snacks." Statista: Global Snack Food Market (January 26, 2022). https://www.statista.com/chart/26699/favourite-snacks-uk/ (accessed November 16, 2022).

Bland, Archie. "Scotch egg is definitely a substantial meal, says Michael Gove." *The Guardian: Coronavirus* (December 1, 2020). https://www.theguardian.com/world/2020/dec/01/scotch-egg-is-definitely-a-substantial-meal-says-michael-gove (accessed November 20, 2022).

Butler, Sarah. "Chocolate sales soar as UK shoppers comfort eat at home amid Covid." *The Guardian: Retail Industry* (October 31, 2020). https://www.theguardian.com/business/2020/oct/31/chocolate-sales-soar-uk-shoppers-comfort-eat-at-home-covid (accessed November 20, 2022).

Fone, Martin. "Curious questions: Why is the pork pie associated with Melton Mowbray?" CountryLife.co.uk: Food and Drink (September 22, 2022). https://www.countrylife.co.uk/food-drink/curious-questions-why-is-the-pork-pie-associated-with-melton-mowbray-247309 (accessed November 17, 2022).

The Grocer. "The UK's 10 most popular chocolate bars and brands 2022" (September 20, 2022). https://www.thegrocer.co.uk/confectionery/the-uks-10-most-popular-chocolate-bars-and-brands-2022/671419.article (accessed November 20, 2022).

Havelock, Laurie. "Chocolate sales are melting away from pandemic highs, as cost of living and rising cocoa prices bite." *INews: Money: Business* (July 16, 2022). https://inews.co.uk/news/business/chocolate-sales-melting-cost-of-living-cocoa-prices-1744999 (accessed November 20, 2022).

Lister, Kate. *A Curious History of Sex*. London: Unbound, 2021.

Mackenzie, Lois. "The UK's favourite biscuits have been revealed—do you agree?" Yahoo Finance (May 28, 2022). https://uk.finance.yahoo.com/news/uk-favourite-biscuits-revealed-agree230100919.html?guccounter=1&guce_referrer=aHR0cHM6Ly93d3cuZ29vZ2xlLmNvLnVrLw&guce_referrer_sig=AQAAAKMqeRIwTcv1GeJ-o3f5SVcK7ZsLuRP8WF6c39ttq3Ds7wWo2EnCy0oWlwlGUWmEz09ZxUsE19MeOpnrS2xelnoixxuE6D2DMPZrGFSaj9E7EgWO67gyBQvC42oSOIwudqOQ8b_fmzMNALy9sDgHzr6bNo615whg17CBZelqlSV9 (accessed November 20, 2022).

Melton Mowbray Pork Pie Product Specification: SPECIFICATION COUNCIL REGULATION (EC) No 510/2006 'MELTON MOWBRAY PORK PIE' EC No: UK/PGI/005/0335/ PDO () PGI (X) (January 4, 2021) https://assets.publishing.service.gov.uk/media/5fd36515e90e076637bb5a40/pfn-melton-mowbray-pgi.pdf (accessed November 17, 2022).

Nationwide Caterers Association. "What is street food?" Streetfood (2016). https://www.streetfood.org.uk/foodies.html (accessed November 1, 2022).

Porter, David. *A Life of Pie* (September 14, 2011). https://deptfordpudding.com/2011/09/14/a-life-of-pie/ (accessed November 17, 2022).

Sim, Keren. "This is the UK's favourite flavour of crisps" *Good Housekeeping* (November 7, 2019). https://www.goodhousekeeping.com/uk/food/a29723082/this-is-the-uk-favourite-flavour-of-crisps/ (accessed November 17, 2022).

Simply Oysters. "Oyster history" (2013–2022). https://simplyoysters.com/oyster-history (accessed November 16, 2022).

Tait, Amelia. "So long, salt and vinegar: How crisp flavours went from simple to sensational." *The Guardian* (January 14, 2020). https://www.theguardian.com/food/2020/jan/14/so-long-salt-and-vinegar-how-crisp-flavours-went-from-simple-to-sensational (accessed November 20, 2022).

Tensley, Brandon. "How the potato chip took over America." *Smithsonian Magazine: Arts & Culture* (January 2022). https://www.smithsonianmag.com/arts-culture/curious-history-potato-chip-180979232/ (accessed November 17, 2022).

9

Dining Out

Britain has long been a melting pot of myriad cultures. For this reason, in modern Britain, it is possible to find dining options from virtually every corner of the world—while French, Italian, Indian, and Chinese restaurants are ubiquitous, in big cities, it is possible to find an even greater range of cuisines. For example, in London, it is possible to visit everything from Afghan ice-cream parlors and Argentinian steakhouses to Korean noodle bars and Yemeni restaurants. Modern European restaurants, which take their inspiration from multiple European cuisines and modern British eateries, which emphasize high-quality, locally sourced ingredients to create traditional British dishes with a modern twist, are also popular. Britain is also home to increasing numbers of vegetarian and vegan eateries that range from tiny takeaways to fine dining experiences. Vegetarian and vegan dishes are also widely available at establishments that are not exclusively vegetarian or vegan. Gluten-free food and drink options are also available at many food outlets. In Britain, establishments that sell or provide food directly to customers must display allergen information in writing either as information on a menu, chalkboard, or in a special information pack. To this end, it is very common in Britain for diners to be asked if they have any allergies prior to ordering their food. Relatedly, in 2010, the Food Hygiene Rating Scheme (FHRS) was launched in partnership between the British government's Food Standards Agency and local councils. The scheme provides British consumers with information about hygiene standards found in businesses at the time the premises were inspected by local authorities—the FHRS scheme covers all businesses supplying or serving food directly to consumers, including restaurants, pubs, cafés, hotels, and take-outs, as well as shops that sell food. The FHRS ratings go from 0, which is applied when urgent improvement is required to a food outlet's food hygiene standards to 5, where the hygiene standards are very good.

In Wales, businesses selling food directly to customers are required by law to display their FHRS ratings in a prominent place on their premises, while in England, businesses are not legally required to display their FHRS rating but are encouraged to do so. In Scotland, all food outlets must undergo a food hygiene inspection undertaken by their local authority. After this inspection, the food outlet is awarded a Food Hygiene Information Scheme (FHIS) rating based on the findings of the inspectors. The FHIS ratings go from Pass, meaning a food outlet meets the legal requirements for food hygiene, to Improvement Required, which means a business must make improvements to meet the legal requirements for food hygiene, and Exempt Premises. This last rating is applied to businesses that meet the Pass criteria for food hygiene, but do not meet the criteria to be part of the FHIS scheme. These businesses are deemed low risk to consumer health with regard to food safety as they are not primarily food outlets, for instance, attractions that sell tins of biscuits to visitors.

Eating establishments in Britain range from the humblest roadside shack serving burgers and soft drinks to multi-award-winning fine dining establishments such as Le Manoir aux Quat'Saisons in Oxfordshire and The Waterside Inn in Berkshire. In 2010, The Waterside Inn became the only restaurant located outside of France to hold the maximum three Michelin stars for 25 years—Michelin stars are awarded to restaurants that the *Michelin Guide* of restaurant reviews considers offers outstanding cooking—therefore, three Michelin stars is often regarded as the highest accolade any restaurant can receive.

Pubs and gastropubs are among Britain's most popular types of restaurant. While both types of establishment offer informal dining, pubs tend to sell traditional British "pub grub," that is, dishes such as sausages and mash, fish and chips, and Sunday roasts, while gastropubs are pubs that specialize in serving particularly high-quality food. While Britain is home to myriad independent restaurants, some of Britain's most visited restaurant chains include such brands as Pizza Express, Pizza Hut, and the peri peri chicken chain Nando's. McDonald's and Subway are extremely popular with Britons as is the British bakery chain Greggs, which is renowned for selling millions of sausage rolls every week.

In Britain, it is possible to dine out not just at pubs, cafés, and restaurants for art galleries such as Tate Britain and the National Portrait Gallery in London have restaurants as do London skyscrapers such as The Shard and 20 Fenchurch Street (nicknamed the Walkie-Talkie), while sports venues such as Lord's cricket ground in London offer food evenings hosted by famed restauranteurs. Fine dining experiences are also available in unusual locations including on boats traveling along the River Thames, steam trains that travel through the British countryside, and in a giant treehouse in Northumberland, northern England. Dining at such venues are a popular treat chosen by Britons to mark special occasions such as birthdays and wedding anniversaries.

At informal eateries such as pubs and cafés, it is common for Britons to order just one dish though pubs will offer diners a choice of starters, main courses, and desserts so it is possible to have a three-course meal in a pub. Many pubs also offer sharing plates such as charcuterie plates or cheese boards, or such bar snacks as Scotch eggs and pork pies, as well as packets of nuts and crisps (chips). At fine dining restaurants, it is usual for diners to order a starter, main course, and dessert—particularly high-end restaurants may also serve additional courses including *amuse-bouches* (complimentary, bite-sized appetizers) served with pre-meal drinks, pre-desserts (small, sweet dishes served after the main course but before the dessert course), and petit fours (bite-sized sweet treats served with tea or coffee). In addition to an *à la carte* menu, many restaurants offer *prix fixe* meals (meals consisting of several courses served for a set total price), while fine dining restaurants may also offer a tasting menu. A tasting menu consists of a variety of dishes created by a restaurant's chef that are served as smaller, individual courses in order to showcase the chef's skill—often the tasting menu will have to be ordered by all diners sat at a table. Some British restaurants also offer a chef's table experience that sees diners sit in an area of a restaurant's kitchen so that they can observe the preparation of their meal before eating.

In Britain, many restauranteurs and head chefs are major celebrities that front television and radio shows and write best-selling cookbooks. Celebrity is not confined to head chefs, however, for celebrity chef and food campaigner Jamie Oliver was discovered by the BBC while working as a sous-chef at The River Café in west London, while Fred Sirieix, the general manager at London's Michelin-starred restaurant Galvin at Windows, presents numerous television programs. Elsewhere, such television shows as *The Great British Menu*, *Masterchef: The Professionals*, *Saturday Kitchen*, and *Saturday Morning* are not only presented by chefs and restauranteurs but they also feature restaurant chefs cooking restaurant-style dishes for the viewing public. Many chefs have regular columns in national newspapers and in popular food magazines including *BBC Good Food*, *Olive*, and *Delicious*. Additionally, particularly famous chefs have created food ranges for supermarkets. For example, for 12 years Heston Blumenthal, owner of the highly innovative three Michelin-starred restaurant The Fat Duck (located a short walk from The Waterside Inn in Berkshire), collaborated with the Waitrose supermarket chain on an eponymous gourmet food range. Such was the cache of buying food endorsed by Blumenthal that when in 2010, Waitrose's Heston line launched the Hidden Orange Christmas Pudding, the pudding sold four times more than any of the chain's previous Christmas pudding lines and was sold out of puddings by November that year.

The Early History of British Dining

The Norman Conquest of England (the military conquest of England by William, duke of Normandy, in 1066) resulted in the growth of British towns that in turn resulted in a growing demand for eateries to feed both residents and travelers. In medieval times, eateries known as cookshops combined the function of restaurant and take-out by selling ready-made meals that could be eaten either at the establishment or at home. The cookshops performed an important role as Britons living in overcrowded accommodation tended to lack cooking facilities. The food offered by cookhouses included roast, boiled, and fried meat, fish and poultry, as well as sweet and savory pies. By the Tudor era (1485–1603), Britain's growing population of artisans and merchants had started to increase demand for dining establishments. Consequently, inns, taverns, and alehouses that had previously exclusively sold drink now started to sell such foods as cakes, toast, pies, and fish dishes too. Some eateries also began to allow customers to bring their own meat with them so that diners could cook the meat over the eatery's fire. By the start of the seventeenth century, many taverns and cookshops had morphed into so-called ordinaries—eateries that served as the forerunner of the modern restaurant by offering a fixed price menu offering meat dishes, vegetables, and bread until midday. This was a time when British industries such as the wool trade were making Britain increasingly wealthy, and the newly rich were happy to indulge in the novel entertainment form of dining out.

Since the sixteenth century, wealthy British households had employed French chefs to produce meals elaborated by sauces and vegetables cooked using French techniques. The French chefs also produced food in smaller, daintier portions than were traditional in Britain up to this time. Therefore, where once a British chef might have roasted a whole animal, now under the influence of French chefs, Britons were served delicately prepared cuts of meat as part of the ongoing process of the sophistication of British cuisine. By the time of the Restoration in 1660 (when King Charles II returned from exile in Europe), a version of French cuisine was available in some inns and taverns, though most inns and taverns continued to serve large portions of such traditional British food as haunch of venison, mutton, ox tongue, many types of fish, pies, pasties, and sausages. Meanwhile, early restaurants in London started to serve French dishes such as *boeuf a la mode* (beef casserole) or *pigeons a l'esteuve* (stewed pigeon) in small portions to the British gentry who were willing to pay high prices for food.

Eighteenth-Century Dining

By the mid-eighteenth century, the British population had started to grow rapidly while innovations in industry and farming had made England one of Europe's richest nations. England's growing wealth created a demand for leisure activities including the enjoyment of gastronomy. Consequently, a finely dressed dining table resplendent with silverware and fine china became a hallmark of sophistication. At the same time, cookbooks such as Eliza Smith's *The Compleat Housewife; or, Accomplish'd Gentlewoman's Companion* (1727), Hanna Glasse's *The Art of Cookery Made Plain and Easy* (1747), and Richard Briggs's *The English Art of Cookery* (1785) became essential reading for fine ladies, as did translations of landmark French cookbooks such as Menon's *The Art of Modern Cookery* (1767) and *The French Family Cook* (1793). Many of the cookbooks ran to several editions, for example, by 1758, *The Compleat Housewife* had reached sixteen editions.

Hannah Glasse

Born in London in 1708, Glasse was the illegitimate daughter of a Northumbrian landowner. Despite her illegitimacy, Glasse was raised on her father's estate and her half-brother later helped fund the publication of her books. When her father became ill, Glasse went to live in London where she secretly wed John Glasse and gave birth to ten children. The couple struggled financially, and this led Glasse to write *The Art of Cookery*, which she hoped would bring the family money. The book was an immediate success as it was aimed at housewives and domestic servants belonging to the burgeoning middle classes. After Glasse's husband died, she became bankrupt and spent time in debtor's prison. To pay debts, Glasse was forced to auction the copyright of *The Art of Cookery*. In 1770, Glasse died in Newcastle.

In the eighteenth century, enjoyment of dining out was fueled by a lust for travel as Britons traveled more often and further afield than ever before, both for business and pleasure. At this time, travel by stagecoach was commonplace and involved overnight stays at inns located along major roads. The inns tended to serve hot beef, pies as well as oysters and various types of freshwater fish, and cold meats that were enlivened by homemade sauces, which is how the iconic British condiment Worcestershire sauce originated. Puddings offered by inns ranged from trifles to fruit tarts and fools.

Inns were distinguished by serving elaborate meals to the traveling upper classes, and when staying at inns, wealthy ladies would be served their meals in their rooms rather than in the inns' dining rooms. In contrast to inns, taverns specialized in serving wine with meals but offered little in the way of accommodation. Alehouses were more basic than taverns for they served ale, beer, and the simplest of foods to lower class travelers.

By the eighteenth century, most British towns included an inn that could accommodate a banquet while several of London's 3,000 inns had gained a reputation for serving excellent food. Moreover, some London inn owners had started to write cookbooks—for example, in 1783, John Farley, the head chef at the London Tavern published the *London Art of Cookery*, which was one of the first restaurant cookbooks.

Nineteenth-Century Dining

By the start of the nineteenth century, some inns had started to rebrand themselves as hotels and as such served food only to those staying at the establishment. These hotels tended to have names that suggested they served foreign food. For instance, London was home to German Hotel and La Sablonniere. Meanwhile, spa towns in English towns including Harrogate in the northern county of Yorkshire, Weymouth in the southwest county of Dorset, and Bath in the southwest county of Somerset were frequented by royalty and thus attracted wealthy visitors. The wealthy tourists viewed inns as insufficiently luxurious and instead stayed in purpose-built lodging houses on a self-catering basis that saw the visitors eat at local taverns. The spa towns started to become home to grand hotels offering elaborate meals as well as to sizeable public dining rooms where guests could mingle. Contrastingly, in London, hotels started to offer private dining suites where members of the social elite could meet without fear of encountering those they wished to avoid. For example, King Louis XVIII of France stayed at London's Grillion's Hotel while in exile on his way back to France in 1814. Despite the Europeanization of British food, Britons of all social classes still enjoyed traditional British foods such as roast meats, game, poultry, and fish, served simply.

In the nineteenth century, wealthy Britons could choose to dine out for pleasure, but the poor often had to dine out due to necessity and thus in actuality dined out more often than the rich. Indeed, nineteenth-century farm workers dined outside in all weathers whilst tending fields and harvesting crops. Since the workers were toiling too far from home to return home for meals, the workers would eat in the fields. Elsewhere, the growth of the tourist industry in Britain together with the spread of the railways meant increasing numbers of British railway termini became equipped with dining areas. Another factor in the trend for dining out in Britain was that British women began to experience greater freedom outside of the home. The greater freedom meant women started to dine out in unchaperoned groups and so dining out became a fashionable pleasure for nineteenth-century women. Meanwhile, the Great Exhibition of 1851 (a major event held in London to celebrate global industry, technology, and culture) strengthened the trend for restaurant dining in London. Previously, London's major hotels had served simple meals to their guests but with the coming of the Great Exhibition, grand hotels equipped with luxurious restaurants became attached to railway stations in order to serve wealthy visitors. By the 1880s, these London hotels had started to offer meals to allcomers rather than just to guests. The meals were served *a la Russe* with courses brought to the table in a specific order with food then portioned by the servers on individual plates from a sideboard standing in the dining room. Another boon to London's growing restaurant industry was the advent of street lighting, which allowed people to travel more easily at night for entertainment purposes including dining out. By 1890, eating in restaurants was a common treat enjoyed by Britons and was also an option for Britons who did not wish to entertain friends at home. Some restaurant proprietors sought to capitalize on Britain's increasingly multicultural populace by offering dishes from across Europe including Italian and French. Vegetarian food was also popular in London at this time, especially in restaurants that were frequented by women. By the late nineteenth century, dining out was an extremely popular pastime with British women who could afford to do so. Previously, genteel British women would not have dined in public alone—at that time, men would have assumed that any woman dining alone was a prostitute, and some establishments would not admit women even if they were accompanied by a male chaperone. Other eateries had women-only sections where women could eat in private. By the end of the 1890s, however, many British women had taken jobs outside of the home and embraced the concept of dining out alone with gusto.

The end of the nineteenth century also saw teashop chains become popular. Teashops served inexpensive, basic meals consisting of hot and cold dishes, tea, coffee, cakes, and bread with all courses placed on the dining table simultaneously. In this way, dining *a la Russe* gradually became confined to only the grandest British restaurants. Probably the most famous British teashop chain was that owned by the company J. Lyons & Co. In 1894, J. Lyons & Co opened a teashop in London's Piccadilly which from 1909 developed into a chain of teashops called Lyons' Corner Houses that went on to number some 200 branches. During the 1920s and 1930s, visiting a Lyons Corner House was the way many Britons were introduced to the concept of dining out. This was true particularly for office workers who wanted a quick, inexpensive meal for lunch. Thus, such teashops helped spread the enjoyment of dining out as a leisure experience to the British lower middle classes.

Modern British Dining

Since the 1920s, dining out for dinner at a grand hotel had been a fashionable way to spend an evening among the British upper classes, but now, dining out was open to more sections of the society. It was also around this time that foreign food, viewed with some suspicion after the First World War, became fashionable again though in some areas, suspicions about the foreignness of food that was not traditionally British lingered. Such suspicions were compounded by the fact that restaurant menus used increasing amounts of foreign words in their restaurant descriptions, which alienated some Britons and led to Britons having to learn a new culinary vocabulary.

During the Second World War, British Restaurants (also known as community kitchens, community meal centers, or similar) were not-for-profit communal eateries established to help feed Britons who had been bombed out of their homes and so lacked cooking facilities, who did not have access to a workplace canteen, who had run out of food ration coupons, and so on. British Restaurants were the brainchild of Britain's minister of food, Lord Woolton, and by 1944, ten such restaurants had formed to serve food to people in Bristol, southwest England.

The restaurants were led by local authorities and volunteer groups some of whom had led similar initiatives during the First World War. Britons did not require coupons to eat at British Restaurants, so the restaurants allowed people to supplement their food rations by buying a healthy, filling meal. In 1943, *The Times* newspaper reported that there were over 2,000 British Restaurants and that the establishments were so popular that their number increased at a rate of ten per week. Indeed, the meals served by British Restaurants represented about 10 percent of the total British civilian food supplies.

Most British Restaurants were located in such buildings as church halls, schools, hospitals, and private houses but the Ministry of Food also developed prefabricated huts that could be erected if there were no suitable buildings available to house a British Restaurant at a certain location. The organizers of British Restaurants also ran mobile canteens that could be set up at bombsites. Around one-third of British Restaurants were supplied with meals from the Ministry of Food central kitchens or from kitchens run by local authorities while the remainder created meals in their own kitchens. British Restaurants were fully self-supporting, and any profit made by the restaurants was taken by the Ministry of Food. Typically, British Restaurants served three-course meals of filling, comforting foods such as soup followed by meat, fish and vegetarian main meals accompanied by vegetables, then a dessert plus tea or coffee. The restraints on Britain's wartime food supply meant, however, that Britons did sometimes have to eat unfamiliar dishes that they found unappealing. For instance, as meat became scarce, the Ministry of Food created the Woolton pie made from vegetables and oatmeal, which soon became a staple dish of British Restaurants.

Most British Restaurants offered a self-service, cafeteria-style set-up, rather than being served by waiting staff, and the majority of the restaurants also had a till from which people could buy food that they could take away in their own containers to eat at home—this was particularly useful for the poorest Britons as they could eke out the portions at home and divide them as they wished. In the countryside, a so-called pie scheme, which was very similar to the British Restaurants' concept was coordinated by the Women's Voluntary Services (WVS), which offered social care to civilians. The Women's Voluntary Services also provided volunteer staff to roughly one-third of British Restaurants though many British Restaurants preferred to pay their staff so as not to undercut privately run restaurants. For many Britons, British Restaurants were their first experience of dining out. However, despite their popularity with the public, British Restaurants were disbanded in 1947. A few British Restaurants did, however, continue to operate as eateries run by local councils until the mid-1950s.

Postwar, the foreign influence on British restaurants continued to increase. For example, while Britain's first Chinese restaurant had opened in London in 1908, in the late 1950s and 1960s, a wave of refugees from Hong Kong led to a slew of Chinese restaurants opening across Britain. The 1960s also saw a steep rise in the number of Indian restaurants in Britain, especially in London and southeast England. Birmingham in central England has been synonymous with curry houses since at least 1945, when Bangladeshi immigrants began to settle in the city and opened eateries selling curry with rice. Today, Birmingham is also home to restaurants influenced by the cuisines of Pakistan, Nepal, India, and Sri Lanka. Famously, Birmingham is the city from which balti originated. Balti is a type of curry both cooked and served in a flat-bottomed steel bowl equipped with two handles. Since the balti bowl is made of steel, it heats up fast and allows the curry to cook quickly. An authentic balti is cooked using vegetable oil rather than ghee (a type of clarified butter often used in Indian cooking), meaning a balti can be far healthier than a standard curry.

So many Birmingham restaurants serve balti that an area to the south of Birmingham city center is nicknamed the Balti Triangle. From 1948 to 1971, immigrants from the Caribbean, known in Britain as the Windrush Generation (named after the ship *Windrush* that brought one of the first groups of Caribbean immigrants to Britain) brought with them many West Indian recipes and helped to make Caribbean food popular across Britain. Many Windrush migrants established their own social spaces where Caribbean food acted as a unifying entity between people displaced from various Caribbean islands. Social gatherings held by Windrush migrants celebrated both the food and music of the Caribbean and in time created a carnival culture in Britain. Many of the Caribbean restaurants of modern Britain originate from the Windrush Generation.

Despite the plethora of new cuisines available to eat in Britain, postwar debt meant many Britons could not afford to eat out often. This situation started to change in 1954, however, when the first Wimpy Bar burger restaurant opened in London in order to cater to Britain's newest consumer group—teenagers. A year after the first Wimpy opened, another American-inspired chain of eateries opened in Britain, for in 1955, the Berni Inn chain of steakhouses was established by Italian British restaurateurs Frank and Aldo Berni, who modeled their restaurants on steakhouses they had encountered while in the United States.

At the end of the 1960s, the British economy boomed meaning Britons experienced a dramatic rise in their standard of living. Consequently, Britons of all social classes started to holiday abroad and in so doing encountered new foods and ingredients that they then sought out at restaurants. By the mid-1970s, Britons had begun to eat out regularly. It was not, however, until the early 1990s that Britain, and most especially London, became a major destination for foodlovers. The reopening of the historic art deco London restaurant Quaglino's in 1993 following a makeover by famous interiors designer and restauranteur Terence Conran was a watershed moment in the history of British food.

This is because the reopening of Quaglino's ushered in a new era of London restaurant that combined slick service, good food, and a certain modern glamor that created a template for media-friendly eateries to which top British restaurants have adhered ever since. The early 1990s was also a time when British chefs, particularly those in London, rediscovered a love of local produce that was given impetus by food scandals such as the outbreak of so-called mad cow disease. Such scandals led Britons to question the origins and quality of the food served to them by restaurants, and so restaurants started to go out of their way to source high-quality, often organic, ingredients. Moreover, the 1990s was a time when Britons began to delay starting families, and so young professionals found they had a greater disposable income on which to spend on dining out. Growing urban populations also resulted in greater demand for more restaurants. For example, while London's geographic boundaries remained unchanged, the city's population grew rapidly leaving London a captive market for food entrepreneurs.

Television's increasing obsession with cooking programs was also crucial to the growth of Britons' fascination with food and dining out as shows such as the BBC program *Ready Steady Cook* (on which two members of the public provided two celebrity chefs with a bag of mystery cooking ingredients that had to be transformed into meals against the clock—first broadcast in 1994) captured the public's imagination and made household names of previously obscure cooks. The more telegenic chefs achieved superstar status with the likes of Gary Rhodes and Jamie Oliver fronting their own shows, while in 1995, 33-year-old *enfant terrible* of the British restaurant scene, Marco Pierre White made headlines for becoming both the first British chef to be awarded three Michelin stars and the youngest chef to achieve three stars. The growing fame of such chefs allied with the rise of so-called Cool Britannia, a period of increased optimism and pride in British culture that lasted throughout the mid- to late 1990s. Cool Britannia was inspired by the London of the Swinging Sixties and coincided with the rise of the Spice Girls, the rivalry between "Brit pop" bands Blur and Oasis, and the UEFA Euro 1996 international soccer tournament held at stadia across England (commonly referred to as Euro '96). In many ways, in '90s Britain cooking was the new rock and roll.

Prior to the London Olympics of 2012, restaurants in London's West End (a loosely defined area of central London that is home to many of the city's major attractions) were the city's go-to food destinations. However, following the Olympics, the east of London, which is seen traditionally as poorer than other parts of the city, became the home of numerous trendy and high-end restaurants. Today, new restaurants open frequently across both central London and in the city's outer boroughs, as they do across Britain on the whole. Today, London is the area of Britain with the most three-starred Michelin restaurants—in 2023, London was home to five restaurants with the maximum number of Michelin stars as well as twelve restaurants with two stars and fifty-seven restaurants boasting one Michelin star. However, Cumbria in the very far north of England is the English county with the most Michelin-starred restaurants—there are eleven Michelin-starred restaurants earning thirteen stars altogether. Since Cumbria has only a population of fewer than 500,000 people, it has more Michelin stars per person than anywhere else in Britain. The most famous Cumbrian restaurant is L'Enclume, which was awarded a third Michelin star in 2022 and holds five AA Rosettes (a nationwide scheme for assessing restaurant food quality in Britain). Scotland is home to twelve Michelin-starred restaurants while Wales has eight Michelin-starred restaurants.

The Covid-19 pandemic had an immense impact on Britain's hospitality sector. Lockdown orders issued between March 20, 2020, and July 4, 2020, meant all pubs, cafés, and restaurants across Britain were ordered to close. During this time, Britain's entire hospitality industry came to an almost complete halt as 81 percent of hospitality businesses were shut temporarily by the spring 2020 lockdown. While some eateries could stay open to sell takeaway, the hospitality sector became a shadow of its former self. Indeed, consumer expenditure data revealed that UK restaurant spending by households in April/May 2020 was 30 percent of that for the same period in 2019. During the month of August 2020, the British government launched the controversial *Eat Out to Help Out* scheme that saw diners at participating restaurants receive a 50 percent discount on food items up to £10 purchased in restaurants, pubs, and cafés every Monday, Tuesday, and Wednesday from August 3 to August 31. The scheme was intended to help establishments earn money and likely did as restaurants that entered the scheme saw dining on Mondays to Wednesdays increase by 50–100 percent over the same period in 2019, and the scheme is credited with making diners feel comfortable with eating out again. However, this return to dining out was not universal for in London, the *Eat Out to Help Out* scheme only had a modest impact—even by September 2020, London restaurants still saw footfall down 25–50 percent below 2019 levels. One of the key reasons for this difference was that Covid-19 had changed the employment activity of central London. With more people working from home rather than entering London to work in offices, shops, and so on, restaurants, cafés, and pubs had far fewer potential customers. Moreover, some critics of the *Eat Out to Help Out* scheme have suggested that encouraging Britons to dine out contributed to the spread of Covid-19. Nonetheless, the reopening of restaurants and other establishments following a lifting of most lockdown restrictions on July 4, 2020, was followed by a gradual return to dining out across Britain. Since all Covid-19 restrictions were lifted, the British hospitality sector has experienced a modest recovery. This recovery has been endangered by the cost-of-living crisis, however, for the crisis has seen both ingredients and energy needed for cooking and heating buildings increase in price.

In July 2022, it was reported that restaurant insolvencies in the UK had risen by 64 percent year-on-year as rising costs meant restaurants could not pay their bills, while in August 2022, it was reported that 60 percent of the UK's Top 100 restaurants were operating at a loss. One of the key reasons for this situation was that animal feed, particularly grain-based feeds eaten by poultry and pigs, had risen sharply in cost due to Russia's invasion of Ukraine. The cost of fruits, dairy, and fats in 2022 also rose more than 20 percent year-on-year. The rise in prices has forced many eateries in Britain to increase the price of the foods they offer. Indeed, not only have small and independent eateries been forced to raise their prices for in July 2022, McDonald's increased the price of its cheeseburger from 99p to £1.19—the first McDonald's price rise in Britain for 14 years. Meanwhile, in April 2023, the well-established Italian restaurant chain Prezzo announced that it would close a third of its restaurants because of the rising costs of the ingredients needed to make pizza and pasta such as mozzarella and tomato sauce, as well as rising energy costs. The restaurant closures would affect 46 of the chain's loss-making restaurants and place 810 staff at risk of redundancy. The Prezzo announcement followed an announcement in March 2023 by The Restaurant Group, the owner of the restaurant chains Frankie and Benny's and Chiquito, which said the chains would close thirty-five restaurants due to a combination of soaring running costs and diners spending less. In the long term, however, many restaurant groups expect to return to profitability, not only by closing unprofitable branches but also by restructuring their businesses to reduce their debts and renegotiating their premises' rental agreements. Indeed, it is predicted that the British restaurant industry revenue will recover fully by 2024.

The rise in costs of certain ingredients means some restaurants have reduced the number of dishes they serve. For example, some restaurants have stopped serving roast lamb as the meat is now too expensive to make a profit. Similarly, some restaurants have started to switch to using cheaper ingredients, for instance, using sea trout instead of salmon or coley instead of cod. Restaurants have also begun to focus even more on using local ingredients that are not only easier to source but also cheaper to transport than ingredients from abroad. In March 2023, however, the hospitality industry saw food inflation drop to 18.9 percent, which was a fourth consecutive fall in year-on-year inflation and the first time in 5 months that food inflation had fallen below 20 percent. The fall in food inflation resulted both from improved availability of milk products and a fall in the price of cooking oils. A fall in the price of crude oil, which in turn impacts the cost of supplying food, also fell. As well as trying to reduce food costs, some British restaurants have also started to look at energy-saving measures such as improving the double-glazing on their window to cut down on heating bills and replacing electric hand-driers with paper towels. Some establishments have also reduced their opening times in order to cut energy costs and staffing costs.

Brexit has also caused issues for some British restauranteurs for Britain's exit from the European Union has impacted the ability of British hospitality businesses to find staff. Many British restaurateurs have reported that they face ongoing staff shortages because for as long as Britain was part of the EU, the British hospitality industry relied heavily on Europe as a pool of skilled hospitality workers as Britons tended to shun hospitality work as they did not wish to work long, often unsociable, hours. Some restauranteurs in Britain have devised schemes to offset the loss of workers from the EU by implementing their own in-house training programs, which enable staff to be recruited and trained.

Further Reading

Broomfield, Andrea. *Food and Cooking in Victorian England: A History*. Westport, CT: Praeger, 2007.

Burnett, John. *England Eats Out: A Social History of Eating Out in England from 1830 to the Present*. Abingdon, UK: Routledge, 2014.

Jones, Stephen. "Why Waitrose cut ties with Heston—and why it might be a strategic win." *The Grocer* (February 27, 2023). https://www.thegrocer.co.uk/waitrose/

why-waitrose-cut-ties-with-heston-and-why-it-might-be-a-strategic-win/676748. article (accessed May 11, 2023).

Lloyd, Gary. "Food inflation drops below 20% for first time in five months." *Morning Advertiser* (May 12, 2023). https://www.morningadvertiser.co.uk/Article/2023/05/12/CGA-Prestige-index-shows-foodservice-inflation-falls-below-20 (accessed May 17, 2023).

Lyon, Phil. "Dining out: Restaurants and British society in the 1930s." *Journal of Culinary Science & Technology* 18, no. 3 (2020): 177–91.

Matheson, Jesse. "How has coronavirus affected pubs, cafes and restaurants?" *Economic Observatory: Business Big & Small* (July 2, 2020). https://www.economicsobservatory.com/how-has-coronavirus-affected-pubs-cafes-and-restaurants (accessed May 16, 2023).

Naylor, Tony. "Restaurants v the cost of living crisis: How will they cope?" *The Observer: Restaurants* (September 18, 2022). https://www.theguardian.com/food/2022/sep/18/restaurants-v-the-cost-of-living-crisis-how-will-they-cope (accessed May 16, 2023).

Office for National Statistics. "Coronavirus and its impact on UK hospitality: January 2020 to June 2021." (July 19, 2021). https://www.ons.gov.uk/businessindustryandtrade/business/activitysizeandlocation/articles/coronavirusanditsimpactonukhospitality/january2020tojune2021 (accessed August 17, 2023).

Panayi, Panikos. *Spicing Up Britain: The Multicultural History of British Food*, London: Reaktion Books, 2008.

Partington, Richard. "Dining out in UK at lowest level since May amid Omicron fears." *The Guardian: Food and Drink Industry*. December 2, 2021. https://www.theguardian.com/business/2021/dec/02/dining-out-in-uk-at-lowest-level-since-may-amid-omicron-fears (accessed April 30, 2023).

Statista Research Department. "Restaurants in the UK—statistics & facts." *Statista: Travel, Tourism & Hospitality: Food & Drink Services* (February 8, 2022). https://www.statista.com/topics/3131/restaurant-industry-in-the-united-kingdom-uk/#topicOverview (accessed May 17, 2023).

Sugg Ryan, Deborah. "The curious history of government-funded British Restaurants in World War 2." Find My Past: History Hub (June 22, 2020). https://www.findmypast.co.uk/blog/history/british-restaurants (accessed May 15, 2023).

Warde, Alan, Jessica Paddock, and Jennifer Whillan. *The Social Significance of Dining Out: A Study of Continuity and Change*. United Kingdom: Manchester University Press, 2020.

10

Food Issues and Dietary Concerns

Food and soft drinks represent Britain's largest manufacturing sector and is the fourth largest such sector globally. Nonetheless, Britain faces a number of food issues ranging from the impact of climate change, soil depletion, and loss of biodiversity on British farming ability to potential labor shortages in the agricultural sector resulting from conflict in Ukraine. Britain also faces several issues arising from people's poor diets.

In 2022, the National Farmers Union Scotland (NFU) warned that Britain will soon experience food security issues not seen since the Second World War due to a combination of the Covid-19 pandemic, Brexit, and Russia's invasion of Ukraine. The same year, the British government set out its first national food strategy. The strategy was focused on increasing domestic output of some foods in order to boost domestic food security. At the same time, the government rejected a recommendation to tackle obesity by introducing taxes on salt and sugar in processed food arguing that Britain already taxes sugar in soft drinks. The environmental group Greenpeace UK criticized the government's food strategy, arguing that the plan did not do enough to tackle greenhouse gas emissions created by the meat and dairy sectors.

Climate Change

The most severe medium- to long-term risk to Britain's domestic food production comes from interlinked environmental factors, chiefly not just climate change but also soil degradation, and the loss of biodiversity. Climate change will cause Britain to suffer greater spells of extreme weather, especially drier summers followed by warmer, wetter winters. Such weather would likely impact British farming by reducing crop yields and endangering livestock through excessively high temperatures and increased risk of disease. Indeed, modeling by the Met

Office (the UK's national weather service) suggests that the main environmental risks facing Britain's food production in the future include heat stress to livestock, drought, increased threat from pests and pathogens, and increased soil erosion.

The implementation of sustainable farming methods will help combat some of these threats and ensure Britain's long-term food security. The danger to British food supplies as a result of unusual weather patterns linked to climate change was evident in 2018, which suffered England's hottest ever summer and was the joint hottest summer ever in the UK. That year, British wheat yields were 7 percent below the 2016–20 average, while in 2020, when June, July, and August experienced spells during which maximum daily temperatures reached a record high of 37.8°C in England, wheat yields were 17 percent down on average. While the wheat harvest bounced back in 2021, the poor wheat yields resulting from the spells of hot weather are an indicator of the effect that increasingly unreliable weather patterns may have on Britain's future food production.

Two areas of British food production that are at particular risk of climate change are dairy farming and potato growing. Heat stress in dairy cattle (when cows feel discomfort at being unable to cool leading to lower milk production and a higher risk of disease) is likely to increase greatly in key dairy-producing parts of Britain, especially southwest England, which is home to 750,000 dairy cattle. The Met Office records that currently in the UK, cattle experience heat stress conditions around 2 to 3 days annually on average, and that it is expected that in the period 2051–70, heat stress conditions could occur for 1 month per year on average. Meanwhile, it is predicted that cattle in eastern and southeast England will likely suffer around 1.5 to 2 months of heat stress per year on average as opposed to the 1 week of heat stress that cattle in these regions suffer

The Founding of the Met Office

The Met Office was founded in 1854 by Vice-Admiral Robert Fitzroy (1805–1865). When the passenger ship the *Royal Charter* sank off the coast of Wales during a violent storm, Fitzroy decided to establish a new storm-warning service, which is now known as the shipping forecast. In operation since 1861, the shipping forecast is the world's oldest national forecasting service and still plays daily on BBC Radio 4. To create the new forecasting system, Fitzroy established a network of coastal weather stations providing gale warnings to ships at sea via telegrams. In 2002, the shipping forecast sea area Finisterre was renamed Fitzroy in honor of the Met Office's founder.

at present. Dairy cattle in England's West Midlands and East Midlands areas are also expected to experience prolonged periods of heat stress.

The Met Office has also looked at how climate change would influence incidents of late blight on British potato farming. Late blight is a disease caused by the organism *Phytophthora infestans*, which causes the decay of potato foliage and tubers in humid weather. Late blight is the most serious disease affecting potatoes and can also affect tomatoes (in which case, the disease is known as tomato blight). In around 50 years' time, the British climate will almost certainly have become wetter and warmer meaning potentially late blight will occur more often in Britain with the greatest increase in outbreaks of the disease occurring in western and northern areas. Instances of phoma stem canker that affects oilseed rape are also expected to increase for higher temperatures have been linked to more severe phoma stem canker in winter oilseed rape crops while higher temperatures combined with increased rainfall may cause more severe stem canker. Climate change could also cause more problems with pesticide resistance for warmer temperatures could result in the need for more frequent applications of pesticide that in time may cause resistance to pesticides to build up. Warmer temperatures could also make it more likely for pests to survive in the British winter.

British-grown crops used as food for humans and animals will also be threatened by future droughts for it is expected that Britain may experience extremely high summer temperatures every 1 in 2 years. In August 2022, areas of England were declared to be experiencing drought with temperatures exceeding 40°C for the first time in British history. In England especially, river levels were lower than in previous hot summers, reservoirs were depleted, and soil moisture reached its lowest level since at least 2013. The lack of water caused farmers many problems as they lost entire plantings of water-loving crops such as peas, salad, broad beans, and spinach. At the same time, animals started to go hungry as grazing vegetation withered. Following the drought declaration, some British farmers have adopted measures to combat the drier weather. These measures include building new pipelines that redistribute water from the wettest regions of Britain to the driest and planting new crops. For instance, farmers in eastern England have started to grow alfalfa, a deep-rooted crop used in countries such as South Africa for livestock, because alfalfa roots are able to reach water deposits held deep within the soil. Farmers have also started to grow so-called cover crops such as clover, vetch, and fodder radish. These crops are not planted for harvesting, but rather to reverse soil erosion and increase water permeation. Many farmers have also started to plant trees on arable land as trees can help slow moisture loss by increasing the rate at which water infiltrates the soil while leaf litter and tree roots uphold soil structure thereby reducing surface water run-off. Therefore, planting trees can not only improve soil quality, but the ground is also more able to hold water. In turn, this helps keep crops irrigated during spells of dry weather.

While British agriculture is impacted by global climate change, British farming also contributes to emissions of nitrous oxide, methane, and carbon dioxide that contribute to global warming. For instance, British farming is a major source of both nitrous oxide and methane emissions produced in Britain though it accounts for only a small amount of Britain's total carbon dioxide emissions. The emissions from British agriculture derive from factors including livestock, agricultural soil, and off-road machinery. However, these emissions are reducing. For instance, between 1990 and 2020, greenhouse gas emissions from farming fell by around 16 percent with most of the decrease coming during the 2000s when there was a reduction in the number of farm animals as well as a decrease in the amount of synthetic fertilizers used by British farmers. Over the last 20 years, emissions of nitrous oxide from agriculture have also fallen. Most agricultural nitrous oxide emissions originate from soil, especially soil to which nitrogen fertilizer application and manure have been applied. Therefore, the fall in nitrous oxide emissions derives from a substantial reduction in the application of nitrogen fertilizer, chiefly to grassland (the amount of nitrogen fertilizer applied to arable land has remained fairly similar). A fall in the number of cattle kept by British farms has also contributed to a decrease in the amount of nitrogen used on grassland. In 2020, farming was estimated to have caused almost half of the UK's total methane emissions. Methane is a by-product of enteric fermentation, a natural part of the digestive process in animals such as cattle and sheep, as well as from the decomposition of manure. The amount of methane caused by farming fell by 15 percent between 1990 and 2020 because the number of cattle and sheep kept by UK farmers reduced. However, since 2009, the falling trend has stalled meaning British methane emissions have remained constant. That said, in 2020, only 1.7 percent of carbon dioxide emissions (equivalent to 5.5 $MtCO_2e$) in the UK could be attributed to farming. Agriculture's contribution to the UK's CO_2 emissions related chiefly to fuel use. The 2022 Farm Practices Survey, which asks farmers about how farming practices in England are affected by current agricultural and environmental issues, showed that 64 percent of farmers thought it important to consider greenhouse gases when making business decisions. This figure was down slightly from 67 percent in 2021. In 2022, 44 percent of farmers asked believed that reducing agricultural emissions would improve the profitability of farming, which was a slightly lower percentage than in 2021. Dairy farmers were most likely to agree that reducing emissions would improve their profit margins, while livestock farmers were less convinced. The most common action taken by British farmers to reduce emissions related to agriculture included recycling waste materials on site, improving farms' energy efficiency, and more accurate application of nitrogen fertilizer.

As well as affecting the ability of British farmers to grow crops, global climate change will also impact Britain's food imports. For instance, rising temperatures in countries such as Spain that export fruit to Britain will impede Britain's supply of fruit. At present, Britain imports £1.8 billion of its fruits and vegetables from Spain—in 2020, the UK was the fourth largest importer of Spanish citrus fruit, importing roughly 288,000 tonnes of such fruit annually, of which around 200,000 tonnes were clementines and mandarins. While citrus fruits enjoy warm weather, the optimal temperature for growing citrus fruits is between 22°C and 34°C. Higher temperatures lead to fruit abscission (when trees lose their leaves and detach ripe fruit) and smaller sized fruit. Both abscission and smaller sized fruit will reduce the commercial value of Spain's citrus fruit yield and would mean a reduction in exports to Britain.

One potential solution to the impact of climate change on fruit supplies to Britain is for Britain to reinvigorate its domestic fruit production through initiatives such as the Our Food 1200 project in Wales that aims to renew the local food economy through building a network of small-scale fruit and vegetable-growers. Ultimately, the Our Food 1200 project should be able to produce sufficient seasonal fruit and vegetables to feed 56,000 households.

Soil Degradation

British agriculture relies on the land; thus, a reduction in soil health poses an underlying threat to Britain's food security. At present, estimates suggest that soil degradation, erosion, and compaction cost Britain over £1 billion per year while reducing the amount of land Britain can use to produce food.

Much of Britain's land area is used for agriculture with most of this land being grassland used for grazing animals rather than for growing crops. This is because not all land is suitable for growing crops while some land is suitable for cultivating specific crops only. Modern farming practices can damage soil. For example, ploughing the soil and using heavy machinery on wet soil can harm the structure of soil. Once the soil is degraded, it is more liable to being washed away by rain, meaning the topsoil needed for crop growth is lost. Monocropping of wheat and barley (where farmers grow the same crop each year) is also problematic for the practice extracts nutrition from the soil resulting in farmers using artificial fertilizers to replenish the soil.

Britain has fairly deep soils, and while most soil erosion occurs slowly, in erosion hotspots, Britain is losing up to 2 cm of soil per year. Although British soil loss occurs slowly, it is nonetheless heavily degraded through overuse, erosion, compaction, and pollution. In particular, British soil is losing the organic matter that makes soil resilient to weathering. For instance, throughout much of British history, British soils have suffered deforestation and more recently have felt the effects of intensive farming. Modern intensive farming methods mean organic matter often fails to return to the soil (through crop residues, manure, and compost), something that leaves the soil less fertile. Britain's arable land, which comprises much of Britain's farmland, is also greatly depleted of carbon. Indeed, such is the British government's concern about the state of Britain's soil that the House of Commons Environment, Food, and Rural Affairs Committee has launched an inquiry to investigate how authorities can meet the government's aim of ensuring all British soil is managed sustainably by 2030. In recent years, scientists have highlighted the importance of soil's role in capturing carbon from the atmosphere. For this reason, there is a move to transform arable fields into pastures or forests as well as to support farming methods that are less carbon-intensive for such measures prevent carbon from being released from soils. In Wales, in order to meet the Welsh government's aim of reducing greenhouse gas emissions by 95 percent by 2050, a variety of methods are encouraged including planting more hedgerows and trees on farms, silvo-pastoral agroforestry that sees livestock graze under trees and in return creating animal-enriched soils, and silvo-arable agroforestry, which sees crops grown under trees. Silvo-arable agroforestry creates shade beneficial to heat-sensitive crops and provides wildlife corridors (tracts of land that connect wildlife habitat). Other methods being introduced to farms in Wales and elsewhere in order to capture carbon in soil include the prevention of overgrazing by livestock, the regeneration of grasslands, and maintaining soil's biodiversity by protecting wildlife such as earthworms that can transport carbon deeper into the soil.

Biodiversity Loss

Society's desire for cheap, year-round food supplies has caused an intensification of British farming that includes greater use of herbicides and artificial fertilizers as well as intensively managed grasslands to ensure good crop yields. This intensive agriculture has led to another problem facing Britain's food production—a decline in Britain's biodiversity (the variety of plant and animal life). In particular, the populations of such pollinating insects as various types of bee (e.g., honeybees, bumblebees, and solitary bees), wasps, hoverflies, moths, butterflies, and beetles have reduced. If British crop yields fall significantly because of a decline in pollinating insect populations, then Britain's food exports will reduce, the number of Britons employed in farming will fall, and food prices will rise. According to a Department for Environment, Food, and Rural Affairs report published in 2014, a severe fall in the population of pollinating insects in Britain would cost the British food industry a loss of £100 billion. Subsequently, a 2019 study revealed that one-third of British bees and hoverflies are in decline, and if current trends continue, some species will become extinct in Britain. It is therefore vital to British food security and larger economy that Britain preserves its biodiversity.

While about 10 percent of Britain's pollinating insect populations have grown recently, including the bees that pollinate crops such as oilseed rape, many species have declined overall. Such a decline puts Britain's long-term food security at risk because if anything happens to the remaining pollinating insects in the future, there will be fewer remaining species to fill the void and pollinate crops. Populations of hoverflies, which are among the most important pollinators, have declined due to habitat loss, climate change, and the use of pesticides in intensive agriculture. Another threat to Britain's pollinating insects is the spread of non-native species such as the Asian hornet, which is invasive and is a major threat to native British honeybees and other insects. Asian hornets have been seen on the Channel Islands (an archipelago in the English Channel, off the

Bees in Britain

Britain is home to over 270 bee species. Most of these are solitary bee species, of which there are around 250 species. Solitary bees exist only in the wild. The European honeybee is Britain's only species of honeybee, but within this species are numerous different types. Though Britain has some wild honeybee colonies, most British honeybees are domesticated and live in hives of 20,000–60,000 bees. Britons who find a bee swarm in an unsuitable place are now able to contact the British Beekeeping Association, which will collect the swarmed bees and relocate them somewhere safe.

northern French coast) and in Gloucestershire (a county in southwest England), leading the Department of Environment, Food, and Rural Affairs to produce a National Pollinator Strategy (2014) that highlights the severity of the threat that Asian hornets pose to British bees. The arrival of Asian hornets is a worry as honeybees are particularly important pollinators of British crops as their hives can be moved easily to be placed near crops thereby providing a pollinating service for the plants. Britain also needs populations of wild pollinators such as wild bee species to ensure high levels of crop pollination because some crops are better pollinated by insects other than honeybees. The number of honeybees in Britain is not sufficient to pollinate all British crops, however. Therefore, while honeybees are one of Britain's most important pollinating insects, at least 1,500 insect species pollinate British plants.

As much of British land is used for agriculture, the management of the agricultural landscape is very important for maintaining pollinator populations. Such crops as oilseed rape provide food for pollinating insects, but they represent only a seasonal food source. Therefore, other insect food sources including pesticide-free hedges, wild grassland, dung-rich pasture, and wildflower margins provide insects with food the rest of the year.

Organic farming (farming that does not use synthetic fertilizers and pesticides) is especially important to pollinators for organic farms support roughly 50 percent more pollinators than nonorganic farms. Organic farming benefits pollinating insects for organic fields are rich in wildflowers and pollinator habitats such as hedgerows. Organic farms also practice crop rotation and mixed farming and so provide a wide range of food sources that pollinating insects can enjoy throughout the seasons.

In order to protect Britain's biodiversity, there are numerous agri-environmental schemes in place that encourage pollinating insects to frequent farmland. For example, there is now a move in Britain to offset the loss of wildflowers in fields and grasslands caused by intensive farming by growing wildflowers such as cow parsley, clovers, and vetches at field margins, on grass banks, and woodland edges so that they can provide food for pollinating insects. Flowering arable plants such as poppies and dead-nettles are also left alone increasingly as they provide insects with nectar and pollen. Farmers are also being urged not to use nitrogen fertilizer as this type of fertilizer stimulates grasses and results in grass outcompeting wildflowers.

Despite the need to protect British bees, in January 2023, the British government gave emergency authorization for the use of the seed treatment thiamethoxam even though this insecticide is banned because it is harmful to bees. Permission was given to use the pesticide on sugar beet seeds in order to protect the British sugar beet crop from the virus yellows disease, a virus spread by aphids that can cause the sugar beet crop to reduce by 80 percent. The government's sanction for the use of thiamethoxam was given against the advice of an independent panel of experts.

Disease

Diseases such as avian flu (commonly referred to in Britain as bird flu), bluetongue, and African swine fever (ASF) threaten to devastate British livestock farming. For example, in the future, it may no longer be possible for British farmers to produce free-range chickens and eggs because of a dramatic increase in the number of avian flu outbreaks in Britain. At the end of 2021, Britain, like the rest of Europe, suffered its largest outbreak of avian flu resulting in millions of farm birds being culled. Indeed, in one outbreak at a farm in Suffolk, eastern England, 80,000 ducks were culled after contracting a highly infectious variant of avian flu. In October 2022, the UK's Chief Veterinary Officer declared the UK (Britain and Northern Ireland) an Avian Influenza Prevention Zone due to an increased number of avian flu cases. The declaration meant that all bird keepers in the UK had to adhere to strict biosecurity measures in order to ensure their birds' safety and prevent the virus spreading. Then, in November 2022, the British government introduced mandatory housing measures across all of England that are in place until further notice. Under these conditions, all bird keepers must keep all birds indoors and uphold biosecurity measures to protect their birds. These biosecurity measures include restricting access to farms by non-essential people, ensuring farm workers change clothing and footwear before entering areas in which bird are kept, and cleaning and disinfecting vehicles regularly to prevent avian flu from spreading. Farmers can still call their birds "free-range" despite being kept indoors as long as their egg-laying birds are not housed for more than 16 weeks. This is important as many British shoppers choose free-range as they feel it is kinder to birds as the birds are able to enjoy time outdoors.

Bird flu is a particularly visible virus in that sick wild birds such as swans can be found on British waterways, in parks, and so on. For this reason, health officials have warned Britons not to go near infected or dead birds for fear the disease could transmit to humans.

Indeed, in February 2023, British authorities announced that public health surveillance surrounding avian flu (increased genomic surveillance and testing of humans exposed to the virus) would be increased because cases of avian flu had been detected in mammals including otters, seals, and foxes located in Durham in northern England; Cornwall in far southwest England; Powys in Wales; and the Inner Hebrides, Shetland, and Fife in Scotland that had probably scavenged infected wild birds. British health experts want to check that the infection does not jump to humans.

Bluetongue virus is a disease that is transmitted by a biting midge and affects ruminants, mostly sheep but also cattle and deer. The first British case of bluetongue virus was detected in England in September 2007, in a cow on a farm in Suffolk. Since then, in Britain, the virus has spread from cattle to sheep with the transmissions of the virus helped by increasing global temperatures that meant the geographical distribution of the midge has grown northward. While the development of a vaccine helped prevent major outbreaks over subsequent years, saving an estimated £460 million and 10,000 British jobs, scientists warn it will be impossible to prevent bluetongue from becoming established in Britain, something that would cause British lamb and beef exports to decline. The culling of infected animals would also cause the price of lamb and beef to rise. Jobs in British farming and food preparation will also be lost. The culling of sheep or cattle would also have an indirect effect on the price of other meats, driving prices upward. If bluetongue were to strike at the same time as another disease, such as one that attacks wheat, the combined impact on both the British food supplies and the economy could be disastrous. The newly emerged Ug99 wheat stem rust fungus is already present in the wheat of several African and Middle Eastern countries and has been detected in parts of Mediterranean Europe. The Ug99 fungus is resistant to the three main anti-rust genes used to protect most wheat, so if the fungus were to reach Britain, the fungus could infect healthy British wheat in mere hours, turning the wheat to mulch in just days. Consequently, scientists are racing to develop a new strain of wheat that is resistant to Ug99.

African swine fever is a highly contagious virus characterized by symptoms including fever, vomiting, and lack of energy that can cause sudden death in wild and farmed pigs. As of 2023, the virus is not found in Britain, but it is spreading around the world including in parts of Europe. As the virus can have a death rate of 100 percent and there is no effective vaccine against it, ASF can have a devastating impact on pig farming. In order to try to stop ASF from entering Britain, Britons must not bring any pork or pork products back to Britain if they are returning from non-EU (European Union) countries. Additionally, British pig owners must register their animals and their animals' location so that if an outbreak of ASF occurs, British authorities are able to track the disease. The ASF virus can survive on clothing, vehicles, and in pork products including sausages and bacon, but at present the virus cannot transmit to humans.

Food Supply Issues and Price Increases

Most of Britain's food is produced domestically by the agriculture and food manufacturing sectors, but Britain also has a wide range of overseas suppliers that allow British consumers to enjoy a range of food products that either cannot be grown domestically or can be grown only seasonally in Britain. At present, the UK (Britain plus Northern Ireland) produces approximately 60 percent of its own food consumption by economic value. In particular, the UK produces 88 percent of all the cereals consumed in the UK, 86 percent of its beef, and around 90 percent of its eggs. The UK is fully self-sufficient in milk and produces more lamb than is consumed in the UK. The UK is also almost fully self-sufficient in poultry and vegetables such as carrots and swedes. As well as producing much of its own food, Britain enjoys well-established trade links that meet consumer food demand year-round. Trade is dominated by countries within the EU, but it is too early to say what lasting effect, if any, Brexit will have on Britain's ability to acquire food from EU countries.

In 2020, around half of British food was imported from a range of countries. This makes Britain's food supply resilient for if one country's food production is disrupted, another can meet demand. Indeed, no one country provides more than 11 percent of British imports. The overwhelming majority of food imported to Britain comes from Europe. The rest is supplied by Africa, Asia, North America, and South America. This has been the case for the last decade. Despite Brexit, EU countries continue to be Britain's main source of food imports. The Netherlands, Republic of Ireland, Germany, and France are the EU's biggest food suppliers to Britain. However, following Brexit, the relationship between Britain and the EU is in a state of flux, and so Britain is forging new trading relationships with other parts of the world. According to the Food and Drink Federation (the organization representing the UK's food and drink manufacturers), the UK's food imports are 13 percent higher than before the Covid-19 pandemic with imports from Canada growing in particular. Canada has become a main source of ingredients for the UK food manufacturing sector.

Food seasonality is complex with Britain depending on some countries for certain foods at specific times of the year because of growing seasons across the world. Consequently, although there is a growing preference in Britain for buying local, seasonal foods, Britain still relies on various supply lines to meet increasing consumer demand for out-of-season foods especially year-round access to unseasonal fresh fruit and vegetables. For this reason, longer, more complex supply chains are forming for out-of-season fresh produce. While in 2020, 50 percent of the fresh vegetables eaten in the UK were produced by British growers, only 16 percent of the fresh fruit eaten in Britain was grown domestically. Instead, most of the fruit eaten in Britain came from a wide range of countries in the EU, Africa, and the Americas, as well as some British growers. Additionally, some parts of the world are especially important to Britain's supply of particular fruits, for example, bananas from the Caribbean and Central America. This regional reliance endangers the supply of these particular products.

In order to support British farmers, the British government has pledged £270 million ($333 million) of investment in farming until 2029. This investment is aimed at promoting new technologies so that Britain can grow more food produced domestically thereby creating jobs and boosting the British economy. The NFU welcomed the investment, saying that Russia's invasion of Ukraine in 2021 had underlined the importance of domestic food production and highlighted the fragility of the global food network. The Russian invasion of Ukraine has hampered domestic British food supplies. Between April 2020 and March 2022, 67 percent of temporary agricultural workers in Britain were Ukrainians issued with Seasonal Worker visas, a figure that equated to some 20,000 workers who perform vital tasks such as planting and picking crops and packing and grading harvested produce. Many of the Ukrainian workers had themselves filled vacancies left by EU workers who had not come to work in Britain post-Brexit. Following Russia's invasion of Ukraine, the number of Ukrainians using the visa scheme dwindled because martial law meant Ukrainian men had to stay in Ukraine. This development meant farms had to look much further afield for seasonal workers resulting in a rise in seasonal farm workers from Indonesia, Nepal, Vietnam, Kyrgyzstan, and Kazakhstan. Despite this rise, British farms still struggled to find seasonal workers, something the NFU believes has resulted in around £60 million worth of food going to waste in the first half of 2022 as there was a lack of workers to pick crops.

Costs to British farms vary each year so there are always significant risks to farming economies, and consequently to Britain's food security and the price of food to the British consumer. The biggest cost to British farmers is that of buying feed, but feed is also the cost with the least stable price. The fertilizers, pesticides, seeds, and fuel used by farms can also vary in price due to many domestic and international factors. In August 2022, the price of fresh food in Britain rose by 10.5 percent, the highest rate since 2008 as food producers passed on the rising cost of fertilizer, wheat, and vegetable oils, much of which are produced in Ukraine and Russia. The increase in shop prices added to the pressure on British households already struggling to pay much higher household energy bills and high petrol prices. Britons on the lowest incomes were hit hardest by the price rises as they spend a larger proportion of their household budget on such essentials as food and fuel.

In response to the price rises, British shoppers started to stretch their budgets by shopping in bulk, at discount stores, and swapping premium brand products in favor of supermarket own label value ranges. British shoppers also returned to food shopping in person rather that shopping online as they sought to reduce unnecessary spending by looking for in-store bargains and cutting back on food delivery costs. Despite such measures, in 2022, the average annual British grocery bill rose by £380, meaning grocery bills were the highest they have been since 2009. Since low-income British households spend a larger proportion than average on food, they feel price increases more acutely than wealthier households. Consequently, British food banks have noted an increase in demand for help with obtaining food. For example, during the period April–September 2022, the Trussell Trust provided almost 1.3 million emergency food parcels. This figure was a third more than during the same period in 2021.

Wastage

Wastage by both the food manufacturing sector and British consumers is another issue facing British food supplies. Food wastage by British food producers reduces both the amount of food available to eat in Britain and the quantity that can be exported. Food wastage also means that resources such as energy are used unnecessarily during production thereby creating unnecessary carbon emissions. The British government estimates that the total yearly wastage within the British food manufacturing sector equates to around 3.6 metric tonnes, a figure that represents between 6 and 7 percent of Britain's total food production. Meanwhile, British households together with the hospitality sector waste approximately 7.7 metric tonnes of food, while the British manufacturing and retail industries waste 1.8 metric tonnes of food. Further, the British charity Waste and Resources Action Programme (WRAP), which works to help Britain achieve a circular economy by promoting sustainability and using resources efficiently, estimates that UK households waste 1.1 million tonnes of food annually as they prepare, cook, or serve too much food—wastage that costs the households £700 per year.

Long-term trends show Britons are aware of food wastage, however, as they become increasingly concerned about the need to reduce greenhouse gas emissions, conserve resources, and save money during the cost-of-living crisis. The concern about food wastage is fueled by initiatives such as Love Food Hate Waste and Food Waste Action Week that target food wastage by consumers. At the onset of the Covid-19 pandemic, British household food wastage fell sharply because Britons were unable to shop as easily. While Britons stockpiled long-life foods in the run-up to the first Covid-19 lockdown in March 2020, the volume of shopping sales reduced sharply the following week as Britons encountered difficulty in purchasing some foods due to a lack of supply and the introduction of lockdown restrictions that made movement outside of the home difficult even though food shopping was listed as one of the legitimate reasons to leave home during lockdown. Additionally, some Britons felt unsafe entering enclosed spaces such as shops alongside non-household members and thus went food shopping less frequently than pre-lockdown. As Britons shopped less frequently, their food management skills improved, and they began to waste less food. This decline in food wastage has started to falter, however, as Britons return to their pre-pandemic lifestyles. Consequently, despite increased awareness of food wastage, British food wastage levels have returned to pre-pandemic levels as people become busier and so have less time to prepare food for batch-cooking, defrosting meals prepared in advance, and mealtimes becoming displaced resulting in more Britons eating takeaways. According to the Waste and Resources Action Programme, Britons most likely to waste food are those aged 18 to 44 who may be less confident at preparing and cooking meals, have young children, or order fruit and vegetable boxes from online companies only to find they do not like some of the items included in the boxes. In order to combat the rise in food wastage, some British food manufacturers and supermarkets including Marks & Spencer, Asda, and Tesco no longer place "best before" dates on products such as fruit and vegetables but instead allow consumers to judge whether food is safe to eat or get shop staff to check the freshness of the fruit and vegetables. Additionally, an increasing number of British food retailers, manufacturers, and other food-related businesses redistribute food that would otherwise go to waste. Indeed, between 2015 and 2021, the UK food manufacturing, retail, and hospitality industries redistributed 426,000 tonnes of surplus food valued at more than £1.3 billion, which is the equivalent of more than one billion meals.

Diet and Health Issues

According to the British Medical Association, in 2018, 63 percent of adults in the UK were overweight, while 27 percent were classified as obese. Similarly, 20 percent of children in the UK were obese by the time they reach 10 years of age, though there was considerable variation between regions and social groups—26 percent of 10-year-old children in the most deprived areas were obese, compared with 11 percent in the least deprived areas of the UK. Meanwhile, according to the National Food Strategy for England (commissioned by the government in 2019), poor diets contribute to an estimated 64,000 deaths every year in England, while more than half of over-45s in the UK live with diet-related health conditions including obesity, type II diabetes, and heart disease. This ill-health costs the English economy £74 billion through factors such as lost workforce productivity.

Various ways have been suggested to combat poor diets and diet-related health issues in Britain. For instance, the National Food Strategy for England called for the introduction of Sugar and Salt Reformulation Tax (which would have been a world first) that would have seen some of the money obtained in tax spent to expand healthy free school meals in England and support healthy eating in deprived communities. The National Food Strategy for England also suggested food education to be made central to the national school curriculum in order to teach children the importance of eating a healthy diet. Other recommendations included schemes to improve the diets of low-incomes households, improving food education in general, the trial of a scheme called "Community Eatwell" that would see family doctors prescribe fruit and vegetables to people with poor diets, and urging the government to establish a target to reduce England's meat consumption by 30 percent over the next decade.

The National Food Strategy for England also stressed the need to help farmers change to using more sustainable farming methods by allocating land equally to high-intensity agriculture and more environmentally friendly types of farming. However, food manufacturers argued that introducing taxes on sugar and salt would lead to consumers paying more for their food, and the British government rejected the introduction of extra taxes on foods high in salt and sugar arguing that such a move would be wrong at a time when living costs were already rising. Instead, the government said more research was needed to determine the link between processed food and obesity and suggested that the food industry needed to better promote the consumption of healthy food.

Further Reading

BBC. "Food bills are set to soar by £380 this year." *BBC: Business* (June 21, 2022). https://www.bbc.co.uk/news/business-61878062 (accessed August 17, 2023).

Briggs, Helen. "Food strategy criticised by government's own adviser." *BBC News: Science & Environment* (June 13, 2022). https://www.bbc.co.uk/news/science-environment-61778967 (accessed August 17, 2023).

Business Wales. Carbon Capture Technology—12 methods that can be incorporated on your farm (November 8, 2019). https://businesswales.gov.wales/farmingconnect/news-and-events/technical-articles/carbon-capture-technology-12-methods-can-be-incorporated-your-farm (accessed January 23, 2022).

Department for Environment Food and Rural Affairs. *Agricultural Statistics and Climate Change*, 10th edn. September 2020. https://assets.publishing.service.gov.uk/government/uploads/system/uploads/attachment_data/file/941991/agriclimate-10edition-08dec20.pdf (accessed August 17, 2023).

Department for Environment Food and Rural Affairs. "National Statistics: Chapter 11: Environment" (October 21, 2022). https://www.gov.uk/government/statistics/agriculture-in-the-united-kingdom-2021/chapter-11-environment (accessed August 17, 2023).

Department for Environment Food and Rural Affairs. "Official Statistics: Agri-climate Report 2022" (October 27, 2022). https://www.gov.uk/government/statistics/agri-climate-report-2022/agri-climate-report-2022 (accessed January 18, 2022).

Department for Environment Food and Rural Affairs. "United Kingdom Food Security Report 2021: Theme 4: Food security at household level" (December 22, 2021). https://www.gov.uk/government/statistics/united-kingdom-food-security-report-2021/united-kingdom-food-security-report-2021-theme-4-food-security-at-household-level (accessed August 17, 2023).

Department for Environment Food and Rural Affairs. "United Kingdom Food Security Report 2021: Theme 2: UK food supply sources" (December 22, 2021). https://www.gov.uk/government/statistics/united-kingdom-food-security-report-2021/united-kingdom-food-security-report-2021-theme-2-uk-food-supply-sources (accessed August 17, 2023).

Environment Agency. "The state of the environment: Soil" (June 2019). https://assets.publishing.service.gov.uk/government/uploads/system/uploads/attachment_data/file/805926/State_of_the_environment_soil_report.pdf (accessed January 10, 2022).

FarmingUK Team. "UK on verge of food security concerns 'not seen since WWII.'" FarmingUK: News: Politics. April 27, 2022. https://www.farminguk.com/news/uk-on-verge-of-food-security-concerns-not-seen-since-wwii-_60282.html (accessed August 17, 2023).

Garry, Freya K., Dan J. Bernie, Jemma C. S. Davie, Edward C. D. Pope. "Future climate risk to UK agriculture from compound events." *Climate Risk Management* 32

(2021): 100282. https://www.sciencedirect.com/science/article/pii/S2212096321000115 (accessed January 18, 2023).

Global Food Security. "UK threat" (2022). https://www.foodsecurity.ac.uk/challenge/uk-threat/ (accessed January 10, 2022).

Levitt, Tom. "The end of free-range eggs? Year-round bird flu outbreaks may keep hens inside." *The Guardian: News: Environment: Wildlife* (March 25, 2022). https://www.theguardian.com/environment/2022/mar/25/the-end-of-free-range-eggs-year-round-bird-flu-outbreaks-may-keep-hens-inside (accessed February 1, 2023).

"National Food Strategy: Independent review: Chapter 16." https://www.nationalfoodstrategy.org/wp-content/uploads/2021/07/National-Food-Strategy-Chapter-16.pdf (accessed August 17, 2023).

Noel, Katherine, Aiming Qi, Lakshmi Harika Gajula, Craig Padley, Steffen Rietz, Yong-Ju Huang, Bruce D. L. Fitt, and Henrik U. Stotz. "Influence of elevated temperatures on resistance against phoma stem canker in oilseed rape." *Frontiers in Plant Science* 13 (March 2, 2022): 785804. doi: 10.3389/fpls.2022.785804. PMID: 35310658; PMCID: PMC8924614 (accessed January 10, 2023).

Powney, G. D., Claire Carvell, Mike Edwards, Roger K. A. Morris, Helen E. Roy, Ben A. Woodcock, and Nick J. B. Isaac. "Widespread losses of pollinating insects in Britain." *Nature Communications* 10 (2019): 1018. https://doi.org/10.1038/s41467-019-08974-9 (accessed August 17, 2023).

Public Health England. "Impact of COVID-19 pandemic on grocery shopping behaviours" (2020). https://assets.publishing.service.gov.uk/government/uploads/system/uploads/attachment_data/file/932350/Grocery_Purchasing_Report.pdf (accessed February 5, 2023).

Rowlatt, Justin. "National Food Strategy: Tax sugar and salt and prescribe veg, report says." *BBC News: UK* (July 15, 2021). https://www.bbc.co.uk/news/uk-57838103 (accessed August 17, 2023).

Shelley, Fred M. *The World's Population: An Encyclopedia of Critical Issues, Crises, and Ever-Growing Countries*. Santa Barbara, CA: ABC-CLIO, 2015.

Waste and Resources Action Programme (WRAP). "Returning to Normality after Covid-19: Food Waste Attitudes and Behaviours in 2021" (August 2021). https://wrap.org.uk/sites/default/files/2021-08/food-trends-report-august-2021.pdf (accessed February 5, 2023).

Glossary

Afternoon tea: an afternoon meal consisting of small sandwiches, cakes, and a hot beverage.

Alban buns: precursor to the hot cross bun that is topped by a cross cut into the dough before baking.

Ale: a type of beer brewed using a warm fermentation method.

Angostura bitters: concentrated aromatic bitters typically used to flavor drinks.

Aqua Vitae: a distilled wine popular in Elizabethan times.

Arbroath Smokies: a type of smoked haddock hailing from Scotland.

Aurochs: extinct wild European oxen.

Balti: a type of curry both cooked and served in a flat-bottomed steel bowl.

Bangers and mash: sausages served with mashed potato.

Bank holiday: a type of public holiday.

Bara brith: a rich fruit loaf made with tea.

Best before dates: a date placed on packaging to indicate when a food is at its best to eat. Foods can still be eaten safely after this date.

Black Jack: an Elizabethan leather cup made waterproof by the application of pitch.

Black pudding: sausage made from a mixture of blood, milk, animal fat, onions, and oatmeal.

Black treacle: a thick syrup made during the refining of sugar.

Brandy butter: a sweet, rich dessert sauce combining butter, sugar, and alcohol typically served with Christmas pudding.

Bread and butter pudding: a traditional dessert featuring stale bread, custard, spices, and dried fruit.

Bread sauce: a sauce made with milk and spices, which is thickened with breadcrumbs and eaten with roast game or turkey as part of Christmas dinner.

Brexit: the term commonly used to refer to the withdrawal of the UK from the European Union (EU) in January 2020.

Brine pit: a pit of salt water where salt is formed by a process of crystallization.

Bubble and squeak: leftover cooked vegetables mixed with mashed potato and fried as individual cakes.
Buttermilk: the liquid left behind after churning butter.
Cadbury Creme Egg: a milk chocolate shell filled with soft white and yellow fondant to resemble a real egg that is sold by the million during Easter.
Cawl: a hearty Welsh meat and vegetable soup.
Christingle: a symbolic object used during an Advent church service comprising an orange, dried fruits, sweets, a candle, and a red ribbon.
Christmas pudding: a sweet pudding made using dried fruit, spices, suet, and alcohol that is steamed or boiled in advance to eat at Christmas.
Clootie dumpling: a steamed Scottish pudding made with dried fruit and spices cooked in a linen cloth called a cloot.
Cock-a-leekie: a Scottish soup made from leeks, chicken barley, and prunes.
Coconut ice: a soft candy colored white and pink made from coconut, condensed milk, and sugar.
Collop: a thin slice of meat.
Cornish pasty: a meat and vegetable pastry synonymous with the English county of Cornwall.
Coronation chicken: cold cooked chicken bound in a creamy, lightly curried mayonnaise often used as sandwich filling, which was invented for the queen's coronation.
Cottage pie: minced beef topped with mashed potato and baked.
Cranachan: a layered Scottish dessert combining toasted oats, raspberries, whipped cream, whisky, and honey.
Crumble: the topping for sweet or savory dishes used instead of pastry.
Cullen Skink: a thick Scottish soup made of smoked haddock, potatoes, and onions. An authentic Cullen skink is made from finnan haddie (cold-smoked haddock from northeast Scotland).
Cumberland sausage: a coiled, peppery sausage from the English county of Cumbria.
Dripping: fat that has dripped from roasting meat and is reused in cooking.
Dry January: when people abstain voluntarily from drinking alcohol.
Dundee cake: a traditional Scottish cake made with glacé cherries, dried fruit, orange peel and zest, and ground almonds that is topped with a pattern of whole blanched almonds.
Eton mess: a traditional dessert comprising strawberries, meringue, and whipped cream.

Fairtrade: a certification system that ensures defined standards are met in the creation and supply of a commodity, including workers' rights, fair pay, and ethical, sustainable production.

Finnan Haddie: cold-smoked haddock from northeast Scotland.

Flesh-eater's license: a permit bought to allow an individual to eat meat on a day specified as a fish-eating day in Elizabethan times.

Food miles: the distance over which food travels from its place of production to the consumer.

Forced rhubarb: when rhubarb plants are grown in the dark to prevent light from reaching them thereby causing the rhubarb stalks to grow faster.

Full English: a substantial dish comprising fried bacon and eggs together with some combination of fried tomatoes and mushrooms, a sausage, black pudding, and fried or toasted bread accompanied by tea or coffee.

Game chips: an accompaniment to roast game birds consisting of thinly sliced, deep-fried potato.

Guy Fawkes Night (or Bonfire Night): A British custom celebrated on November 5 to commemorate the failure of the Gunpowder Plot (1605).

Haggis: a pudding made from the minced liver, heart, and lungs of a sheep (or other animal) combined with suet and oatmeal, then seasoned with onion and spices such as cayenne pepper. The mixture is packed into an animal's stomach before being boiled.

High tea: a more substantive meal than afternoon tea, in which meat, fish, and egg dishes, as well as breads and desserts, are served as an early evening meal.

Himalayan rock salt: rock salt from the Punjab region of Pakistan that is usually a pinkish color due to the inclusion of trace minerals.

Hot cross bun: a sweet, spiced, fruity bun on top of which is piped a cross.

Inn: an establishment where travelers lodge and dine. Typically, inns are located in rural areas along busy roads.

Irn Bru: A Scottish non-alcoholic carbonated drink made to a secret recipe.

Jam roly-poly: a steamed or baked suet pudding spread with jam and rolled in the manner of a Swiss roll.

Jellied eels: a dish strongly associated with London's East End comprising eels boiled in a spiced stock that sets to form a jelly.

Kedgeree: a traditional British breakfast dish comprising boiled rice, smoked haddock, hard-boiled eggs, curry powder, and sometimes sultanas.

Kippers: smoked herrings usually eaten at breakfast.

Lamb's wool: apple drink topping consumed during wassailing.

Lammas: from the Anglo-Saxon *loaf-mass*, a Christian celebration during which loaves of bread made from newly collected grain are consecrated.

Lancashire hotpot: a meat and vegetable baked stew originating in northwest England.

Lava bread: a traditional Welsh food made from edible seaweed.

Leporaria: Roman enclosures containing rabbits.

Liquorice Allsorts: assorted confectionery sold as a jumbled mixture. The sweets are made of liquorice, sugar, coconut, aniseed, fruit flavorings, and gelatin.

Lugnasad: Celtic festival in celebration of the summer harvest.

Madeira cake: a rich cake similar to a pound cake that originated in the nineteenth century to accompany sweet Madeira wine.

Malting: the process of steeping, germinating, and drying barley to convert it into the malt used for brewing, whisky and vinegar making, and malt extract production.

Manchet (or Pandemain): a light, refined, textured bread, eaten in the Middle Ages and Tudor times, made of stoneground wheat sieved twice through a cloth.

Marks & Spencer: a retail chain that revolutionized lunchtimes when it introduced prepacked sandwiches to the British public.

Maslin: a medieval bread made from a combination of grains such as rye and barley.

Mead: an alcoholic drink made of fermented honey and water.

Megrim: a deep-water flatfish.

Metheglin: mead made with herbs.

Mince pies: small sweet mincemeat pies eaten at Christmas.

Mothering Sunday: the fourth Sunday of Lent when traditionally children give their mothers gifts and cards.

National Food Strategy for England: an independent report commissioned by the British government into the food system in England compiled by restauranteur Henry Dimbleby.

Neeps and tatties: Scottish term for the mashed swede and potato served with haggis.

***Noson Gyflaith*:** A Welsh Christmas and New Year tradition that sees families invite friends to their homes for dinner followed by making toffee, games, and storytelling.

Ordinaries: a type of Elizabethan tavern.

Pantries: boxes equipped with air-holes in which foods such as cheese were stored.

Parkin: a dark, spicy gingerbread from northern England eaten on Guy Fawkes Night.

Pease pudding: a savory dish made from boiled split yellow peas, water, salt, and spices that is typically cooked around a ham joint.

Perry: an alcoholic drink made from fermented pears.

Pigs in blankets: small sausages wrapped in bacon.

Ploughman's lunch: a cold dish typically comprising cheese, salad, bread, and a pickled onion eaten at lunchtime.

Plygain: a traditional Welsh Christian worship service held at Christmas.

Pollinating insects: insects that transfer pollen between flowers.

Pork scratchings: salted, deep-fried pig skin served as a snack.

Porridge: oats cooked slowly with water or milk, eaten for breakfast either by itself or with salt, sugar, or dried fruit added.

Pottage: a thick stew-soup of boiled vegetables, grains, and, if available, meat or fish commonly eaten by medieval peasants.

Queen's Platinum Jubilee pudding: a lemon and Swiss roll amaretti trifle that in May 2022 won a competition to become the official pudding of the Queen's Platinum Jubilee.

Rock salt: Rock salt (or halite) is the remains of inland seas or lakes that evaporated millions of years ago. The large size of rock salt crystals means that typically it is not used in cooking as it takes too long to dissolve in food. Instead, rock salt is used to flavor food or for decorative purposes. Some food-grade rock salt is used to make brines.

Rock: often known after its place of origin, for example, Blackpool rock or Brighton rock, a type of hard stick-shaped boiled sugar confectionery typically flavored with peppermint. Rock tends to be sold at British seaside resorts. Sticks of rock have a pattern embedded throughout their length that spells out the name of the resort where the rock is sold—the place name can be read on both ends of the stick and remains readable even after pieces are bitten from the stick.

Royal warrant: a mark of recognition to businesses that supply goods or services to members of the royal family or their households.

Rumbledethumps: a Scottish cheese and potato dish.

Scotch broth: a hearty soup made from barley, dried peas, and vegetables.

Scotch egg: a boiled egg wrapped in sausage meat, coated in breadcrumbs, then deep-fried.

Shepherd's pie: minced lamb topped with mashed potato and baked.

Shrove Tuesday (or Pancake Day): a feast day before Lent begins on Ash Wednesday.

Simnel cake: a fruit cake featuring two layers of marzipan, one on top of the cake and one running through the middle. On top of the cake, sitting on the layer of marzipan, are eleven marzipan balls each representing one of Jesus's disciples (it is not usual to include Judas).

Sotiltees (or subtleties): elaborate Elizabethan ornamental sugar sculptures.

Spotted dick: a steamed pudding made with suet and currants or raisins typically served with custard.

Stargazy pie: Cornish fish pie with sardines poking out the top, looking at the stars.

Sticky toffee pudding: a dessert comprising sponge cake, dates, and toffee sauce usually served with custard or ice cream.

Suet: the fat found around beef and mutton kidneys used in cooking.

Sugar beet: a sucrose-rich plant grown commercially for sugar production.

Summer pudding: an English dessert of summer berries encased in sliced bread that is chilled overnight in a basin.

Sunday roast: a meal typically comprising roast meat with various vegetables served as lunch on Sundays.

Superfood: a food reputed to provide health benefits to the consumer due to its exceptional nutrient content.

Syllabub: a wine (or sometimes cider) drink sweetened with nutmeg, milk, and cream.

Table salt: Table salt is mined from natural salt deposits (dried-up areas of seawater) before being processed into smaller crystals. Unlike sea salt, table salt production involves chemicals for after mining it is purified before being infused with anti-caking agents. Table salt is used in cooking and as a seasoning. Sea salt is used to season and preserve foods as well as in cooking.

Teetotalism: a movement advocating complete abstention from alcohol.

Temperance movements: social movements advocating the use of alcohol in moderation.

Tiffin: fridge-cake made from crushed biscuits, sugar, butter, golden syrup, raisins, glacé cherries and melted chocolate.

Tipsy laird: a Scottish trifle flavored with whisky or the whisky-based liqueur Drambuie.

Toad-in-the-hole: sausages baked in Yorkshire pudding batter.

Treacle: a syrup made during the refining of sugar.
Treacle toffee: slightly bitter toffee associated with Guy Fawkes Night and in Wales with Christmas.
Veganuary: when some people decide not to eat animal-derived products.
Verjuice: a highly acidic liquid made from unripe fruit such as crab apples used for cooking.
Victoria sandwich: a cake comprising two layers of light sponge sandwiched together with jam named after Queen Victoria.
Wassailing: the ancient custom of visiting orchards in order to sing to the trees thereby ensuring a bountiful harvest.
Whey: the liquid by-product created after milk has been curdled and strained during cheese making.
Whitstable: a seaside town in Kent, southeast England, famous for its oysters.
Yorkshire pudding: a savory batter pudding typically served alongside Sunday roasts.
Yule log: a Christmas dessert consisting of chocolate sponge and cream rolled to resemble a wooden log.

Selected Bibliography

Arndt Anderson, Heather. *Breakfast: A History*. Lanham, MD: Rowman & Littlefield. 2013.

Broomfield, Andrea. *Food and Cooking in Victorian England: A History*. Westport, CT: Praeger, 2007

Burnett, John. *England Eats Out: A Social History of Eating Out in England from 1830 to the Present*. Abingdon, UK: Routledge, 2014.

Burnett, John. *Liquid Pleasures: A Social History of Drinks in Modern Britain*. London: Routledge, 1999.

Chrystal, Paul. *The History of Sweets*. Yorkshire, UK: Pen and Sword History, 2021.

Collingham, Elizabeth M. *Curry: A Tale of Cooks and Conquerors*. Oxford: Oxford University Press, 2007.

Corbin, Pam. *River Cottage Handbook No. 8: Cakes*. London: Bloomsbury, 2011.

Davidson, Alan. *The Oxford Companion to Food*, 2nd edn. Tom Jaine (ed.). Oxford: Oxford University Press, 2006.

Fort, Tom. *Casting Shadows: Fish and Fishing in Britain*. London: William Collins, 2020.

Freeman, Bobby. *First Catch Your Peacock: The Classic Guide to Welsh Food*. Ceredigion: Y Lolfa Cyf, 1996.

Gant, Andrew. *Christmas Carols: From Village Green to Church Choir*. London: Profile Books, 2014.

Goldstein, Darra, ed. *The Oxford Companion to Sugar and Sweets*. Oxford: Oxford University Press, 2015.

Gooding, Mike J., and Peter R. Shewry. *Wheat: Environment, Food and Health*. Chichester, UK: John Wiley & Sons, 2022.

Grigson, Jane. *Jane Grigson's Fruit Book*. New York: Atheneum, 1982.

Guzey, Demet. *Mustard: A Global History*. London: Reaktion Books, 2019.

Jennings, Paul. *A History of Drink and the English, 1500–2000*. Abingdon: Routledge, 2016.

Lister, Kate. *A Curious History of Sex*. London: Unbound, 2021.

Lyon, Phil. "Dining out: Restaurants and British society in the 1930s." *Journal of Culinary Science and Technology* 18, no. 3 (2020): 177–91.

Mason, Laura. *Food Culture in Great Britain: Food Culture around the World*. Ken Albala (ed.). Westport, CT: Greenwood Press, 2004.

Mason, Laura. *Roasts*. London: National Trust Books, 2019.

Mortimer, Ian. *The Time Traveller's Guide to Elizabethan England*. London: The Bodley Head, 2012.

Palmer, Ned. *A Cheesemonger's History of the British Isles*. London: Profile Books, 2019.

Panayi, Panikos. *Fish and Chips: A History*. London: Reaktion Books, 2022.

Panayi, Panikos. *Spicing Up Britain: The Multicultural History of British Food*. London: Reaktion Books, 2008.

Roufs, Timothy G., and Kathleen Smyth Roufs. *Sweet Treats around the World: An Encyclopedia of Food and Culture*. Santa Barbara, CA: ABC-CLIO, 2014.

Shanahan, Madeline. *Christmas Food and Feasting: A History*. Lanham, MD: Rowman & Littlefield, 2019.

Shelley, Fred M. *The World's Population: An Encyclopedia of Critical Issues, Crises, and Ever-Growing Countries*. Santa Barbara, CA: ABC-CLIO, 2015.

Spencer, Colin. *British Food: An Extraordinary Thousand Years of History*. London: Grub Street, 2002.

Vogler, Pen. *Scoff: A History of Food and Class in Britain*. London: Atlantic Books, 2020.

Walton, John K. *Fish and Chips, and the British Working Class, 1870–1940*. London: Leicester University Press, 2000.

Warde, Alan, Jessica Paddock, and Jennifer Whillan. *The Social Significance of Dining Out: A Study of Continuity and Change*. United Kingdom: Manchester University Press, 2020.

Williams, Victoria. *Celebrating Life Customs around the World: From Baby Showers to Funerals*, volumes 1–3. Santa Barbara, CA: ABC-CLIO, 2017.

Williams, Victoria. *London: Geography, History and Culture*. Santa Barbara, CA: ABC-CLIO, 2022.

Yates, Annette. *English Traditional Recipes: A Heritage of Food and Cooking*. London: Hermes House, 2010.

Ysewijn, Regula. *Pride and Pudding: The History of British Puddings, Savoury and Sweet*. London: Murdoch, 2016

Electronic Sources

Armstrong, Martin. "The UK's favourite snacks." January 26, 2022. *Statista: Global Snack Food Market*. https://www.statista.com/chart/26699/favourite-snacks-uk/ (accessed November 16, 2022).

Barber, Harriet. "Britain is one shock away from a food crisis, experts warn." *The Telegraph: News: Global Health Security*. June 1, 2022. https://www.telegraph.co.uk/global-health/terror-and-security/britain-one-shock-away-food-crisis-experts-warn/ (accessed August 21, 2022).

Barrie, Josh. "Banana bread had a serious moment in lockdown, and it might be about to have another one." *INews: Lifestyle*. September 25, 2020. https://inews.co.uk/inews-lifestyle/food-and-drink/banana-bread-baking-craze-lockdown-second-wave-660901 (accessed August 22, 2022).

BBC. "1953: Sweet rationing ends in Britain". *BBC: On This Day*. 2008. http://news.bbc.co.uk/onthisday/hi/dates/stories/february/5/newsid_2737000/2737731.stm (accessed September 27, 2022).

BBC. "Cambridge University study finds Anglo-Saxon kings were mostly vegetarian." *BBC News: UK: Cambridgeshire*. April 22, 2022. https://www.bbc.co.uk/news/uk-england-cambridgeshire-61178452 (accessed August 17, 2023).

BBC. "Food bills are set to soar by £380 this year." *BBC: Business*. June 21, 2022. https://www.bbc.co.uk/news/business-61878062 (accessed August 17, 2023).

BBC. "How to eat like a Victorian." *BBC News*. October 16, 2016. https://www.bbc.co.uk/news/magazine-37654373 (accessed August 17, 2023).

BBC. "'Mad cow disease': What is BSE?" *BBC News: UK*. October 18, 2018. https://www.bbc.co.uk/news/uk-45906585 (accessed August 17, 2023).

BBC. "Why do the French call the British 'the roast beefs'?" *BBC News*. April 3, 2003. http://news.bbc.co.uk/1/hi/2913151.stm (accessed August 17, 2023).

BBC Bitesize. "The bittersweet history of confectionery." 2022. https://www.bbc.co.uk/bitesize/articles/zm2q4xs (accessed August 17, 2023).

Bilton, Sam. "A history of the Christmas pudding: The origins of a Christmas favourite." *English Heritage*. https://www.english-heritage.org.uk/visit/inspire-me/history-of-the-christmas-pudding/ (accessed August 17, 2023).

Bland, Archie. "Scotch egg is definitely a substantial meal, says Michael Gove." *The Guardian: Coronavirus*. December 1, 2020. https://www.theguardian.com/world/2020/dec/01/scotch-egg-is-definitely-a-substantial-meal-says-michael-gove (accessed November 20, 2022).

Bossart, Celine. "The complete and slightly insane history of gin in England." VinePair. May 21, 2018. https://vinepair.com/articles/england-gin-history/ (accessed August 23, 2022).

Breville. "The UK's favourite desserts revealed." *Breville: Blog*. 2019. https://www.breville.co.uk/blog/UK-favourite-desserts-revealed.html (accessed August 17, 2023).

Brewers Journal. "UK brewery numbers increase 7.5%, surpassing 3,000." March 15, 2021. https://www.brewersjournal.info/uk-brewery-numbers-increase-7-5-surpassing-3000/ (accessed August 17, 2023).

Briggs, Helen. "Food strategy criticised by government's own adviser." *BBC News: Science and Environment*. June 13, 2022. https://www.bbc.co.uk/news/science-environment-61778967 (accessed August 17, 2023).

British Beer and Pub Association. "Beer through the ages." British Beer and Pub Association: Beer History. https://beerandpub.com/passions/beer-through-the-ages/ (accessed September 11, 2022).

British Coffee Association. "Coffee consumption." 2022. https://britishcoffeeassociation.org/coffee-consumption/ (accessed August 17, 2023).

British Sea Fishing. "The big five fish species." https://britishseafishing.co.uk/the-big-five-fish-species/ (accessed September 27, 2022).

British Sea Fishing. "Brexit and Britain's Fisheries." https://britishseafishing.co.uk/brexit-and-britains-fisheries/ (accessed October 3, 2022).

British Sugar. "Back British sugar." https://www.britishsugar.co.uk/back-british-sugar (accessed September 26, 2022).

Brooks, Stephanie, Christopher T. Elliott, Michelle Spence, Christine Walsh, and Moira Dean. "Four years post-horsegate: An update of measures and actions put in place following the horsemeat incident of 2013." *npj Science of Food* 1, no. 5 (2017). https://doi.org/10.1038/s41538-017-0007-z (accessed August 17, 2023).

Buettner, Elizabeth. "'Going for an Indian': South Asian restaurants and the limits of multiculturalism in Britain." *Journal of Modern History* 80, no. 4 (2008): 865–901. https://doi.org/10.1086/591113 (accessed August 17, 2023).

Bule, Guise. "The traditional Full English Breakfast." *English Breakfast Society: Research*. 2012–2023. https://englishbreakfastsociety.com/full-english-breakfast.html (accessed April 2, 2023).

Business Wales. "Carbon Capture Technology—12 methods that can be incorporated on your farm." November 8, 2019. https://businesswales.gov.wales/farmingconnect/news-and-events/technical-articles/carbon-capture-technology-12-methods-can-be-incorporated-your-farm (accessed January 23, 2022).

Butler, Sarah. "Chocolate sales soar as UK shoppers comfort eat at home amid Covid." *The Guardian: Retail Industry*. October 31, 2020. https://www.theguardian.com/business/2020/oct/31/chocolate-sales-soar-uk-shoppers-comfort-eat-at-home-covid (accessed November 20, 2022).

Campaign for Real Ale. "What we stand for." CAMRA.org.uk. 2022. https://camra.org.uk/about/about-us/what-we-stand-for/ (accessed September 12, 2022).

Carling. "The current market and future trends of cider: Part 2—the current market and future trends." *Carling: Insights*. https://www.carlingpartnership.com/insights/where-is-cider-going-2/ (accessed September 8, 2022).

Clark, Peter. "The 'Mother Gin' controversy in the early eighteenth century." *Transactions of the Royal Historical Society* 38 (1988): 63–84. JSTOR, https://doi.org/10.2307/3678967 (accessed August 23, 2022).

Cocks, Simon. "Brits buy over 3 million ready meals each day." *Good Housekeeping*. February 24, 2016. https://www.goodhousekeeping.com/uk/food/food-reviews/a669695/brits-buying-over-3-million-ready-meals-each-day/ (accessed August 17, 2023).

Coe, Sarah, Xameerah Malik, Felicia Rankl, Paul Bolton, and Iona Stewart. "House of Commons Library: The effect of the war in Ukraine on UK farming and food production." July 18, 2022. https://researchbriefings.files.parliament.uk/documents/CDP-2022-0147/CDP-2022-0147.pdf (accessed August 17, 2023).

Cohen, Billie. "The true story behind England's tea obsession." *BBC Travel: Food and Hospitality*. August 28, 2017. https://www.bbc.com/travel/article/20170823-the-true-story-behind-englands-tea-obsession (accessed September 13, 2022).

Conway, Jan. "Ice cream and frozen desserts in the UK—statistics and facts." *Statista: Food and Nutrition*. January 19, 2023. https://www.statista.com/topics/7237/ice-cream-in-the-uk/#dossier-chapter1 (accessed February 23, 2023).

The Cornish Pasty Association. "About the pasty." 2023. https://cornishpastyassociation.co.uk/about-the-pasty/ (accessed April 17, 2023).

Coulson, Jim. "Nutty northern Easter traditions." *Northern Life*. March 23, 2021. https://northernlifemagazine.co.uk/nutty-northern-easter-traditions/ (accessed January 2, 2023).

CountryFile. "British harvest: How long does the season last, when is harvest day, plus history and traditions." *CountryFile: Food and Recipes*. October 5, 2020. https://www.countryfile.com/how-to/food-recipes/british-harvest-how-long-does-the-season-last-when-is-harvest-day-plus-history-and-traditions/ (accessed August 17, 2023).

Countryside Online. "British sugar: All you need to know." January 13, 2021. https://www.countrysideonline.co.uk/food-and-farming/feeding-the-nation/sugar/ (accessed September 26, 2022).

Crown. "Fluoride." NHS: Health A to Z. August 21, 2021. https://www.nhs.uk/conditions/fluoride/ (accessed September 11, 2022).

Crown. "National Statistics: Chapter 7: Crops." Department for Environment, Food and Rural Affairs. July 27, 2022. https://www.gov.uk/government/statistics/agriculture-in-the-united-kingdom-2021/ (accessed October 6, 2022).

Cuff, Madeleine. "Kippers, the breakfast dish that fell out of favour, are back on British menus." *The Guardian: Business: Retail: Fish*. April 7, 2012. https://www.theguardian.com/lifeandstyle/2012/apr/07/food-kippers-smoked-fish-sales-revival (accessed April 24, 2023).

Davey, James. "Life in lockdown Britain means fewer shopping trips but bigger bills." *Reuters: Business News*. April 28, 2020. https://www.reuters.com/article/uk-health-coronavirus-britain-supermarke/life-in-lockdown-britain-means-fewer-shopping-trips-but-bigger-bills-idUKKCN22A0V7?edition-redirect=uk (accessed August 21, 2022).

Davis, Laura. "Revealed: Liverpool's favourite Scouse ingredients." *The Liverpool Echo*. February 27, 2018. https://www.liverpoolecho.co.uk/whats-on/food-drink-news/revealed-liverpools-favourite-scouse-ingredients-10953251 (accessed April 19, 2023).

DEFRA. "Foot and mouth disease control strategy for Great Britain." November 2011. https://assets.publishing.service.gov.uk/government/uploads/system/uploads/attachment_data/file/69456/fmd-control-strategy111128.pdf (accessed February 2, 2023).

Department for Environment Food and Rural Affairs. *Agricultural Statistics and Climate Change*, 10th edn. September 2020. https://assets.publishing.service.gov.uk/government/uploads/system/uploads/attachment_data/file/941991/agriclimate-10edition-08dec20.pdf (accessed August 17, 2023).

Department for Environment, Food and Rural Affairs. "Drinking water quality in England: A triennial report 2017–2019." December 2021. https://assets.publishing.service.gov.uk/government/uploads/system/uploads/attachment_data/file/1042163/drinking-water-quality-england17-19.pdf (accessed September 11, 2022).

Department for Environment, Food and Rural Affairs. "Farming Statistics—final crop areas, yields, livestock populations and agricultural workforce at 1 June 2020 United Kingdom." December 22, 2020. https://assets.publishing.service.gov.uk/government/uploads/system/uploads/attachment_data/file/946161/structure-jun2020final-uk-22dec20.pdf (accessed October 4, 2022).

Department for Environment, Food and Rural Affairs. "Official Statistics: Agri-climate Report 2022." October 27, 2022. https://www.gov.uk/government/statistics/agri-climate-report-2022/agri-climate-report-2022 (accessed January 18, 2022).

Department for Environment, Food and Rural Affairs. "National Statistics: Chapter 11: Environment." October 21, 2022. https://www.gov.uk/government/statistics/agriculture-in-the-united-kingdom-2021/chapter-11-environment (accessed August 17, 2023).

Department for Environment, Food and Rural Affairs. "United Kingdom Food Security Report 2021: Theme 2: UK food supply sources." December 22, 2021. https://www.gov.uk/government/statistics/united-kingdom-food-security-report-2021/united-kingdom-food-security-report-2021-theme-2-uk-food-supply-sources (accessed August 17, 2023).

Department for Environment, Food and Rural Affairs. "United Kingdom Food Security Report 2021: Theme 4: Food security at household level." December 22, 2021. https://www.gov.uk/government/statistics/united-kingdom-food-security-report-2021/united-kingdom-food-security-report-2021-theme-4-food-security-at-household-level (accessed August 17, 2023).

Department for International Trade and The Rt Hon Liam Fox MP. "UK wine exports pouring into overseas markets." Gov.uk. May 30, 2019. https://www.gov.uk/government/news/uk-wine-exports-pouring-into-overseas-markets. https://www.gov.uk/government/news/uk-wine-exports-pouring-into-overseas-markets (accessed August 23, 2022).

Easter Brand Fact Sheet. CadburyWorld.co.uk. https://www.cadburyworld.co.uk/schoolandgroups/~/media/CadburyWorld/en/Files/Pdf/factsheet-easterbrands (accessed November 14, 2022).

Eating Better. "Ready Meals Snapshot Survey 2020." https://www.eating-better.org/uploads/Documents/2019/ready-meal-survey-final.pdf (accessed August 17, 2023).

El-Beih, Yasmin. "How coffee forever changed Britain." *BBC Travel: Food and Hospitality: History: London*. November 19, 2020. https://www.bbc.com/travel/article/20201119-how-coffee-forever-changed-britain (accessed August 31, 2022).

English Heritage. "Why do we have Easter eggs?" *English Heritage: History at Home: Blog.* April 6, 2020. https://www.english-heritage.org.uk/visit/inspire-me/blog/articles/why-do-we-have-easter-eggs/ (accessed November 14, 2022).

Environment Agency. "The state of the environment: Soil." June 2019. https://assets.publishing.service.gov.uk/government/uploads/system/uploads/attachment_data/file/805926/State_of_the_environment_soil_report.pdf (accessed January 10, 2022).

FarmingUK Team. "UK on verge of food security concerns 'not seen since WWII.'" *FarmingUK: News: Politics.* April 27, 2022. https://www.farminguk.com/news/uk-on-verge-of-food-security-concerns-not-seen-since-wwii-_60282.html (accessed August 17, 2023).

Fetzer, Thiemo. "Subsidizing the spread of COVID19: Evidence from the UK's Eat-Out-to-Help-Out scheme." October 29, 2020. https://warwick.ac.uk/fac/soc/economics/research/centres/cage/manage/publications/wp.517.2020.pdf (accessed August 21, 2022).

Fone, Martin. "Curious questions: Who invented the Ploughman's Lunch?" *Country Life: Food and Drink.* April 9, 2022. https://www.countrylife.co.uk/food-drink/who-invented-the-ploughmans-lunch-241426 (accessed April 12, 2023).

Fone, Martin. "Curious questions: Why is the pork pie associated with Melton Mowbray?" CountryLife.co.uk: *Food and Drink.* September 22, 2022. https://www.countrylife.co.uk/food-drink/curious-questions-why-is-the-pork-pie-associated-with-melton-mowbray-247309 (accessed November 17, 2022).

French, Phoebe. "Record 15.6m bottles of wine produced in England and Wales last year." *The Drinks Business.* February 1, 2019. https://www.thedrinksbusiness.com/2019/02/record-15-6m-bottles-of-wine-produced-in-england-and-wales-last-year/ (accessed August 23, 2022).

Garry, Freya K., Dan J. Bernie, Jemma C. S. Davie, and Edward C. D. Pope. "Future climate risk to UK agriculture from compound events." *Climate Risk Management* 32 (2021): 100282. https://www.sciencedirect.com/science/article/pii/S2212096321000115 (accessed January 18, 2023).

Global Food Security. "UK threat." 2022. https://www.foodsecurity.ac.uk/challenge/uk-threat/ (accessed January 10, 2022).

The Grocer. "Pandemic bake-offs, banana bread fever and social recipes: 10 charts explaining UK attitudes to home baking." May 11, 2021. https://www.thegrocer.co.uk/trend-reports/pandemic-bake-offs-banana-bread-fever-and-social-recipes-10-charts-explaining-uk-attitudes-to-home-baking/655954.article (accessed August 22, 2022).

The Grocer. "The UK's 10 most popular chocolate bars and brands 2022." September 20, 2022. https://www.thegrocer.co.uk/confectionery/the-uks-10-most-popular-chocolate-bars-and-brands-2022/671419.article (accessed November 20, 2022).

Hall, Daniel. "The curious tradition of blessing the River Tweed's salmon and the story behind it." *Chronicle Live.* February 6, 2022. https://www.chroniclelive.co.uk/news/

north-east-news/river-tweed-norham-berwick-salmon-22973681 (accessed August 17, 2023).

Harkness, Caroline, Mikhail A. Semenov, Francisco Areal, Nimai Senapati, Miroslav Trnka, Jan Balek, and Jacob Bishop. "Adverse weather conditions for UK wheat production under climate change." *Agricultural and Forest Meteorology* 282–283 (March 15, 2020): 107862. https://www.sciencedirect.com/science/article/pii/S01681 92319304782 (accessed October 4, 2022).

Havelock, Laurie. "Chocolate sales are melting away from pandemic highs, as cost of living and rising cocoa prices bite." *INews: Money: Business*. July 16, 2022. https://inews.co.uk/news/business/chocolate-sales-melting-cost-of-living-cocoa-prices-1744999 (accessed November 20, 2022).

The Herald Scotland. "Runny eggs declared safe to eat 30 years after Edwina Currie's salmonella scare." October 11, 2017. https://www.heraldscotland.com/news/15587 982.runny-eggs-declared-safe-eat-30-years-edwina-curries-salmonella-scare/ (accessed September 26, 2022).

Irvine, Susannah, Aleksandra Gorb, and Brigid Francis-Devine. *House of Commons Library: Food Banks in the UK*. July 14, 2022. https://researchbriefings.files.parliam ent.uk/documents/CBP-8585/CBP-8585.pdf (accessed August 21, 2022).

Jane Austen's World. "Food—to die for: Food preparation in the Georgian era." August 5, 2012. https://janeaustensworld.com/2012/08/05/food-to-die-for-food-preparat ion-in-the-georgian-era/ (accessed August 17, 2023).

Janovich, Adriana. "Lamb and mint: A classic pairing." *Washington State Magazine*. Spring 2021. https://magazine.wsu.edu/2021/02/17/lamb-mint-a-classic-pairing/ (accessed June 1, 2023).

Jeffreys, Henry. "Smoked salmon." *The Spectator*. December 16, 2017. https://www.spectator.co.uk/article/smoked-salmon/ (accessed May 25, 2023).

Johnson, Ben. "The great British pub." *Historic-UK*. June 1, 2015.https://www.histo ric-uk.com/CultureUK/The-Great-British-Pub/ (accessed August 17, 2023).

Jones, Stephen. "Why Waitrose cut ties with Heston—and why it might be a strategic win." *The Grocer*. February 27, 2023. https://www.thegrocer.co.uk/waitrose/why-waitrose-cut-ties-with-heston-and-why-it-might-be-a-strategic-win/676748.article (accessed May 11, 2023).

Knight, Sam. "How the sandwich consumed Britain." *The Guardian: News: The Long Read*. November 24, 2017. https://www.theguardian.com/news/2017/nov/24/how-the-sandwich-consumed-britain (accessed August 17, 2023).

Levitt, Tom. "The end of free-range eggs? Year-round bird flu outbreaks may keep hens inside." *The Guardian: News: Environment: Wildlife*. March 25, 2022. https://www.theguardian.com/environment/2022/mar/25/the-end-of-free-range-eggs-yea r-round-bird-flu-outbreaks-may-keep-hens-inside (accessed February 1, 2023).

Liverpool John Moores University. "Direct and indirect impacts of COVID-19 on health and wellbeing." *Rapid Evidence Review*. July 2020 (Version 2). https://www.

ljmu.ac.uk/~/media/phi-reports/2020-07-direct-and-indirect-impacts-of-covid19-on-health-and-wellbeing.pdf (accessed August 17, 2023).

Lloyd, Chris. "'Spectacular' 6,000 year old salt-making site found on Teesside." *The Northern Echo: News*. March 31, 2021. https://www.thenorthernecho.co.uk/news/19200577.spectacular-6-000-year-old-salt-making-site-found-teesside/ (accessed September 25, 2022).

Lloyd, Gary. "Food inflation drops below 20% for first time in five months." *Morning Advertiser*. May 12, 2023. https://www.morningadvertiser.co.uk/Article/2023/05/12/CGA-Prestige-index-shows-foodservice-inflation-falls-below-20 (accessed May 17, 2023).

MacEacheran, Mike. "The contentious origins of England's famous pudding." *BBC: Hidden Britain: Food and Drink: Lake District*. July 16, 2021. https://www.bbc.com/travel/article/20210715-the-contentious-origins-of-englands-famous-pudding (accessed March 8, 2023).

MacEacheran, Mike. "The strange story of Britain's oldest sweet." *BBC: Food and Hospitality: Food and Drink: England*. July 11, 2019. https://www.bbc.com/travel/article/20190710-the-strange-story-of-britains-oldest-sweet (accessed March 8, 2023).

Mackenzie, Lois. "The UK's favourite biscuits have been revealed—do you agree?" Yahoo Finance. May 28, 2022. https://uk.finance.yahoo.com/news/uk-favourite-biscuits-revealed-agree230100919.html?guccounter=1&guce_referrer=aHR0cHM6Ly93d3cuZ29vZ2xlLmNvLnVrLw&guce_referrer_sig=AQAAAKMqeRIwTcv1GeJ-o3f5SVcK7ZsLuRP8WF6c39ttq3Ds7wWo2EnCy0oWlwlGUWmEz09ZxUsE19MeOpnrS2xelnoixxuE6D2DMPZrGFSaj9E7EgWO67gyBQvC42oSOIwudqOQ8b_fmzMNALy9sDgHzr6bNo615whg17CBZelqlSV9 (accessed November 20, 2022).

Marine Management Organization. "UK Sea Fisheries Statistics 2020." https://assets.publishing.service.gov.uk/government/uploads/system/uploads/attachment_data/file/1020837/UK_Sea_Fisheries_Statistics_2020_-_AC_checked.pdf (accessed September 27, 2022).

Marine Stewardship Council. "UK and Irish fisheries spotlight." Marine Stewardship Council: UK and Irish Fisheries. https://www.msc.org/uk/what-we-are-doing/uk-irish-fisheries (accessed October 3, 2022).

Matheson, Jesse. "How has coronavirus affected pubs, cafes and restaurants?" *Economic Observatory: Business Big and Small*. July 2, 2020. https://www.economicsobservatory.com/how-has-coronavirus-affected-pubs-cafes-and-restaurants (accessed May 16, 2023).

Melton Mowbray Pork Pie Product Specification: SPECIFICATION COUNCIL REGULATION (EC) No 510/2006 "MELTON MOWBRAY PORK PIE" EC No: UK/PGI/005/0335/ PDO () PGI (X). January 4, 2021. https://assets.publishing.service.gov.uk/media/5fd36515e90e076637bb5a40/pfn-melton-mowbray-pgi.pdf (accessed November 17, 2022).

Miller, Norman. "The UK's heritage apple renaissance." *BBC Travel: Forgotten Foods*. July 6, 2022. https://www.bbc.com/travel/article/20220705-the-uks-heritage-apple-renaissance (accessed October 6, 2022).

Mitchell, Ian. "Taking the pledge." *Whisky Magazine: History*. https://whiskymag.com/story/taking-the-pledge (accessed September 13, 2022).

Morris, Steve. "Hats off to the great British greasy spoon." *The Critic*. March 27, 2012. https://thecritic.co.uk/hats-off-to-the-great-british-greasy-spoon/ (accessed April 5, 2023).

Mukherjee, Debabrata. "The British curry." *History Magazine: History UK: Culture UK*. November 2, 2017. https://www.historic-uk.com/CultureUK/The-British-Curry/ (accessed August 17, 2023).

National Federation of Fish Friers. "Everything you need to know about fish and chips." National Federation of Fish Friers: Fish and Chips. https://www.nfff.co.uk/pages/fish-and-chips (accessed April 24, 2023).

National Food Strategy: Independent Review: Chapter 16. https://www.nationalfoodstrategy.org/wp-content/uploads/2021/07/National-Food-Strategy-Chapter-16.pdf (accessed August 17, 2023).

Nationwide Caterers Association. "What is street food?" *Streetfood*. 2016. https://www.streetfood.org.uk/foodies.html (accessed November 1, 2022).

Naylor, Tony. "How to eat: A ploughman's lunch." *The Guardian: Lifestyle*. March 31, 2014. https://www.theguardian.com/lifeandstyle/wordofmouth/2014/mar/31/how-to-eat-a-ploughmans-lunch (accessed April 12, 2023).

Naylor, Tony. "Restaurants v the cost of living crisis: How will they cope?" *The Observer: Restaurants*. September 18, 2022. https://www.theguardian.com/food/2022/sep/18/restaurants-v-the-cost-of-living-crisis-how-will-they-cope (accessed May 16, 2023).

Noel, Katherine, Aiming Qi, Lakshmi Harika Gajula, Craig Padley, Steffen Rietz, Yong-Ju Huang, Bruce D. L. Fitt, and Henrik U. Stotz. "Influence of elevated temperatures on resistance against phoma stem canker in oilseed rape." *Frontiers in Plant Science* 13 (March 2, 2022): 785804. doi: 10.3389/fpls.2022.785804. PMID: 35310658; PMCID: PMC8924614 (accessed January 10, 2023).

Office for National Statistics. "Coronavirus and its impact on UK hospitality: January 2020 to June 2021." July 19, 2021. https://www.ons.gov.uk/businessindustryandtrade/business/activitysizeandlocation/articles/coronavirusanditsimpactonukhospitality/january2020tojune2021 (accessed August 17, 2023).

PA Media. "Number of pubs in England and Wales falls to record low." *The Guardian: Hospitality Industry*. July 4, 2022. https://www.theguardian.com/business/2022/jul/04/number-of-pubs-in-england-and-wales-falls-to-record-low-covid-19-soaring-costs (accessed September 14, 2022).

Partington, Richard. "Dining out in UK at lowest level since May amid Omicron fears." *The Guardian: Food and Drink Industry*. December 2, 2021. https://www.theguard

ian.com/business/2021/dec/02/dining-out-in-uk-at-lowest-level-since-may-amid-omicron-fears (accessed April 30, 2023).

Porter, David. "A life of pie." September 14, 2011. https://deptfordpudding.com/2011/09/14/a-life-of-pie/ (accessed November 17, 2022).

Power, M., B. Doherty, K. Pybus, and K. Pickett. "How COVID-19 has exposed inequalities in the UK food system: The case of UK food and poverty." *Emerald Open Research* 2 (May 13, 2020): 11. doi: 10.35241/emeraldopenres.13539.2. PMCID: PMC7219559 (accessed August 21, 2022).

Powney, G. D., Claire Carvell, Mike Edwards, Roger K. A. Morris, Helen E. Roy, Ben A. Woodcock, and Nick J. B. Isaac. "Widespread losses of pollinating insects in Britain." *Nature Communications* 10 (2019): 1018. https://doi.org/10.1038/s41467-019-08974-9 (accessed August 17, 2023).

Public Health England. "Impact of COVID-19 pandemic on grocery shopping behaviours." 2020. https://assets.publishing.service.gov.uk/government/uploads/system/uploads/attachment_data/file/932350/Grocery_Purchasing_Report.pdf (accessed February 5, 2023).

Public Health England. "Salt reduction targets for 2024." September 2020. https://assets.publishing.service.gov.uk/government/uploads/system/uploads/attachment_data/file/915406/2024_salt_reduction_targets_070920-FINAL-1.pdf (accessed September 26, 2022).

Rivard, Christopher, Jeffrey Thomas, Miguel A. Lanaspa, and Richard J. Johnson. "Sack and sugar, and the aetiology of gout in England between 1650 and 1900." *Rheumatology* 52, no. 3 (March 2013): 421–6. https://doi.org/10.1093/rheumatology/kes297 (accessed August 17, 2023).

Robinson, Robb. "The evolution of railway fish traffic policies, 1840–66." *Journal of Transport History* 7, no. 1 (1986): 32–44. https://doi.org/10.1177/002252668600700103 (accessed October 2, 2022).

Rowlatt, Justin. "National Food Strategy: Tax sugar and salt and prescribe veg, report says." *BBC News: UK*. July 15, 2021. https://www.bbc.co.uk/news/uk-57838103 (accessed August 17, 2023).

Salt Association. "The history of salt." https://saltassociation.co.uk/education/salt-history/ (accessed September 23, 2022).

The Scotch Whisky Association. "Facts and figures." https://www.scotch-whisky.org.uk/insights/facts-figures/ (accessed September 6, 2022).

The Scotch Whisky Association. "Story of scotch." Scotch Whisky Association: Discover. https://www.scotch-whisky.org.uk/discover/story-of-scotch/ (accessed September 6, 2022).

The Scotsman. "When sea salt was Scotland's white gold." March 10, 2017. https://www.scotsman.com/sport/football/when-sea-salt-was-scotlands-white-gold-60156 (accessed September 25, 2022).

Seafish Industry Authority. "The economic impacts of the UK sea fishing and fish processing sectors: An input-output analysis." 2017. https://www.sff.co.uk/wp-content/uploads/2017/03/Seafish-2006_I-O_Key_Features_Final_090108.pdf (accessed August 17, 2023).

Seal, Rebecca. "Deconstructing cawl, the hearty Welsh stew." *National Geographic: Travel*. October 14, 2021. https://www.nationalgeographic.co.uk/travel/2021/09/deconstructing-cawl-the-hearty-welsh-stew (accessed April 19, 2023).

Searl, Fred. "Raspberry volumes set for big rise as season begins." *Fresh Produce Journal*. June 23, 2021. https://www.fruitnet.com/fresh-produce-journal/raspberry-volumes-set-for-big-rise-as-season-begins/185604.article (accessed October 10, 2022).

Secret Smokehouse. "London cure smoked salmon." 2023. https://secretsmokehouse.co.uk/pages/london-cure-smoked-salmon (accessed August 17, 2023).

Sim, Keren. "This is the UK's favourite flavour of crisps." *Good Housekeeping*. November 7, 2019. https://www.goodhousekeeping.com/uk/food/a29723082/this-is-the-uk-favourite-flavour-of-crisps/ (accessed November 17, 2022).

Simply Oysters. "Oyster history." 2013–2022. https://simplyoysters.com/oyster-history (accessed November 16, 2022).

Speciality Food Magazine. "How Brexit will impact the food sector in 2022." *Speciality Food Magazine: Brexit*. January 13, 2022. https://www.specialityfoodmagazine.com/news/brexit-impact-food-sector-in-2022 (accessed August 22, 2022).

Specification Council Regulation (EC) No 510/2006 on Protected Geographical Indications and Protected Designations of Origin. "Cornish pasty." https://assets.publishing.service.gov.uk/media/5fd34f3dd3bf7f3059ef3cd2/pfn-cornish-pasty-pgi-pdf.pdf (accessed April 24, 2023).

Statista Research Department. "Restaurants in the UK—statistics and facts." *Statista: Travel, Tourism and Hospitality: Food and Drink Services*. February 8, 2022. https://www.statista.com/topics/3131/restaurant-industry-in-the-united-kingdom-uk/#topicOverview (accessed May 17, 2023).

Sugg Ryan, Deborah. "The curious history of government-funded British Restaurants in World War 2." *Find My Past: History Hub*. June 22, 2020. https://www.findmypast.co.uk/blog/history/british-restaurants (accessed May 15, 2023).

Tait, Amelia. "So long, salt and vinegar: How crisp flavours went from simple to sensational." *The Guardian*. January 14, 2020. https://www.theguardian.com/food/2020/jan/14/so-long-salt-and-vinegar-how-crisp-flavours-went-from-simple-to-sensational (accessed November 20, 2022).

Taylor, Elise. "How gin bounced back from decades of decline to become London's latest It drink." *Vogue: Food*. June 11, 2018. https://www.vogue.com/article/how-gin-became-londons-it-drink-again (accessed September 4, 2022).

Tensley, Brandon. "How the potato chip took over America." *Smithsonian Magazine: Arts and Culture*. January 2022. https://www.smithsonianmag.com/arts-culture/curious-history-potato-chip-180979232/ (accessed November 17, 2022).

The Tewkesbury Mustard Company. "History of Tewkesbury mustard." 2014. https://www.tewkesburymustard.co.uk/history-of-tewkesbury-mustard/ (accessed May 30, 2023).

Thomas, Louis. "The 10 most popular beer brands in the UK". The Drinks Business July 5, 2022. https://www.thedrinksbusiness.com/2022/07/the-10-most-popular-beer-brands-in-the-uk/ (accessed August 29, 2022).

Thomas, Louis. "The 10 most popular wine brands in the UK". The Drinks Business. July 12, 2022. https://www.thedrinksbusiness.com/2022/07/most-popular-uk-wine-brands/ (accessed August 29, 2022).

UK Fisheries Ltd. "UK's distant waters fishing fleet." 2022. https://ukfisheries.net/uk-fish-consumption (accessed September 23, 2022).

UK Tea and Infusions Association. "FAQs about tea." Tea.co.uk. 2022. https://www.tea.co.uk/tea-faqs (accessed August 30, 2022).

Waste and Resources Action Programme (WRAP). "Returning to normality after Covid-19: Food waste attitudes and behaviours in 2021." August 2021. https://wrap.org.uk/sites/default/files/2021-08/food-trends-report-august-2021.pdf (accessed February 5, 2023).

The Whiskey Exchange. "Glenlivet: Single malt scotch whisky." *The Whiskey Exchange: Scotch Whisky: Single Malt Scotch Whisky*. 1999–2022. https://www.thewhiskyexchange.com/b/40/glenlivet-single-malt-scotch-whisky (accessed September 7, 2022).

William Reed Ltd. "Tea addicts, gender splits and the love of a traditional cuppa: 10 charts explaining UK attitudes to hot beverages." *The Grocer: Trend Reports*. September 16, 2019. https://www.thegrocer.co.uk/trend-reports/10-charts-explaining-uk-attitudes-to-hot-beverages/597574.article (accessed August 17, 2023).

Wood, Zoe. "One in three Britons drink plant-based milk as demand soars." *The Guardian: Food and Drink Industry*. September 17, 2021. https://www.theguardian.com/business/2021/sep/17/britons-drink-plant-based-milk-demand (accessed October 9, 2022).

Wright, Fraser. "A history of Clapshot, including a recipe for making your own." *The Scotsman: Food and Drink*. December 21, 2015. https://foodanddrink.scotsman.com/food/a-history-of-clapshot-including-a-recipe-for-making-your-own/ (accessed May 30, 2023).

Yorkshire Pudd. "The Yorkshire pudding—where did it all begin?" Yorkshire.Pudd: The Yorkshire Pudding. 2023. https://www.yorkshirepudd.co.uk/yorkshire-pudding-history/ (accessed May 29, 2023).

Index

abolition of slavery xvii, 37–8, 103
adulteration of food and drink xviii, 9, 44, 118–19, 125, 131, 166
afternoon tea x, xviii, 8, 107, 108, 121–2
Allhallowtide foods 145–6
Anglo-Saxons ix, xv, 3, 27, 28, 114, 126, 144
animal diseases
   African swine fever xii, 198–9
   avian flu xii, xxii, 197–8
   bluetongue xii, xxi, 197, 198
   bovine spongiform encephalopathy (BSE) xii, xxi, xxii, 17
   foot-and-mouth disease xii, xxi, 17–18
American influence on British food and drink 9, 12, 14, 15, 133, 150, 161, 182, 199

beer xvi, xviii, xix, 77–8, 112, 114–18, 129, 130, 131, 132, 146, 166, 178
   lager xix, 40, 116–17
biscuits 6, 13, 31, 41, 97–8, 99, 100, 108–9, 161, 165–9
   shortbread 105–6, 168
brandy xvii, 118, 128–9, 131, 132, 152
bread ix, xi, xx, 4, 5, 6, 8, 9, 11, 13, 14–15, 27, 29, 31, 38, 39, 41, 42, 59, 61, 64, 71, 77–8, 79, 86, 90, 144
   bread sauce 65, 150
   in desserts 8, 96, 98–9, 100–3, 107, 151
breakfast x, xi, xix, 6, 8, 10, 31, 38, 41, 45, 52, 71–6, 98, 103, 111, 120, 124, 125, 164
   English breakfast xi, 10, 71, 72–4
   kippers x, xix, 8, 72, 75–6
   porridge 4, 6, 10, 71, 72, 74–5
Brexit xii–xiii, xxii, 20, 22, 35–6, 47, 80, 186, 199–200
British Empire xi, xv, xviii, 9, 119, 124, 128, 132

East India Company xvii, xviii, 9–10, 115, 121, 124, 162
Burns Night 102–3, 104, 139–40

cake 5, 8, 13, 21, 31, 37, 41, 45, 96, 106, 107, 120, 121, 122, 139, 141, 145–7, 152, 153–6, 176, 180
   gingerbread 6, 97, 147, 153, 166, 167
   wedding cakes 155–6
celebrity chefs xv, xxi, 11, 62, 76, 88, 99, 175–6, 183–4
   Blumenthal, Heston 62, 175–6
   Oliver, Jamie 76, 175, 183
cereals and grains x, xvii, xx, 2, 3, 4, 6, 12, 14, 42, 75, 79, 118, 129, 144, 147, 151, 185, 199
   wheat xv, xix, 2, 4, 12, 14, 39–41, 42, 75, 139, 141, 144, 166, 190, 193–4, 198, 201
cheese xvi, xx, xxi, 3, 5, 6, 9, 10, 13, 15, 22, 27, 42–3, 57–8, 60, 62, 64, 71, 77–8, 86, 95, 142, 152, 153–4, 156, 175
   British cheeses 46–9
   Cheddar xxi, 46–7, 57, 64, 77–8, 152
   Stilton xxi, 47–9, 60, 64, 77
children and teenagers xi, 13, 14, 15, 17, 20–1, 38, 44, 45, 81, 115, 139, 143–6, 149–50, 167, 182, 202
   childhood health xix, 11, 15, 44–5, 203
Chinese restaurants xix, 15, 173, 182
Christmas foods 57, 65, 103, 106, 137–8, 139, 146, 148–53, 165, 176
chocolate xvii, xviii, xix, 9, 99, 106, 143, 148, 153, 161, 168, 169–70
   hot chocolate 8, 43, 120
cider 8, 77, 126–7, 138
climate change xiii, 6, 189–93, 195
   drought xiii, 190–2
   emissions from food production 189, 192–4, 201–2

coffee xvii, 8, 9, 37, 43, 45, 73, 111, 120, 121, 122, 123–5, 132, 175, 180, 181
cookbooks ix, xv, xvi, xvii, xviii, 2, 11, 63, 65, 67, 68, 77, 84, 88, 90, 98, 99, 100, 102, 103, 104, 141, 145, 152, 153, 165, 175, 177, 178
　Modern Cookery for Private Families xviii, 11, 153
　Mrs Beeton's Book of Household Management xviii, 11, 64, 153
　The Forme of Cury xvi, 98, 151, 152, 164
Cool Britannia xv, 183–4
convenience foods xi, xii, 16, 121
Cornwall 28, 47, 74, 122, 126, 144, 149, 198
　Cornish fairings 97–8
　Cornish pasty 79–82
cost of living crisis xii, 1, 20, 22–3, 98, 170, 185, 201, 202, 203
Covid-19 xii, xiii, xxii, 20–2, 40, 100, 117, 130, 159, 163, 169–70, 184–5, 189, 199, 202
　Eat Out to Help Out scheme xxii, 21–2, 184–5
Crusades ix, xv, xvi, 3, 36, 96

desserts xvi, 8, 10, 16, 38, 39, 45, 50, 95–109, 167, 168, 175
　English desserts: xx, 63, 96–102, 108
　ice cream xvii, 8, 27, 99–101
　pancakes x, xvi, 7, 108, 140–1
　Scottish desserts: 102–6, 108, 140
　Welsh desserts: 106–9
dinners 83–92
　cawl 60, 85–7, 88
　Lancashire hotpot 71, 84–5, 87, 88
　Scouse 87–8
disease and illness in humans 8, 15, 17, 19, 44, 45, 115, 203
　cholera xviii, 112, 115
　malnutrition 11, 13
　obesity xv, 189, 203
drinking water xviii, 44, 111–14, 115, 119

Easter and Lent xvi, 6, 63, 140–3, 152
　Easter eggs xix, 142–3, 163
edible flowers x, 6, 7, 98
eggs xi–xii, xx, xxi, 14, 15, 16–17, 42, 59, 97–8, 103, 107, 108, 139, 141–3, 147, 149, 154, 164, 197, 199

　as breakfast food 8, 10, 72–4
　Scotch eggs 162–3, 175
Elizabethan food and drink x, 5–7, 37, 97, 115, 131, 155–6
European Protected Designation of Origin (PDO) status xxi, xxii, 47, 48, 89, 164
European Union xxi, xxii, 18, 22, 34, 61, 79, 133

farming ix, x, xvii, 2, 5, 7, 8, 12, 18, 23, 38–44, 52, 54, 118, 144, 177, 200
　dairy farming and cattle 12, 42–3, 189–93, 198
　soil degradation xiii, 42, 189–91, 193–4
　sustainability xiii–xiv, 189–97, 203
First World War xi, 12–13, 44, 179, 116, 122, 129
　rationing xi, xix, 13
fish and seafood xv–xvi, 3, 4, 5, 6, 8–9, 13, 27, 29, 31–6, 50, 57, 59–60, 61, 69, 71, 132, 141, 144–5, 149, 162, 166, 176–9, 181
　Cod Wars xx, xxi, 33–4
　kippers x, xix, 8, 72, 75–6
　oysters 5, 8, 10, 60, 85, 159–60, 178
　smoked fish 3, 8, 57, 58–9, 60, 92, 140
　sustainable fishing 31, 34, 60, 76, 190
fish and chips xi, xix, 10, 31, 57, 63, 65, 89–91, 174
fishing industry and trade ix, xvi, xviii, xix–xxii, 3, 6, 30, 31–4, 35, 82
folklore and customs 66, 82, 103, 108, 111, 138–9, 141, 144–9, 151, 153–4, 156
　superstition 81, 143
　Welsh folklore and traditions 138–9, 146–8
food banks xii, xiii, xv, xxi, 19, 20–3, 201
food hygiene schemes xxi, 173–4
food preservation x, xi, xviii, 5, 10, 29, 30, 37, 58, 65, 166
　freezing xi, xviii, 16, 27, 32, 99–100
　pickling 10, 65
　refrigeration: x, xix, 9, 10, 30
　smoking xvi, 3, 58–9, 76
food scandals xi–xii, 16–19, 183
　horsemeat scandal xii, 18–19
　salmonella egg scandal xi–xii, xxi, 16–17
food supply chain issues xiii, 20, 22–3, 44, 193, 199–201, 202

food wastage 13, 201–2
foraged food ix–x, 1–2, 4, 6, 115
French influence on British food x, xvi, 4, 7, 8, 29, 50, 80, 101, 104–5, 130–1, 156, 160, 166, 173, 176–7, 179
　Norman Conquest of Britain ix, xv, xvi, 3, 28, 50, 69, 96, 114, 126, 176
fruit x, xi, 1, 2, 5, 6, 7, 10, 12, 13, 14, 20, 22, 38, 49–52, 53–4, 58, 61, 67, 69, 80, 82, 100, 101–2, 106–7, 123, 131, 132, 140, 144, 149–50, 168, 178, 185, 193, 200, 202, 203
　apples xviii, 6, 10, 49, 50–2, 69, 77, 78, 83, 96, 107, 126–7, 138–9, 146, 147, 154
　bananas 14, 21, 49, 102, 200
　citrus fruits xx, 14, 66, 67, 73, 97, 149–50, 152, 176, 193
　dried fruit 97, 99, 103, 142, 145, 150, 151, 161
　fruitcakes 139, 152–6
　raspberries 6, 53–4, 101, 102, 104
　redcurrants 65, 67–9
　rhubarb xix, 49–50, 107

gastropubs 57, 162, 174
Georgian era xvii, 7–9, 72, 99, 112
gin x, xvi, xvii, xviii, 7, 50, 65, 118–20, 129, 131, 165
Glasse, Hannah xvii, 63, 67, 177
Guy Fawkes Night 146–8

Hallowe'en 145–6
harvest x, 22, 126, 138, 144–5, 148, 200
　crop failures and poor harvests x, xvi, xix, 4, 6, 12, 87, 119, 190
　harvest celebrations xviii, 53, 102, 137, 144–5
herbs 2, 6, 19, 59, 64–5, 68, 85, 88, 104, 115, 132
Hogmanay 103, 104, 106, 140

immigration x, xi, xv, 7, 15, 22, 182
Indian influence on British food and drink xi, xvii, xx, 9–10, 57, 60, 67, 99, 121–3, 162, 165, 173, 182
　chicken tikka masala xxi, 88–9
　restaurants xi, xx, 15, 182
Industrial Revolution 7, 30, 32, 73, 84, 99

Jewish food in Britain xi, 10, 58, 89–90

kitchen equipment xi, 5, 10–11, 79, 86, 99, 107, 108, 151

Lancashire hotpot 84–5, 88
land enclosure ix, x, xvi, 2, 7, 42–3, 87
London x, xvi, xvii, xviii, 4, 5, 8, 12, 15, 19, 21, 28–9, 43, 44, 48, 49, 58–9, 79, 88, 89, 90, 99, 101, 112, 118, 121, 144, 155, 167
　brewers 115–16
　coffee 123–5
　gin 118–20
　markets and shopping x, 4, 5, 8, 43, 50, 52, 54, 122, 144, 162, 164
　restaurants 4, 10, 15, 76, 173, 174, 175, 177, 178–9, 180, 182–4
　street food 8, 124, 159–60
lunch xviii, xxi, 13, 16, 46, 62, 65, 71, 76–83, 86, 89, 160, 163, 180
　ploughman's lunch xviii, 46, 65, 71, 77–8

markets 5, 10, 32, 43
　farmers' markets 51, 160–1
Middle Ages ix, 3–5, 53, 75, 98, 130
middle classes 8, 10–11, 72–3, 116–17, 120, 124, 129, 131–2, 160, 168, 177, 180
Middle Eastern foods in Britain ix, 3, 96, 14, 165, 173
milk ix, xx, 2, 8, 10, 12, 14, 15, 42–8, 62, 65, 74–5, 77, 92, 97, 99, 121, 141, 154, 161, 186, 190, 199
　milk in desserts 102–8
　non-dairy milks 6, 10, 45, 60, 98, 141
monasteries xvi, 46, 50, 111, 114–15
Mothering Sunday 141
mustard xviii, 6, 13, 58, 64, 65, 66–7, 68

Neolithic period ix, 2, 42, 50, 114, 165
New Year 126, 139, 140, 146, 148

organic food 17, 183, 196

pollinating insects and biodiversity loss xiii–xiv, xxii, 42, 50, 194–7
Poor Laws xvii, 6

pubs and inns 116–18, 124, 129, 146, 173, 174–5, 176
   impact of Covid-19 xxii, 20–2, 159, 163, 184–5
   pub food 62, 74, 77–8, 79, 80, 84, 87, 89, 102

rape (rapeseed) xiv, 23, 41–2, 191, 195–6
restaurants and dining out xi, xix–xxii, 4, 15–16, 57, 58, 62, 88–9, 92, 95, 102, 106, 131, 173–86
   greasy spoon café 73–4
   impact of Covid-19 20–1, 159, 163
   Michelin stars xxi–xxii, 174, 175, 183, 184
Roman Britain ix, xv, 2–3, 27–8, 46, 50, 52–3, 75, 86, 111, 114, 141, 148, 165
   foods introduced by Romans to Britain 2, 50, 53, 130
royalty xvi, xvii, xxii, 29, 48, 48, 61, 80, 96, 105, 120, 130–1, 133, 155, 178
   Elizabeth I 6, 68, 142
   Queen Victoria 121, 129, 139, 168–9
   William III and Mary II xvii, 30, 118
Russian invasion of Ukraine xii–xiii, xxii, 22–3, 40, 185, 200–1

salt xv, xvi–xviii, xix, 27–31, 47, 65, 68, 75, 100, 165, 189, 203
sauces x, 5, 10, 65–9, 176, 178
Second World War xv, xx, 13–14, 33, 45, 47, 48, 51, 52, 73, 76, 91, 101, 122–3, 125, 162, 168, 179
   alcohol during Second World War 117, 129, 132
   British Restaurants communal dining facilities 180–1
   Dig for Victory campaign xi, 14
   rationing xi, xx, 13–15, 46, 123, 125, 180–1
snacks 31, 57, 161–70
   crisps 164–5
   pork pie 163–4
soups and stews x, 6, 8, 10, 13, 31, 46, 60–1, 64, 68, 71, 73, 83, 84–8, 92, 140, 159–60, 161, 177, 181
spices ix–x, 3, 6, 8, 19, 37, 60, 68, 88–9, 96–9, 107
   ginger ix, 3, 6, 10, 96, 98, 147, 151–2, 164

pottage ix, 4, 5, 42, 140, 151
street food xxi, 8, 10, 52, 159–61, 165
sugar ix, x, xvi, xvii, xix, xx, 3, 6, 8–9, 13, 36–9, 64, 68, 69, 96–100, 103, 104, 107–8, 119, 121, 139, 141, 147, 156, 166, 168–9, 189, 197, 203
   sugar beet 38–9, 168, 187
   in wartime 13, 15, 21, 101–2
Sunday roast 11, 62, 71, 76, 78–9, 83, 151, 174
superfoods 41, 52
supermarkets xi, 16, 18, 19, 20–1, 23, 47, 53, 57, 64, 76, 83, 88, 106, 117, 130, 132–3, 160, 165, 170, 175–6, 201, 202
sweets xx, 6, 15, 38, 99, 104–5, 146–8, 149, 161

tableware 4, 6, 86, 154, 175, 179
taxes on food and drink xvi–xviii, 29–30, 37, 131–2, 168, 189, 203
   on alcohol 116–19, 127–31
   on tea and coffee 121, 124
tea x, xvii–xx, 8, 13, 15, 37, 43, 73, 111, 112, 115–16, 120–5, 131, 167–8, 180
television xxi, 156, 168, 175, 183
temperance 116, 124, 131
transport ix, xviii, xix, 2, 8, 16, 22, 28, 32, 37, 43, 116, 164, 186
   railways x, xviii, 9, 32, 43–4, 50–4, 175, 179
   steam ships x, xix, 9, 12, 32, 90–1
Twelfth Night foods 137–9

upper-class diet and social elite 3–7, 73, 80, 95–7, 119, 120, 129, 150, 164, 168, 178–9, 180

vegan food 45, 71, 98, 137, 173
vegetables xi, 2, 5, 6, 7, 10, 22, 53, 57, 60, 61, 63–5, 67, 68, 78, 79–82, 141, 144, 146, 150, 176, 181, 193, 200, 202, 203
   mushy peas 61, 63–4, 89
   onions 2, 6, 10, 49, 60, 61, 64–5, 85, 87, 92
   root vegetables including potatoes xix, xxi, 7, 10, 12, 43, 49, 57, 60, 61–2, 64–5, 74, 78, 80, 83, 84–7, 90, 92, 140, 164–5, 190–1, 199
   in wartime 12–15

watercress 52–3, 60
vegetarianism xii, 3, 19, 46, 60, 64, 71, 74, 78–9, 85, 140, 151, 153, 163, 173, 179, 181
Victorian food and drink x–xi, 9–12, 38, 51, 52, 53, 61, 90, 116, 121–2, 129, 145, 160, 167–8, 169
   Victorian breakfasts xi, 10, 72–3
   Victorian Christmas traditions 148–9, 151–2
   Victorian desserts 98–101
Vikings ix, xv, xvi, 3, 9, 102

wassailing 126, 138, 146
weddings 57, 72, 153, 155–6
whisky xvi–xviii, 127–130, 140, 154
wine ix, xvii, 2, 6, 8, 100, 118, 130–3, 151, 178
   in Scottish desserts 102–4
women xi, 16, 17, 21, 29, 38, 63, 90, 122, 123, 146, 153–4, 160, 179–80
   and alcohol 114, 117, 118, 127, 130, 132
   wartime roles xix, 12–13, 14, 15, 181
working classes and the poor x, xvi, 2, 4–8, 10–13, 15, 20, 23, 30, 32, 38, 42–4, 52, 62, 73, 76, 81, 85, 87, 88, 91, 124, 142, 155, 159–60, 179, 181, 184
   alcohol consumption 116–17, 118–19, 126, 129, 132

Yorkshire pudding xvii, 61–3, 78, 83

About the Author

Victoria Williams, PhD, is an independent writer and researcher living in London. She is the author of ABC-CLIO's *Weird Sports and Wacky Games around the World: From Buzkashi to Zorbing* (winner of the 2016 RUSA Outstanding Reference Sources Award); *Celebrating Life Customs around the World: From Baby Showers to Funerals*; *Indigenous Peoples: An Encyclopedia of Culture, History, and Threats to Survival,* and *London: Geography, History and Culture.* She is also the coeditor of ABC-CLIO's *Etiquette and Taboos around the World: A Geographic Encyclopedia of Social and Cultural Customs.* Williams wrote her PhD thesis on fairytales in Victorian literature and art and on film, and has written on a variety of other subjects, including Hollywood film, London society and culture, Mesoamerican mythology, Victorian literature, U.S. folklore, and British folk customs. She has also lectured on Victoria fairy paintings and depictions of childhood in 1940s film. In the past, Williams has worked as an editorial assistant for a leading British food magazine and has run a small business selling traditional British cakes at artisan markets. Currently, alongside her writing, Williams runs a west London market championing local makers, including food producers.

www.ingramcontent.com/pod-product-compliance
Lightning Source LLC
Chambersburg PA
CBHW050325020526
44117CB00031B/1780